Dictionary of
Film
Terms

PETER LANG
New York • Washington, D.C./Baltimore • Bern
Frankfurt am Main • Berlin • Brussels • Vienna • Oxford

Frank Eugene Beaver

Dictionary of
Film
Terms

The Aesthetic Companion to Film Art

PETER LANG
New York • Washington, D.C./Baltimore • Bern
Frankfurt am Main • Berlin • Brussels • Vienna • Oxford

Library of Congress Cataloging-in-Publication Data
Beaver, Frank Eugene.
Dictionary of film terms: the aesthetic companion to film art / Frank Eugene Beaver.
p. cm.
Includes bibliographical references and index.
1. Motion pictures—Dictionaries. 2. Cinematography—Dictionaries. I. Title.
PN1993.45.B33   791.43'03—dc22   2005002249
ISBN 978-0-8204-7298-0

Bibliographic information published by **Die Deutsche Bibliothek**.
Die Deutsche Bibliothek lists this publication in the "Deutsche
Nationalbibliografie"; detailed bibliographic data is available
on the Internet at http://dnb.ddb.de/.

Cover design by Lisa Barfield

The paper in this book meets the guidelines for permanence and durability
of the Committee on Production Guidelines for Book Longevity
of the Council of Library Resources.

Printed in the United States of America

Contents

Preface

A *Dictionary of Film Terms* consists primarily of alphabetically arranged definitions of the techniques, concepts, genres, and styles that have evolved as a part of cinematic expression and analysis. The topical index lists groups of terms that relate to larger concepts of film art, such as editing, cinematography, composition, and lighting.

Together, these elements are intended to present in brief, accessible form a handbook on the methods of a unique, multifaceted, and constantly changing medium of dramatic and non-dramatic storytelling. The handbook offers, through definition, explanation, and, wherever possible, photographic illustration, the commonly used and the not-so-familiar terms which have been employed in describing the cinema in its many aspects.

In an attempt to provide a thorough overview of film aesthetics, *A Dictionary of Film Terms* includes definitions of concepts which are relevant to the historical development of the motion picture (for example, *actualité*, last-minute rescue) as well as those which are applicable to contemporary cinema (for example, animatronics, blue-green-screen process, "buddy" films, digital sound, gross-out film, mocumentary, structural film, etc.). Many film terms have both historical and contemporary value. When this is the case, I have noted the historical continuity by citing earlier as well as more recent films for which the concept or technique has relevance.

Technical terminology has been incorporated freely into the dictionary, but in each entry involving a technological concept, an effort has been made to expand the definition so that it encompasses and suggests the term's value as an aesthetic variant of motion-picture expression. The entry film "grain," for example, carries both a chemical and an aesthetic meaning. In an effort to keep the dictionary focused on film aesthetics, terms that might be considered primarily technical have been eliminated.

I have made an attempt to define each term in the dictionary so that it stands on its own. For easy referencing, however, a term which is used in defining a concept and which appears elsewhere in the dictionary as a separate definition is indicated by boldface type. Other relevant terms, to which the reader might want to refer, are listed at the end of definitions.

No dictionary of film terms can ever be complete or perfect. Yet, it has been my goal to provide one that the filmgoer will find illuminating in the range and clarity of its entries.

A number of people have helped me in this effort, especially Dan Madaj, Damon Zucca, and Lisa Dillon. To these individuals I owe gratitude and thanks.

Frank E. Beaver

Acknowledgments

The photographic stills in this book appear courtesy of the Museum of Modern Art Stills Library and the University of Michigan Photographic Services Library. I would like to thank Columbia Pictures, MGM, Paramount, Warner Bros., RKO, Twentieth Century-Fox, United Artists, and Univeral Studios for their cooperation in making stills available for this dictionary.

A

Absolute film   Another term used to define **abstract**, non-representational expression in cinema which developed as part of the **avant-garde**, **experimental** film movement in Europe in the 1920s. Form in the absolute film is derived from graphic and rhythmic emphases rather than from any narrative or logical ordering of the images.

Abstract film   A type of film which expresses, through its rhythms and visual design, intentions that are essentially non-narrative (photo 1). Abstraction emphasizes form over content. In an abstract film that employs recognizable objects, the images are used not to suggest their usual meanings but for effects that are created by the film's editing, visual techniques, sound qualities, and rhythmic design, that is, form. The rhythmical and mechanical motion of common objects in Fernand Léger's *Ballet Mécanique* (1924) represents a type of abstract film. Many contemporary **animated films** where colors and shapes are the principal interest of the artist can also be described as abstract in quality. The animated **computer films** of John and James Whitney, for example, represent a type of abstract film: *Permutations* (1968), *Lapis* (1963–66). These films consist of abstract configurations that

[ABSTRACT FILM] 1. Francis Thompson's abstract study of a large-city environment, *N.Y., N.Y.* (1957), was realized through the extensive use of prisms and distorting lenses.

are computer-generated. The images are enhanced by optical techniques such as **filter** coloring and **dissolves** to give the works a feeling of totally free, non-associative form. Stan Brakhage in *Mothlight* (1963) created an abstract design in motion by attaching moth wings to mylar tape and then printing the images on film without an accompanying soundtrack. See **Experimental film, Avant-garde.**

Academic editing (see **Invisible cutting**)

Accelerated montage (see **Montage**)

Acting (for film)   The film actor has been defined in many ways: as a nonactor, as a mannequin, as a "maker of faces." These descriptive labels result in part from the mosaic, edited nature of film construction. A film performance, like a film scene, is often "built" rather than shot. It has also been said that the screen actor is more dependent on physical characteristics than the stage actor and that physique and facial features often determine the kinds of roles a film actor plays throughout an entire career.

Because of the possibility for candid, natural acting and because the screen performance does not always demand refined theatrical skills, the film actor has often been described by theorists as an individual whose art is that of effective behaving. "Behaving" in motion-picture acting implies concessions to the piecemeal process of filmmaking. Unlike the stage actor, who enjoys the benefit of a continuous performance, the film actor must usually develop a character in bits and pieces and usually out of story-line sequence. The **director** guides the actors from scene to scene, often giving them on the spot the emotions and actions required in a given situation. Rehearsal time is often kept to a minimum because of both the shooting process and the economics of filmmaking.

A popular theory is that the best film performance is behavioristic—one in which the actor is completely without the airs and self-sufficient qualities of the trained artist. The film actor, some critics argue, must not appear to be acting at all. This claim is based on the assumption that the motion picture is a medium committed to realism. Many directors have, in fact, favored untrained actors, as in the case of Italian **neorealist** films. Film actors of long standing, however, contend that the successful screen performer utilizes skills equal to those of the theatrical performer.

The degree to which an actor is allowed to reflect on characterization and to make the effort to reveal subtleties of character varies from director to director. Michelangelo Antonioni has said: "The film actor ought not to understand, he ought to be." Federico Fellini has told his film actors, "Be yourselves and don't worry. The result is always positive."

Other directors (for example, D.W. Griffith, George Cukor, Arthur Penn, Mike Nichols) have sought closer collaboration with the film actor in developing a character for the screen.

At least four facets of a screen actor's performance can be critically evaluated: (1) The physical dynamics of the character; (2) The inner spirit of the character; (3) The cinematic control of the character; (4) The truth of the character.

A screen performance is physically dynamic when the actor's movements, physique, facial features, and personality traits attract and hold the attention. The inner spirit of the character is the quality of the performance in revealing subtle emotions and character shadings. The truth of the character refers to the success of the actor in revealing a character who seems dramatically believable. Cinematic control of the character refers to a proper use of the medium, the ability of the actor to create a character without overplaying or underplaying. The screen performance in varying degrees demands vocal, facial, and physical restraint because of the more intimate and realistic nature of the film medium. The large size of the motion-picture screen itself creates a demand for actor restraint. See **Method actor, Character.**

Actualité

A term which refers to a **documentary**-like film. Historically, *actualités* are associated with the early work of the Lumière brothers in France. Films of workers leaving a factory, a train arriving at a station, and a mother feeding her child presented "actual" views of the world. Unlike the work of Robert Flaherty (*Nanook of the North*, 1922), the Lumière films were often uninterrupted recordings of events in motion. Flaherty frequently staged or restaged scenes in creating his environmental studies. The motion-picture camera, placed at a single recording position, was the exclusive agent in the Lumière views of everyday life, omitting the expressive role of editing. These short actualités are viewed as the beginning of the documentary impulse in filmmaking and the recognition of the motion-picture camera's penchant for realism.

Contemporary independent filmmakers often return to the concept of the *actualité* in examining subject matter. Andy Warhol's *Sleep* (1963) and *Empire* (1964) can be described as extended *actualités*. In these films Warhol simply photographs a sleeping man in one case and the Empire State Building in another, allowing his camera to run for lengthy periods of time from a single, unvaried **angle of view**. These uninterrupted views of actuality in which the independent filmmaker's involvement is minimal have led to the label **"minimal cinema"** or "minimal film."

Adaptation

A screenplay which has been adapted from another source, such as a play, novel, short story, or biography, and rewritten for the screen. Best-selling novels have been a major source for film adaptations, mainly because of the commercial appeal of an already-popular book title.

Screen adaptations from novels and plays have generated a considerable amount of theoretical discussion about similarities and differences in the storytelling media. Many of the discussions of adaptations center on the differences between the visual nature of film versus the novel's opportunities for expression through descriptive prose and the literary trope (metaphors and similes). To film theorists such as Siegfried Kracauer and George Bluestone, an adaptation of a book for the screen implies the need to translate literary images into visual images. The adaptation is, they say, necessarily different from the original if it is to be an effective screen story. Although film writers will often include forceful dialogue in the script, many of the essential elements of characterization and plot in a film emerge through non-verbal communication: costumes, makeup, physique, and action.

The screenwriter is also usually committed to an economy of expression in adapting stories from another medium. The film story is bound by a time constriction that traditionally has resulted in films of approximately two hours or less in length. What may be richness of detail in a novel can become distracting in a motion picture. The screenwriter usually aims for a swift, economical development of character and plot. Often secondary characters and subplots from a novel are used minimally in a film because they clutter and interrupt the steady development of dramatic crises that are essential to the success of a motion picture. For this same reason screenwriters in adapting a novel will most often select the active parts of the plot and ignore elements that do not directly relate to it. A memorable minor character in a book may be only a background **extra** in a film, and an idea that an author may develop poetically and metaphorically in a novel may be reduced to a passing line of dialogue or an image on the screen.

Theorists do not suggest that either the novel or the motion picture is a more desirable medium than the other. Outstanding screen adaptations can be significantly different from the parental novel and yet be equal to the novel in quality. What The African Queen (1951), a popular descriptive novel, lost in adaptation it gained in the unforgettable performances of Humphrey Bogart and Katherine Hepburn. In adapting The Godfather (1972), screenwriters Mario Puzo and Francis Ford Coppola were able to present a romantic pageant that rivaled the best that the epic screen had ever achieved despite deletions and concessions to action rather than character. Ideas taken from the novel and brought to imagistic life on the screen revealed the heart of Puzo's book, if not its full substance.

Particularly successful in adapting literary works to the screen, Ruth Prawer Jhabvala demonstrated in *The Europeans* (1979), *A Room with a View* (1985), and *Howard's End* (1992) the degree to which an adaptation can retain richly nuanced character details and subtleties of human interaction. These films, directed by James Ivory, were stylish period pieces that focused on the manners and mores of characters defined originally in novels by Henry James (*The Europeans*) and E.M. Forster (*A Room with a View, Howard's End*). Other highly regarded novel-into-film adaptations include *The Hours* (2002) and *House of Sand and Fog* (2003).

Advance   (see **Sound Advance**)

Aerial shot   A shot taken from an airplane or a helicopter, intended to provide views of sky action or expansive, bird's-eye views of a scene below. Aerial shots are often used liberally in treating fast-paced, action stories, for instance the James Bond films. Beautiful aerial shots of African desert terrain, abstract in quality, were included in *The English Patient* (1996). Digitalized virtual-reality enhancement resulted in spectacular aerial shots of Manhattan in the 2004 sequel, *Spider-Man 2*.

Aleatory film (technique) A motion picture in which content is developed entirely or in part through chance conditions rather than through preconceptions of idea and form. The use of aleatory techniques in the filming of an event means that the filmmaker has trusted that the event and the techniques used will reveal meaning despite the uncertainties involved.

The term "aleatory" is from the Latin word *aleator*, meaning "gambler," thus suggesting the risks involved in use of the approach in a filmmaking situation. Aleatory techniques are used commonly by **cinema verité** and **direct cinema** documentarists and by fiction filmmakers who have employed improvisation in the direction of a film narrative, for example, Robert Altman in *A Wedding* (1978).

Another form of the aleatory effect involves an unrehearsed incident which occurs during filming and which is retained as a part of the film's spontaneity. One such incident occurs in *The Great Train Robbery* (1903) when one of the robbers crossing a small stream by rock, slips and falls into the water. In Robert Altman's *Three Women* (1977)

Shelley Duvall was filmed entering an automobile and driving away. In taking the shot Duvall's skirt caught in the car door and was visible dragging the pavement as she drove away. The humor of the spontaneous incident resulted in a decision to repeat it in subsequent automobile scenes. The running gag appropriately fit the quirky character developed by Duvall for the film.

One of the screen's most-noted aleatory moments occurs in *On the Waterfront* (1954), when Marlon Brando, shy and awkward with the woman he loves (Eva Marie Saint), slips onto his hand one of Saint's gloves.

Alienation Effect (see **Ambiguity**)

Allegory A type of story, film, or play in which the objects, characters, and plot represent a larger idea than that contained in the narrative itself. An allegory is an extended narrative **metaphor** achieved by the dual representation of characters, events, or objects. The character (objects) and events are intended to represent both themselves and abstract ideas which lead to a greater thematic significance. The western film *High Noon* (1952) was written so that the marshal (Gary Cooper) might be seen as a personification of individual courage in times of public threats. *High Noon* was intended to evoke an inspirational response to issues surrounding the freedom-threatening activities of McCarthyism during the late 1940s and early 1950s.

Many critics in interpreting the theme of *The Godfather, Part II* (1974) saw the evolution by Michael (Al Pacino) into a "don" who is totally without scruples or patriarchal feelings as having allegorical implications for cut-throat business practice in 20th-century corporate America. Roman Polanski's short non-dialogue film *Two Men and a Wardrobe* (1962) offers a powerful, ironic allegory about discrimination. The allegory evolves through two men who emerge from the sea with a large wardrobe, and are rejected along their journey through "life." Others, possessing a variety of other kinds of objects, are deemed acceptable within the society through which the two men and their wardrobe pass before returning to the sea.

Ambient light Light within the mise-en-scène that appears to originate from natural sources, like windows, lamps, the sun, etc.

Ambient sound Natural background sound which is considered an essential element of the **sound track**. During portions of a film containing no dialogue or music a sound track without ambient sound or a technologically supplied background tone will appear artificially "dead." Sound engineers provide ambient sound in a variety of ways, including background sounds (birds chirping, street noises, wind, etc.) or with "room sound" where a recording is made simply with a "live" microphone placed in an empty room. When mixed with the dialogue track, open-mike ambient room sound—as with other background sounds—prevents any dead spots from occurring on the sound track. Ambient sound also serves the aesthetic function of creating an environmental presence that is complementary to sound effects and character dialogue.

In rare instances ambient sound is removed altogether for narrative effect. In Tony Richardson's *The Loneliness of the Long Distance Runner* (1962) a brief funeral-day scene is accompanied by a perfectly "dead" sound track, startling in its sudden and complete silence.

Similarly, in *All That Jazz* (1979) the sound track goes "dead" during a table-rehearsal scene in which the choreographer (Roy Scheider) experiences a heart attack.

Ambiguity   An approach in theater and film where the meaning of dramatic and character action is intentionally unclear. Inspiration for this approach can be attributed in part to the work of the playwright Luigi Pirandello (*Six Characters in Search of an Author*, 1921). Film directors such as Jean-Luc Godard and François Truffaut have presented screen characters who, in a Pirandellian manner, are searching for personal identity; by making the characters conscious of the medium (theater or film) in which their search is being conducted, an ambiguous theatrical response is effected. Self-conscious awareness of both the "search" and the dramatic medium of expression produces in the audience an uncertainty as to what is real and what is dramatic. Fiction and reality are subtly combined. The philosophy behind such films is that the director must have the right of personal expression and be free to raise questions about life and illusion (art) without necessarily providing answers. In many ways this philosophy grows from both an awareness of cinema's possibilities as well as a rejection of the well-made film of explicit meaning. Haskell Wexler's *Medium Cool* (1969) tackles the thematic question of illusion and reality in the motion picture (dramatic and journalistic) through a story that is highly ambiguous in its narrative form and in its resolution. *The Stunt Man* (1980) was another screen exercise about the ambiguous nature of illusion and reality in the filmmaking process (photo 2). In *The French Lieutenant's Woman* (1981), a film directed by Karel Reisz with a screenplay by Harold Pinter, dramatic ambiguity is achieved through the retelling of a Victorian affair between a gentleman and a promiscuous woman, intercut with a contemporary affair occurring between the actor and actress who are portraying the Victorian couple in a movie.

[AMBIGUITY] 2. Peter O'Toole portrays Eli Cross, a motion-picture director, who is making a film about World War I in *The Stunt Man* (1980). When a young fugitive is hired as a stunt man, he becomes caught up in a game of confusion—deviously carried out.

There is often a political motive behind dramatic approaches that are intentionally ambiguous, particularly with filmmakers like Godard and Wexler. In works by these directors (*Le Gai Savoir*, 1968; *Medium Cool*, 1969), viewers are made aware of the illusory nature of the medium, rather than seduced by it, and thus are thought to be more intellectually alert to the message. See **Reflexive cinema**.

American montage (see **Montage**)

American studio years The period in American filmmaking, roughly between 1925 and 1960, when the studio system dominated production and exhibition. Film production was highly departmentalized, with each stage of the filmmaking process treated in an assembly-line manner. Producers within the studio's units oversaw all aspects of film production—writing, directing, editing, and the release of finished product—and sometimes assumed authoritarian positions within the studio system.

The studio system was geared to the production of motion pictures designed to appeal to mass audiences. It was an era characterized by well-made pictures whose technical quality enhanced their sentiment and romantic appeal. Narrative **conventions** and formulae were repeated from one picture to the next as the studios turned out popular film types: musicals, gangster films, westerns, series films, romances, comedies. Imitation of successful pictures in each genre was standard studio procedure. Production heads argued on the industry's behalf and in support of the studio system by stressing the role of motion pictures in providing diversion and escape for the American people. In addition to this escapist approach, a code of values was employed in the treatment of subject matter that tended to support the American work ethic and right over wrong.

After 1946, a peak year in motion-picture attendance, there began a steady decline in box office grosses and major alterations occurred in the old studio system. The reasons for the changes were varied: (1) World War II was over, tensions abated, and many people who sought emotional release through films during the war ceased to attend them. (2) The period after the war was a time when many Americans moved to the suburbs, away from the metropolitan and neighborhood movie houses. (3) Other diversions began to compete for the budgeted entertainment dollar: racetracks, night baseball, bowling alleys, more extensive travel. (4)

Installment buying became a widely available merchandising practice, thus stimulating more spending on home products. (5) By 1948 television was having a significant impact as an entertainment medium. (6) In 1948, in an antimonopoly move, the United States Supreme Court ruled that the production studios must divest themselves of their theater chains, thus depriving the studios of guaranteed outlets for their releases. The result was a curtailment of **B-picture** production and the dismissal of numerous studio employees, including contract players.

Following these events, the studio system changed dramatically. Independent production increased throughout the 1950s and 1960s, eventually leading the studios out of self-initiated feature-film production and into new roles as administrative overseers for independently produced projects. All production arrangements would be handled by the outside producer, who would then seek investment money from the studios, rent studio space, and negotiate for the studio to handle promotion and distribution of the finished product. This set of operating procedures was common by 1980. See **Studio picture**.

Anamorphic lens An optical lens which allows a scene of considerable width to be photographed onto a standard-sized **frame** area. By using a similar lens on the projector, the narrowed image is increased to an aspect ratio of 2.35:1, or a scene that is more than twice as wide as it is high. The standard aspect ratio for 8-mm, 16-mm, and 35-mm film is 1:33:1. The anamorphic, wide-screen process was introduced commercially by Twentieth Century Fox with *The Robe* in 1953 (photo 3). The device itself was invented by Henri Chrétien in 1927. See **CinemaScope**.

Angle The positioning of a motion-picture camera so as to view a given scene. A camera may be placed straight on to a scene; or it may be placed at a side angle, **high angle**, or **low angle**. Many of the early cinematographers failed to recognize the aesthetic values of camera angles. The tendency was to place the camera in a single straight-on, wide-angle view of a scene. This was particularly true for filming of action on sets. Early sets tended to be theatrical and flat, and, therefore, were limited in the dimensionality that would have allowed angle shooting. To "angle" the camera in the early years of filmmaking meant to risk overshooting the sets.

[ANAMORPHIC LENS] 3. The squeezed-together images in an anamorphic frame from *The Robe* (1953).

The angle of a shot is regarded to have both compositional and psychological values. It also aids in diminishing the "flatness" or two-dimensionality of a scene by placing scenic elements into an oblique relationship to one another. By so doing, the angle provides a varied perspective of the scene. See **Angle of view, Dutch angle**.

Angle of view A photographic term which refers to the scope of a shot as determined by choice of **lens** and camera distance from subject. The angle of view ranges from a wide angle of view (**long shot**) to a narrow angle of view (**close-up**).

Animated film Most commonly a film type in which individual drawings (cels) have been photographed frame by frame. Usually each frame differs slightly from the one that has preceded it, thus giving the illusion of movement when the frames are projected in rapid succession (24 **frames per second**).

"**Pixilation**" is the term used to describe the frame-by-frame animation of objects and human beings as distinguished from the animation of hand-drawn images.

The short animated film has been widely used for curtain raisers and filler material for feature-length live-action pictures. Full-length, animated films, particularly those of Walt Disney (*Pinocchio*, 1940; *Cinderella*, 1950; *Beauty and the Beast*, 1991; *Aladdin*, 1992; *Brother Bear* 2003 *Chicken Little* 2005); and Ralph Bakshi (*Fritz the Cat*, 1972; *Wizards*, 1977), have enjoyed enormous popularity with the film-going public. A violent, Japanese-made animation feature, *Akira* (1988), told a futuristic science-fiction tale in a technologically superior manner, gaining cult-status in the VHS home-video market. In the 21st century, the feature animated film has continued to generate huge audiences, for example, *Chicken Run* (2000), *Shrek* (2001), and *Shrek II* (2004).

Increasingly, many serious artists have used the genre for distinct artistic, social, and information potential. These artists see the animated film as a medium being closer to the graphic and plastic arts than to live-action films. Their films exhibit the expressive possibilities of line and composition available to the graphic artist. Some film theorists, noting these efforts, have maintained that animated films are most aesthetically pleasing when the animator is "graphic" rather than "photographic." The Zagreb School of Animation in Zagreb, Yugoslavia, became a major producer after 1950 of animated films that were principally abstract and graphic in design.

Short animated films have been produced in many different artistic media, among them: clay animation (*Closed Mondays*, 1976); puppet/model animation (*The Hand*, 1965; computer animation (*Permutations*, 1968); kinestatic collage (*Frank Film*, 1975); and pixilation (*Neighbors*, 1952). See **Animation school of violence, Kinestasis**.

Animation school of violence A term applied to animated cartoons which use slapstick, and sometimes extreme violence, as a major comedic element. These cartoons are typified by the work of Tex Avery, a Hollywood animator for Walter Lantz, Warner Brothers, and M-G-M in the 1930s, 1940s, and 1950s. Avery, who created Bugs Bunny, Chilly Willy, and Lucky Ducky, among other characters, employed a bizarre approach in his cartoon gags. A character would often receive a blow on the head, crack into a pile of jigsaw-like pieces, and then reshape itself on the screen. Avery was also intrigued by the cartoon's ability to present grotesque changes in character size and shape. These violent, bizarre approaches led critics to describe Avery as an anarchic film-maker—"a Walt Disney who has read Kafka."

Animatronics   The mechanized, remote-controlled manipulation of model figures or puppets to produce lifelike action. Electric motors, cables, rods, and hydraulic systems are among those devices employed to activate animatronic puppets. The queen in *Alien Resurrection* (1997) was an animatronic puppet, as was the queen's child. Animatronics have been used extensively in science-fiction films, in screen fantasies, and in animal-populated thrillers such as *Jurassic Park* (1993). In the creation and control of the T-rex dinosaur in *Jurassic Park*, Spielberg's film displayed major advancements in the use of animatronic models.

Anime   The term for Japanese animation in all its diverse thematic and stylistic manifestations. Anime are strikingly different from Western cartoon styles because of their attentive allegiance to Japanese cultural traditions and mores. The display of anime outside Japan in recent years has been explosive, in television broadcasts, in festivals, in film theaters, and on the internet. *Pokemon* (1997), hugely popular and commercially successful abroad, helped direct attention to anime. Aesthetically, anime are often characterized by striking comic book imagery and choreographed action. Professional and amateur artists have been attracted to the movement. Anime content ranges from children's fare to intense action thrillers to sci-fi to hard-core pornography to social drama.

Antagonist   That individual or force which opposes the hero (**protagonist**) of a motion picture or a play and imbues the work with dramatic conflict. The antagonist may be another character (Darth Vader in *Star Wars*, 1977) or a more abstract force such as the raw elements of nature in *Nanook of the North* (1922).

Anthology film   A term used to designate a theme film constructed around a variety of existing sources. Various materials are brought together to explore a topic such as the "Who-Dunnit?" detective film genre which is the title of an anthology film in the *Best of British Cinema* (1989) series. An anthology tribute to the M-G-M musical formed the documentaries *That's Entertainment, Part I* (1974) and *That's Entertainment, Part II* (1976). The latter anthology film expanded the M-G-M focus to include excerpts from outstanding comedy and drama films produced at the Hollywood studio. *Celluloid Closet* (1995) combined film clips and interviews in a thematic study of homosexuality in Hollywood movies.

Anticlimax   A concluding moment in a motion picture's dramatic development which fails to satisfy audience expectations. The final plotting mechanism which is used to resolve the film's conflict, for example, may be too trivial, implausible, or uninteresting to be dramatically pleasing. Something more important or more serious was expected at this point in the motion picture. This undesired effect is referred to as an "anticlimax." In mystery and detective films an anticlimax may be an intentional plotting device to place the viewer off guard.

Antihero   A character in a film, play, or novel who is a sympathetic figure but who is presented as a non-heroic individual—often apathetic, angry, and indifferent to social, political, and moral concerns. In film the antihero, as typified by James Dean in the 1955 film *Rebel without a Cause*, and Jack Nicholson in *Five Easy Pieces* (1970), is presented as a tough and resentful character externally, but one who is highly sensitive inwardly. He is motivated by a need for personal truth and justice and struggles to rise from an underdog position to one of control over his own situation.

In screen comedy the antihero usually takes the form of the little man bucking the system, its pettiness and adherence to false, shallow values. Charlie Chaplin, an early antihero type, has been followed in more recent times by the likes of Dustin Hoffman in *The Graduate* (1967) and Woody Allen in *Bananas* (1971) and *Play It Again, Sam* (1972). Charlie Chaplin's antihero persona is the well-intentioned and innocent, yet insecure, bumbler who is aspiring to social stature but who fails constantly. He remains on the edges of society but is content and reasonably happy, and, in being so, is victorious.

In **gangster films** lawless figures for whom sympathy is evoked are also frequently referred to as antiheroes, for example, the main characters in *The Public Enemy* (1931), *Scarface* (1932), *Bonnie and Clyde* (1967), and *Butch*

Cassidy and the Sundance Kid (1969).

Robert De Niro has appeared as a volatile, neurotic antihero in such films as *Taxi Driver* (1976) and *The King of Comedy* (1983). In these films De Niro portrays a societal "loser" seeking a moment of recognition. The British actor Ewan McGregor has portrayed antiheroic characters in *Trainspotting* (1996) and *Young Adam* (2003). Colin Farrell was an antihero figure in the Irish film *Intermission* (2003).

Aperture (lens)   The diaphragmatic opening of a given **lens**. A motion-picture lens can be "opened up" or "stopped down" to regulate the amount of light which passes to the sensitized film surface. A large aperture (open), necessary in adverse lighting situations, permits more light to reach the film; a small aperture (stopped down), necessary when available light is more than adequate for a proper **exposure**, allows less light to pass to the film **emulsion**.

The size of the aperture opening has certain aesthetic implications in photographing a scene. A large aperture opening decreases the **depth of field** in a shot and can cause the blurring of images in parts of the picture. By regulating the aperture opening so that some images in a shot are in sharp focus and others are blurred (**soft focus**), compositional emphasis can be placed on desired elements in a scene. Conversely, a small aperture can increase depth of field and can be employed to keep all elements in a framed shot in sharp focus.

A-picture   A term originating in the 1930s, used to denote the higher-quality film on a double-feature bill. The A-picture was usually made with popular stars and with careful attention to **production values**. Its counterpart, a lower-budget effort, was referred to as the **B-picture.**

Archetype   A literary term, inspired by psychologist Carl Jung, which refers to that element in film, drama, myth, literature, or religion which evokes in the viewer or reader a strong sense of primitive experience. Any image or arrangement of images which activates such primordial responses to literary and dramatic subject matter is referred to as the archetype. Archetypal criticism is the study of those patterns and images in mythic, literary, and dramatic expression which, through repetition, can be recognized as elements which produce an awareness of common, universal conditions of human existence. John Ford's *Stagecoach* (1939), for example, can be studied for its archetypal structure as a mythic journey through "the heart of darkness" to light, with the experience bringing to the vehicle's occupants spiritual cleansing and new knowledge of the conditions for survival through human interaction. The mythic, revealing journey as a dramatic framework is as old as storytelling itself, and its use by Ford in *Stagecoach* or Francis Ford Coppola in *Apocalypse Now* (1979) becomes archetypal. *Apocalypse Now* took much of its narrative inspiration from Joseph Conrad's novel *The Heart of Darkness*—with Coppola redesigning Conrad's tale of an Englishman's journey through Africa to fit an American's journey through war-stricken Vietnam. New knowledge of what so-called civilization is capable was the ultimate intention in the journey-to-awareness archetype employed by Conrad and Coppola. The Coen Brothers' comedy *O Brother, Where Art Thou?* (2000) cleverly updated the mythic journey of Homer's *Odyssey*. Archetype is also a term used to indicate a prototypical literary or dramatic character of recognizable human traits, for example, the character who is torn between feelings of passion and those of duty and responsibility. Jane Eyre of Charlotte Brontë's novel and the screen versions made of it exemplify this character archetype who must reside within conflicting psychological worlds.

Arc shot A moving camera shot in which the camera moves in a circular or semicircular pattern in relation to the object or character being photographed rather than moving in a parallel line. The arc shot provides a varied perspective of the photographed scene by partially or totally circling characters or objects, for example, the filming of the principal characters in a picnic scene in the adult thriller, *Consenting Adults* (1993, photo 4). Circular arc shots were used by Claude Lelouch to intensify the emotion at the end of *A Man and a Woman* (1966) as two lovers are reunited in a long embrace in a train station. Brian De Palma heightened the romantic dance sequence in *Carrie* (1976) with arc shots. The agony of a young woman (Jennifer Connelly) in *House of Sand and Fog* (2003) over ownership of her home is intensified with a dynamic arc shot as she stands at the end of a pier on the California coast. See **Trucking shot**.

Armature The skeletal frame used to build model figures or puppets for animatronic and stop-action filming.

[ARC SHOT] 4. The camera "arcs" in a circular movement around the principal characters in Alan J. Pakula's suspense thriller, *Consenting Adults* (1993), a Hollywood Pictures Company production.

Art director The individual responsible for the set design of a motion picture. The art director works to create settings that are com-
patible with other production elements, like costumes and
furnishings, so that a desired visual style is projected for the
film. The achievements of the art director are often more
readily apparent in the **studio picture** than in a **location
picture**, although the art director's work may be equally
important in the latter type of film where certain interior
work must be matched to exterior scenes. The art director
is sometimes credited as the production designer.

Art theater film A term frequently used in the 1950s and early 1960s to
describe a motion-picture theater which exhibited films that
were for the most part outside the commercial mainstream.
Art theaters exhibited works that were considered important
to the state of film expression regardless of their popular
appeal: films by foreign directors, by **independent filmmakers**, and works not released nationally. Art theaters
also frequently presented programs that included film classics.

During the 1970s the term "art theater" was also often
used by exhibitors who showed, exclusively, pornographic

motion pictures. The adoption of this term by such exhibitors was a promotion gesture that was intended to call attention to specialized subject matter and to suggest serious purpose behind the showing of admittedly candid and controversial films. The "art theater" label implied that films being exhibited there had artistic merit, a criterion which the Supreme Court used in determining whether a motion picture possessed "redeeming social value."

ASA rating (see **Film speed**)

Aspect ratio A term for the comparative relationship of width to height in a projected motion-picture or television image. The standard aspect ratio for a 35-mm film is 1:33:1, or an image that has a width-height relationship of 4 to 3. The standard aspect ratio for 70-mm films is 2:2:1. The **anamorphic** process can produce an aspect ratio of 2.35:1, a projected image which is almost 2 1/2 times wider than it is high. See **Cinemascope**, **Cinerama**.

Asynchronous sound A term for film sound which has not been synchronized with the screen image.

Asynchronous sound also includes aesthetic use of sound for expressive purposes. Because of the composite nature of film art, the element of sound (**music, dialogue, sound effects**) is highly manipulative. The sounds of a clucking chicken can be juxtaposed with a shot of a ranting politician for satirical effect.

A popular variation of asynchronous sound in contemporary filmmaking has been in the use of **sound advances** in the editing of scenes. An asynchronous sound advance can occur when the film editor shows the face of a character screaming in horror, and instead of using the natural sound of the character's horrified voice, inserts the piercing, shrill siren of a police car, to be seen in the following scene.

The device of the sound advance combines asynchronous and **synchronous sound** in a uniquely cinematic way.

Francis Ford Coppola made extensive use of combined synchronous-asynchronous sound in the baptism scene of *The Godfather* (1972). Near the end of the film, shots of a solemn religious ceremony are juxtaposed with scenes of a vendetta occurring simultaneously in various parts of the city. The sounds of the grand church music and priestly intonations of the baptismal rite continue uninterrupted as the gunmen carry out their tasks. Through the use of synchronous-asynchronous sound, and visual **crosscutting**, an ironic, psychological linking of past, present, and future occurs.

Asynchronous sound can serve to create irony between sound and image, to satirize and parody dramatic situations, and to link separate moments of time in expressive ways.

Atmospheric quality A term applied to a motion picture with a special visual appeal that is derived from the dramatic use of natural elements: light, weather conditions, heat, landscape, environment. In Carol Reed's *Odd Man Out* (1947) a correlation is made between changing weather conditions (from fair sky to

[ATMOSPHERIC QUALITY] 5. The constant suggestion of heat and fire imbues Lawrence Kasdan's *Body Heat* (1981) with strong atmospheric qualities which underscore the film's torrid love story.

rain to snow) and mood changes as the protagonist, a doomed fugitive (James Mason) struggles over a day's time to reach friends and relatives before he dies. Dry weather conditions and heat added atmospheric quality to Roman Polanski's *Chinatown* (1974). Fire and heat supplied both atmospheric and symbolic quality to Lawrence Kasdan's 1981 film *Body Heat* (photo 5). *House of Sand and Fog* (2003), set in a coastal location, drew its aura of mystery from atmospheric qualities underscored by compelling music. Expressionistic light and shadow provided such atmospheric quality to a type of detective-mystery film of the 1940s that it was given its own visual label: ***film noir***, or literally "black film." See **Visual effects**.

Auteur (criticism) A critical-theoretical term which comes from the French, meaning "author." As a theoretical concept the term "auteur" has been used to describe motion-picture **directors** whose works were said to have been produced with personal vision. Hence, an auteur is a director who "authors" a film by a driving personality and individual artistic control of the filmmaking process.

The auteur theory denies to some extent the idea that film **criticism** must examine the cinema as a collective art form and view each picture as the end result of a team of artists and technicians. While this is true in many cases, the auteur critics in expounding their theory claimed that many major directors have carried with them from film to film individualized self-expression. As with an author, the filmmaker of vision incorporates into individual pictures a view of life through individual style. Therefore, the auteur critics judge motion-picture art by examining both the filmmaker (director) and the works that the director has produced. A single film by a major director does not stand alone, but is viewed in relation to all the films by that director. The auteur critics claim that this critical procedure allows for the serious examination of lesser works by a given director that might have been previously overlooked.

The auteur theory was first discussed by François Truffaut in an article, "Une certaine tendance du cinéma français," written in 1954 for the French film magazine *Cahiers du Cinéma*. Andrew Sarris, an American critic for *The Village Voice*, is given credit for bringing Truffaut's ideas on auteur criticism to the United States. The French critics, as well as Sarris and other subscribers to the auteur concept, developed lists of directors who were considered to have achieved auteur status. Among those directors: Alfred Hitchcock, Raoul Walsh, John Ford, Max Ophuls, Joseph Losey, Howard Hawks, and many others.

The major opposition to the auteur theory came from critics who pointed out that this procedure of criticism made certain motion pictures acceptable when they were clearly poor films; others have argued that the approach tended toward hero worship and led to a priori judgments.

At the same time, the auteur theory has served a number of useful functions in film criticism: (1) it provided a method for looking at film technique and style rather than content alone; (2) it stimulated, as a result of its controversial nature, provocative discussion of the motion picture as a serious art form; (3) it brought recognition to directors such as Alfred Hitchcock and John Ford who had previously been overlooked by the critics as serious artists; (4) it reestablished the importance of the director in film art and criticism.

Available light Light which comes from existing sources such as daylight or room lighting, and which is used as total or partial illumination in the filming of a motion picture. The term "available lighting" differentiates it from lighting that is supplied by studio lights or transportable lighting instruments that are specifically designed for professional use in location shooting. When available lighting is the only type of illumination for a film scene, and when it is in no way manipulated for special effect, the images can carry a strong realistic quality. See **Ambient light**.

Avant-garde A term used to describe the first **experimental film** movement which began in Europe about 1920. "Avant-garde" is often applied in contemporary criticism to any film that employs new, original techniques and experimental approaches in expressing ideas on film. The first avant-garde filmmakers produced two general types of films: those which employed techniques commonly associated with the **Dada** and **surrealist** movements in literature and art, and those which were non-narrative and **abstract** in quality.

The impetus behind the first film avant-garde movement grew out of a revolt against cinema realism. The filmmakers embraced surrealism because of its "belief in the higher reality of certain hitherto neglected forms of association, in the omnipotence of the dream, in the disinterested play of thought," as stated by surrealism's principal spokesman, André Breton. The surrealist movement also provided filmmakers with opportunities for parody of painting, sex, psychology, contemporary politics, and the motion picture itself. The surrealists seized upon and photographed a variety of material phenomena and arranged these "word pictures" in disparate, illogical ways to effect subjective, dreamlike meanings. They did not want their images to have a mimetic life, but a spiritual life—to become images sprung free of a material existence. Man Ray's films *Emak Bakia* (1927) and *L'Etoile de Mer* (1928) and Luis Buñuel-Salvador Dali's *Un Chien Andalou* (1928) are representative of these surrealist impulses.

Surrealism by no means dominated the film avant-garde, either in practice or in theory. Within the movement there was a group of filmmakers who were advocates of **cinéma pur**, "pure cinema": these artists wanted to return the medium to its elemental origins. At the center of this group was René Clair, who wrote in 1927: "Let us return to the birth of the cinema: 'The cinematograph,' says the dictionary, 'is a machine designed to project animated pictures on a screen.' The Art that comes from such an instrument must be an art of *vision* and *movement*."

The cinema purists—Clair, Viking Eggeling, Fernand Léger, Hans Richter, among others—were interested in the rhythm, movement, and cadence of objects and images within a film—the building of an internal energy through which vision and movement would become both the form and the pleasure of the film.

The film titles of the cinema purists suggest the musical-like emphasis on animated pictures: *Rhythmus 21, Ballet Mécanique, Symphony Diagonale, The March of the Machines, Berlin: The Symphony of a Great City.*

The pure-cinema interests were not limited to rhythmical abstractions alone, but also manifested themselves in the fiction film: in Jean Renoir's adaptation in 1926 of Emile Zola's *Nana*, a film where the original plot is incidental and where Renoir abstractly treats Zola's story; in Carl Dreyer's *The Passion of Joan of Arc* (1928), where the ordered use of extreme close-ups produces a spiritual response to the face; and in Jean Cocteau's *Blood of a Poet* (1930), a film made up almost entirely of visual transformations which take place in the mind of the poet. See **Futurism, Noncamera film**.

B

Background music Music which appears on the **sound track** as accompaniment to a film scene. Background music may be specially supplied accompaniment or it may appear to originate from a source within the scene, for example, an orchestra, a phonograph, or a radio. The latter type of background music is referred to by musical composers as **source music**. Film theorists often refer to source music as diegetic music. In feature films, background music is usually employed to reinforce mood or emphasize action. The amount of background music varies according to the filmmaker's intentions, often appearing liberally in screen **melodramas**, for example, and less noticeably in the works of realist directors.

Back Light   (See **Lighting: Actor light**)

Back Projection   (See **Rear screen projection**)

Backstage musical (See **Musical film**)

Back story   A term for the incorporation of new narrative details within a screenplay as the plot develops, and which enriches the plot and helps further define the characters. The introduction of new information—through dialogue, flashbacks, etc.—as the story progresses is a means by which a screenplay gains in texture and dimension and by which it sustains

audience interest. Back stories are integral to a complex
character-study film such as Stephen Daldry's *The Hours*
(2002), a film which seeks to connect the lives of three
women in three different time periods of the 20th century.

Balance (compositional) "Compositional balance" refers to the harmonious
arrangement of elements in an artistic frame (photo 6).
Balance in a motion-picture frame depends on a variety of
visual elements: placement of objects and figures, light,
color, line, and movement. The aesthetic purpose of frame
balance or imbalance is to direct attention and to evoke psychological responses from images appropriate to the dramatic tone of the film story. See **Composition**.

[BALANCE] 6. A compositionally balanced frame in *Crossfire* (1947). The stronger, dominant right side of the frame (because our eyes scan right) is balanced by having Robert
Young seated while Robert Ryan (on the left) stands. Ryan's height on the left brings balance to a shot which otherwise would be dominated by Young's position. Robert Mitchum's
placement between the other two characters at midlevel further balances the frame.

Biographical film (Biopic) A motion picture based on the life of a public figure, most commonly an individual struggling to achieve goals
against considerable odds (*Gandhi*, 1982) or to recover from
a major setback which threatens an already-successful career

(*Coal Miner's Daughter*, 1980), *Ray* (2004), *Walk the Line*, (2005). The biography film was a popular studio staple at Warner Brothers during the 1930s when the lives of famous people working on behalf of the public good were brought to the screen for their inspirational value, for example, *The Story of Louis Pasteur* (1936), *The Life of Emile Zola* (1937), and *Juarez* (1939). Sports figures have also been popular subjects for screen biographies (*The Babe Ruth Story*, 1948), as have been entertainment personalities (*Chaplin*, 1992). Common characteristics of the biography film are the heroic elements of determination and personal courage. *A Beautiful Mind* (2001) was a particularly complex and emotionally evocative biographical film about the life of mathematician/economic theorist John Forbes Nash, Jr. (Russell Crowe), a man who experiences devastating bouts of schizophrenia and eventually overcomes them. "Biopic" has been the colloquial term frequently used to designate this type of film genre.

Bird's-eye shot   (See **Aerial shot**, **High-angle shot**)

Bit part/Bit player An actor who appears very briefly in a film in a role that usually contains some lines of dialogue. Numerous well-known screen performers appear as bit players in Robert Altman's insider's-view-of-Hollywood satire *The Player* (1992). Bit player is a term distinguishable from that of "extra" or **cameo player**. An extra appears in a film as a non-speaking background figure; a cameo role involves an actor in a brief but important featured part.

Black-and-white film A film that is produced and released on an **emulsion** that renders images in shades of gray.

Almost all films prior to 1935 were produced on black-and-white stock, although it was a common practice to tint films for symbolic effect.

Directors, until the perfection of color emulsions, worked successfully with the aesthetic possibilities of black-and-white film. The use of light and dark images on the screen became a visual art. Black-and-white film stocks permitted considerable opportunities for expressionistic use of light and shadow. Psychological inferences could be made through artistic shadings of the gray scale, and creation of mood was possible through tonal renderings. The luminous images achieved by outstanding directors of the 1930s and 40s led to the use of the phrase "the silver screen." This term clearly and favorably suggested an awareness of the unique aesthetics of black-and-white films.

Although color has been the norm in filmmaking since the mid-1960s, black-and-white emulsions have remained popular with independent filmmakers (*Clerks*, 1994) and have occasionally been used by major feature directors such as Peter Bogdanovich in *The Last Picture Show* (1971) and *Paper Moon* (1973), Mel Brooks in *Young Frankenstein* (1974), Woody Allen in *Manhattan* (1979) and *Zelig* (1983), the Coen Brothers' *The Man Who Wasn't There* (2001), and George Clooney's *Good Night and Good Luck* (2005). A popular contemporary visual effect is one which combines color with black and white imagery, for instance, *Pleasantville* (1998).

Black comedy   A motion picture or a stage play which treats serious subject matter in humorous ways. The tone of the comedy is dark and pessimistic. In the late 1940s, the Ealing Studios in Great Britain began to make black comedies based on bizarre events often lifted from real-life incidents. One of the best known of the Ealing comedies, *Kind Hearts and Coronets* (1949), involved the efforts of a young gentleman (Alec Guinness) to gain the family fortune by murdering all his relatives. *Dr. Strangelove* (1963), a satire about the possibilities of nuclear war, *Catch 22* (1970), an absurd, satirical view of World War II, and *The End* (1978), a humorous character study of a terminally ill man (Burt Reynolds), are later examples of black comedy. In Lawrence Kasdan's *I Love You To Death* (1990) a woman (Tracey Ullman) attempts to murder her husband (Kevin Kline) after she learns he has been unfaithful. The comic efforts by Ullman to commit murder are developed to black proportions. Films by Scottish director Danny Boyle, for example *Shallow Grave* (1994) and *Trainspotting* (1996), have been characterized as black comedies, as was the Academy Award-winning *American Beauty* (1999). See **Comedy**.

Black film   A term used to describe films made about and by filmmakers who are African American, Indian, Pakistani, Caribbean, etc.

Blaxploitation film A commercial-minded film of the 1970s made to appeal specifically to the interests of black audiences. The design of such films drew heavily on the popularity of black actors in screen stories that were often highly sensational. Tough crime plots with a superhero figure (for instance, *Shaft*, 1971) were common ingredients. The enormous commercial success of *Shaft*, directed by black director Gordon Parks, generated many imitations that were made to capitalize on the drawing power of action films with black heroes. Other titles within the genre include *Melinda* (1972), *Superfly TNT* (1973), *Black Belt Jones* (1974), *Three the Hard Way* (1974), and *Coffey* (1974).

Blimp　A camera silencing device which prevents the sound of the camera motor and its gears from being picked up by the recording microphone. ***Cinema verité*** documentarists and feature-film directors who wish to deny illusory experiences will often leave the camera unblimped, employing the motor noise as a self-conscious element of the film's sound track.

Blocking　The arrangement of characters and objects within a film frame. Blocking is a significant element in photographic **composition** and dramatic expression. Blocking may be used to project a sense of depth into the flat, two-dimensional screen. The blocking of an object or character at the edge of the frame in the immediate foreground and the placement of additional characters or objects in midground and background create a sense of compositional depth within the film frame. In most instances of character blocking, where objective **points of view** are desired, the characters do not openly acknowledge the presence of the camera and are blocked in ways to make the viewer less aware that the camera has recorded the action. When shots are angled slightly, even in **close-ups**, the camera's presence is less noticeable because characters do not appear to be looking directly into the lens. For both aesthetic and objective recording purposes, actions are blocked so that close-up shots of actors are usually taken in three-quarter profile.

When a character does actually look directly into the camera lens, as if to "present" himself or herself or to "address" the camera, a form of **presentational blocking** occurs. While neither objective nor subjective as such, presentational blocking brings the character and the viewer into a dynamic relationship. The character seems to be reaching out to make the viewer a more active participant in the drama.

A form of presentational blocking which breaks the illusion of objectivity altogether takes place when a character actually acknowledges the presence of the audience through speech or gestures. In *Tom Jones* (1963), Albert Finney winks at the audience in "knowing" moments and shrugs his shoulders in times of defeat.

Bluescreen/greenscreen process The special-effects process in which a brightly lit blue or green screen is positioned behind the action as it is being filmed in order to produce traveling mattes that can optically combine background location scenery or digitalized imagery with the live-action footage. A brightly lit greenscreen will achieve the same effect as a bluescreen. Bluescreen/greenscreen processes can also be used to remove parts of human bodies. Gary Sinise's missing leg in *Forrest Gump* (1994) was achieved by covering the leg in bluecloth and filming against a bluescreen area of the set. This latter effect is openly demonstrated in *Stuck On You* (2003). To render Matt Damon invisible while his conjoined-at-the-waist twin brother (Greg Kinnear) acts in a television series, Damon is clothed in a blue bodysuit for filming against a bluescreen. See **Traveling Matte**.

Boom shot   (See **Crane shot**)

B-picture   A term describing a film which appeared on **double-feature** bills in the 1930s, 1940s, and 1950s. The B-picture was usually the second movie on a two-picture bill. It was characteristically different from the main picture (**A-picture**): lower budget, lesser-known stars, often employing reworked themes from familiar genres such as the **western, horror**, and **science-fiction** film. Production of B-pictures for theatrical release ceased in the late 1940s, although the characteristics of this type of film have continued in the form of made-for-television movies and low-budget independent films such as *The Blair Witch Project* (1999).

The term is sometimes used in contemporary film criticism in a derogatory manner to describe a low-budget film or a film of inferior quality. However, in recent years many film critics and historians have expressed an intense interest in the study of the B-picture category and its directors. They argue that this class of picture and its artists must be judged alongside the A-picture because of (1) the important role each type played in motion-picture and cultural history, (2) the economic system which produced the B-picture, and (3) the perspective the B-picture provides in terms of both cinematic style and content within an art form that is ever changing.

Buddy films   A type of film also popularly called "the buddy salvation" picture, so named because its stories involve male companionship. The term came into use during the 1960s and early 1970s through the popularity of such films as *Midnight Cowboy* (1969), *Butch Cassidy and the Sundance Kid* (1969), *The Sting* (1973), *The Last Detail* (1973), *California Split* (1974), and *Freebie and the Bean* (1976). These were among the many films of the period dealing with males who bolstered one another in dramatic conflict and crisis. In these pictures women were relatively unimportant as pivotal characters. The popular, highly acclaimed *Thelma & Louise* (1991) revealed the buddy film concept successfully transferred to female protagonists who celebrate companionship and who bolster one another emotionally. Presented in the form of a road picture, *Thelma & Louise* utilized many of the action elements common to male buddy pictures such as *Butch Cassidy and the Sundance Kid* and *Freebie and the Bean*.

C

Caesura   Principally a literary term denoting a rhythmical pause and break in a line of verse. The caesura is used in poetry to diversify rhythmical progress, and thereby enrich accentual verse. The term first gained significance in motion-picture art through the editing experiments of Sergei Eisenstein. In applying his concept of montage as the "collision of shots," Eisenstein often included caesuras—rhythmical breaks—in his films. The acts of *The Battleship Potemkin* (1925) are separated by caesuras that provide a rhythmical contrast to the preceding action. The intense, frenetic action of the mutiny, for example, is followed by the lyrical journey of a dinghy to the shore.

The three Burt Bacharach musical sequences in *Butch Cassidy and the Sundance Kid* (1969) provide contrasting caesuras that separate the major actions of the film. Several intense action sequences in *Master and Commander* (2003), for example, a raging sea storm and fight scenes, are followed by caesuras—quiet, scenic interludes that are often accompanied by melodic cello music.

Cameo role/performance A featured screen role of short but memorable duration, often constituting only a single-scene appearance. The actor performing the cameo role is usually a major film star or entertainment figure. Ava Gardner's appearance in the concluding scene of *The Life and Times of Judge Roy Bean* (1972) was designated a cameo role. Rock performer Alice Cooper made a cameo appearance in *Wayne's World* (1992), a spoof of cable-television programming. Bette Midler appeared in an uncredited cameo role in Nancy Myers' *What Women Want* (2000).

Camera movement The movement of the motion-picture camera for the purpose of following action or changing the view of a photographed scene, person, or object. The camera and the base to which it is affixed may move together in order to: move toward or away from a stationary subject (**dolly shot**); move behind or ahead of a moving person or object (**tracking shot**, photo 7); move alongside a moving object (**trucking shot**); move up or down on an automatic crane for a lower or higher **angle of view** of a scene (**crane shot**). The camera may also be moved while the base to which it is attached remains stationary: a movement of the camera left or right on a fixed base is a **pan**, while one up and down is a **tilt**.

[CAMERA MOVEMENT] 7. The camera tracks ahead of a group of characters as they walk and talk in a scene for Mike Nichols' *Catch 22* (1970).

A **zoom shot** can give the effect of camera movement, although it is the variable **focal length** of the lens rather than a moving camera that creates the effect.

Camera movement, in addition to following action and changing image composition, can be used to suggest a **subjective** point of view by having the moving camera assume character eye or body movements, as in Delmer Daves' *Dark Passage* (1947). A constant use of camera movement in a motion picture is often referred to as **fluid-camera technique**. American director Oliver Stone made the fluid camera a technical trademark of his cinematic style in such films as *Platoon* (1986), *Wall Street* (1987), *Talk Radio* (1988), and *JFK* (1991). In these films Stone's camera often appeared to be charging through the stories' locations. Woody Allen's *Deconstructing Harry* (1999) employed a constantly moving camera with near-dizzying effect, as did *The Bourne Supremacy* (2004).

Camera obscura   A device developed by Leonardo da Vinci in the 16th century which established the basic principle of photographic reproduction. The camera obscura (darkroom) allowed a small ray of light to pass through a hole into a totally dark space. An inverted and laterally reversed image of the outside scene appeared on a surface in the darkened room, thus producing the earliest form of a "camera." Da Vinci's image could be traced by the artist to achieve greater realism in artistic renderings. With the development of a photographic plate by Nicéphore Niépce and Louis J. M. Daguerre in the 1830s, which would preserve the inverted image, still photography became possible.

Camera speed   The speed at which film runs through a motion-picture camera. Usually camera speed is noted in **frames per second** (fps). Motion pictures consist of a series of still photographs (**frames**) which in rapid projection give the impression of movement. Standard projection speed for sound motion pictures is twenty-four frames per second, and for silent film sixteen frames per second. See **Pixilation, Slow motion**.

Caméra stylo   A concept articulated by French critic-director Alexandre Astruc who challenged motion picture directors to strive for a caméra-stylo or "camera pen" approach to filmmaking. Astruc believed the motion picture to be capable of the subtlety and range of expression available to literary writing, thus the charge for a "camera pen."

Canned drama   A term used by early film critics to describe a motion picture. Many turn-of-the-century critics, unable to recognize the unique qualities of the cinema, employed terms and standards taken from the theater. Because early short-film narratives also often resembled stage plays, yet were permanently recorded on celluloid, they were frequently referred to as "canned drama." Similar terms, such as "picture play" and "photo drama," indicated the difficulty early writers had in finding a separate vocabulary for describing motion pictures.

The term "canned" is still used frequently in film criticism to imply that all motion-picture performances are immutable and thus to suggest differences between film and theater. The expression comes from the fact that once a film is completed it is stored in a motion-picture can.

Canted shot   (See **Dutch angle**)

Cartoon   A hand-drawn **animated film**, usually ten to fifteen minutes in length. The term comes from the Italian word *cartone*, meaning "pasteboard," a material on which sketches were made. "Cartoon" was first used to describe satirical newspaper and magazine drawings which commented on public figures or political matters. Early film animators in the 1920s began to apply the term to their short character sketches which were released as motion-picture shorts (for instance, Walt Disney's *Alice in Cartoonland*, 1924). There evolved in the extensive production of these short animated films during the 1920s, 1930s, and 1940s a host of familiar cartoon characters: Mickey Mouse, Donald Duck, Bugs Bunny, Mr. McGoo, etc. Feature films such as *Who Framed Roger Rabbit?* (1988) and *Looney Tunes: The Action Continues* (2003) have celebrated the popularity of familiar Hollywood cartoon characters. See **Anime**.

Censorship (U.S.).   Motion-picture censorship includes three kinds of regulation: (1) the suppression of film material intended for production, (2) the inspection of film material after the motion picture has been produced with the possible intention of denying public access to the material, and (3) the deletion of material from motion pictures by a censor, or the banning of a motion picture in its entirety because of "objectionable" content.

Statutory censorship began in the United States in the first decade of the new medium. By 1922 more than thirty states had pending censorship legislation.

In 1930, the Hollywood industry, under the guidance of Will Hays, drew up a self-regulatory code of moral standards to be used as a film production guide. This code and its administering organization, popularly called the "Hays Office," were designed as an internal means of combating outside statutory censorship. The code contained a list of specific and general production taboos: illicit sex, undue suggestiveness, illegal drug use, pointed profanity, and methods of crime were among the kinds of material forbidden by the code.

First Amendment guarantees of freedom of speech were given to the motion picture for the first time in *"The Miracle Case"* (1952) decision.

The rating system, devised by the Motion Picture Association of America in 1968, replaced Hollywood's self-regulatory code as a means of attempting to obviate statutory censorship of motion pictures. The rating system classified films according to their suitability for various age groups and offered four categories: (G), General audiences; (M), later changed to (PG), Mature audiences, "parental guidance" advised; (R), Restricted, adult accompaniment required for anyone 17 or under; (X), No one admitted under 18 years of age. (PG-13) was added in 1984 as a special warning for very young children and the (X) rating was changed in 1990 to (NC-17), no one 17 and under admitted.

Statutory regulation centered on the issue of obscenity increased in the United States after the Supreme Court ruled in *Miller vs. California* (1973) that community standards, rather than state or national standards, would be applied in interpreting individual cases. See **Rating system**.

Character   Any fictional figure who appears in a motion picture narrative. Also a term for the individualized personality of an imaginary person created by the screenwriter and interpreted by an actor. An actor performing a particular role usually strives to untap the inner qualities of character and reveal them through the artistic methods of dramatic interpretation: action, voice, gesture, physical traits, mannerisms, etc. The character of a screen figure may become all the more provocative when a full understanding of personal/psychological attributes goes begging and the conveyed character remains shrouded in mystery and ambiguity as with the persona of Charles Foster Kane in *Citizen Kane* (1941). The very nature of human character in all its complexity is behind the philosophical rationale of Akira Kurosawa's *Rashomon* (1950).

Character actor A specialized screen actor who usually portrays a particular type of character. The character is often based on an evolved persona derived from the actor's physical qualities and personal mannerisms. Daniel Stern, the lumbering burglar sidekick to Joe Pesci in the *Home Alone* (1990, 1992) comedies, represents character acting in the comic buffoon tradition. Donald Meek, a whiskey drummer in *Stagecoach* (1939), was a character actor who played out his screen career as a shy, stammering screen type. **Typecasting** from picture to picture is common for character actors.

Chase A popular film element characterized by the pursuit of individuals or objects on the screen. The chase has been a significant part of motion-picture storytelling since the advent of the medium. Many early film narratives contained a chase as a means of providing excitement in what were often otherwise static films. A French producer for Pathé, Ferdinand Zecca, was an early master of chase films—producing numerous short pictures made up almost entirely of pursuit sequences (*Slippery Jim*, 1905).

The chase comedy was also a highly popular film genre in the first decades of the motion picture. The Keystone Kop comedies of Mack Sennett invariably ended with a zany chase. The chase was often a significant element in Charlie Chaplin's one-reel comedies. Audiences in the silent film era came to expect the chase as the standard means of bringing a screen comedy to its conclusion.

D.W. Griffith made extensive use of the chase as an element of dramatic tension in his films. Most of Griffith's major films ended with extended chases, carefully edited to build tension and usually concluding with a **last-minute rescue**.

The chase as a thematic element has had a major place in many of the standard film genres: the **western**, the **gangster**-intrigue picture, and the **costume film**.

Film theorists have attributed the popularity of the chase to both the appeal of action on the screen and the motion picture's unique ability to follow complex, intense movement. A film such as *The Fugitive* (1993) is essentially a narrative devised for the screen as an extended chase as is

Transporter 2 (2005). *Transporter 2* consists of an hour-and-a-half of incredulous chase episodes (by automobile, boat, and airplane), each concluding in a miraculous climax reminiscent of chases in James Bond films.

Chiaroscuro lighting A painting term used frequently to describe a type of motion-picture imagery in **black-and-white** and **color films** where the pictorial representations are rendered in terms of light and shade. The artistic arrangement of lights and darks, without regard for strong color values, becomes the primary method of visual presentation of scenic elements. The early interior scenes of *The Godfather* (1972) have a chiaroscuro effect, particularly those involving Don Corleone (Marlon Brando) in conference at his desk while the wedding party dances outside. In these interior scenes Don Corleone, lit in muted **sepia** tones, is set against a dark, **limbo** background.

Cineaste A term from the French, meaning filmmaker or producer. Cineaste is used, however, in France, and recently elsewhere, to describe the serious student of film art or the serious film enthusiast.

Cinema novo A South American film movement that originated in Brazil in the 1960s and which was characterized by a spirited interest in social and political ideology. Nelson Pereira dos Santos (*Barren Lives*, 1963) and Glauber Rocha (*Black Gold, White Devil*, 1964) were two of the important filmmakers who led the movement, mixing in their films social realities of national concern with purely aesthetic interests. The combination of local subject matter and dynamic expression inspired film directors throughout Latin America toward a "new cinema."

***Cinéma pur* (pure cinema)** An **experimental-film** term usually applied to works made during the first **avant-garde** movement which occurred in Europe during the 1920s. Pure cinema enthusiasts were opposed to narrative expression in the motion picture, advocating instead an exploitation of the unique cinematic devices of the medium in order to provide a purely visual and rhythmic experience. **Dynamic cutting, fast and slow motion, trick shots**, and moving camera shots were among the techniques employed to give visual-rhythmic life to subject matter that included inanimate objects as well as people. In Germany, Hans Richter used **stop-action cinematography** for *Rhythmus '21* (1921), a pure-cinema exercise which animated geometric paper designs of various shapes and tones. For *Ballet Mécanique* (1924) Fernand Léger, a French cubist painter, placed people and household objects in non-associative rhythms on the screen. The *cinéma pur* efforts of the first avant-garde movement fall into a type of film now more commonly referred to as **abstract film**.

Other experimental filmmakers who have produced purely abstract films include Francis Thompson (*N.Y., N.Y.,* 1957), Stan Brakhage (*Mothlight,*1963), Larry Cuba's (*3/78,* 1968), and Norman McLaren's (*Synchromy,* 1972).

CinemaScope   A wide-screen process developed and introduced by film technicians at Twentieth Century Fox in the early 1950s. In CinemaScope filming the aspect ratio of images varied from 2:66:1 to 1:66:1. The traditional screen ratio had been 1:33:1. Camera technicians employed **anamorphic lenses**, invented by Henri Chrétien in 1927, to photograph scenes so that they were wider than they were high (approximately 2 1/2 times wider). By using a comparable lens on

[CINEMASCOPE] 8. A CinemaScope image from *How to Marry a Millionaire* (1953), shown above as it looked in the film print and below as it appeared when projected on the screen.

the 35-mm projector, the images could be projected at their original width (photo 8).

Cinematic   A critical term expressing an awareness of that which is peculiar and unique to the film medium. "Cinematic" generally encompasses the full range of techniques available in motion-picture art. When applied to a specific film, the term is used to indicate that the filmmaker has employed the editing and visual devices, themes, or structural approaches that are especially appropriate to the medium.

"Cinematic" can also be defined historically by examining the innovations of early film artists who sought to break the new medium away from the artistic traditions of the legitimate theater. These innovations—peculiar to the film medium—included the use of camera **angles**, realistic decor in dramatic setting, mobile camera, naturalistic **acting**, optical techniques (**dissolves, fades, superimpositions, irises**), and especially the advantages of motion-picture editing which allowed (1) variety in the scope of shots, (2) rhythmical control of dramatic action, and (3) the ability to move freely in time and space through editing.

The exploitation of the unique time-space possibilities of the motion picture has often been a principal factor in a film's being deemed "cinematic."

"Cinematic" has also been used to describe certain kinds of story material which seem especially suited to the film medium. The **chase**, for example, is regarded as a narrative element which is peculiarly cinematic; the motion picture, again because of its free use of time and space, is able to follow intense, complex action with ease.

The term has also been frequently used in literary criticism to describe fictional methods which suggest certain affinities with the motion picture. Likenesses have been drawn between film techniques and the fictional methods of such writers as James Joyce, Marcel Proust, Virginia Woolf, John Dos Passos, William Faulkner, Gustave Flaubert, and many others. Primarily the cinematic analogy has been used because of these authors' temporal (time) arrangement of their material. The goal of the writer may be simultaneous action (**parallel development**) as in Dickens' *A Tale of Two Cities* and Faulkner's *Light in August*; an impressionistic, stream-of-consciousness point of view found in James Joyce's *Ulysses* and Virginia Woolf's *To the Lighthouse*; or the collective narrative with several interweaving stories which was the approach used in John Dos Passos' *USA*. These techniques are viewed as resembling the cutting techniques which are also available to the filmmaker and thus have been labeled cinematic. See **Cinematic time and space, Filmic, Simultaneity**.

Cinematic time and space A term which indicates the relationship of time and space in the motion picture. In a theatrical experience space for the most part remains static and constant. On the other hand, space in the cinema can be altered because the camera serves as a selective intermediary in the screen experience. Individual shots within a motion picture are capable of breaking up the rigid space-time continuum of the "real-world experience."

In the real-world experience a man rises from his armchair where he has been reading an evening newspaper, crosses to the bar, and mixes a drink. His movements from the chair to the bar must be made through actual space and time. In the cinema experience the man can rise and start his movement to the bar. The initial movement can be followed by a brief two-second shot of a startling headline in the newspaper resting on the armchair, followed immediately by a close-up of the man sipping his drink at the bar and contemplating the impact of the headline.

Cinematic space is thus intimately woven with the unique temporal (time) possibilities of the motion picture. A character's movement, for example, can be made to appear unusually prolonged through the addition or repetition of visual space. In *Bonnie and Clyde* (1967), the moment of recognition by the two killers that they are about to be ambushed is extended with unusual effect by intercutting numerous close-ups of the gangsters as they glance at one another.

Through the elimination or addition of visual space in photographing and editing a film, time can be either expanded or contracted. An unusual use of cinematic time-and-space manipulation serves as the basis for *Run Lola Run* (1999) where the heroine's rush to deliver 100,000 German marks to her boyfriend is shown three times, each run affected by slight time changes that alter the action. This device was similar to that employed in *Sliding Doors* (1998), a drama with Gwyneth Paltrow as a young PR executive whose life takes two different paths after she misses a ride home on the Underground. In *She Loves Me, She Loves Me Not* (2003), halfway through the movie everything comes to a stop, rewinds rapidly to the beginning, then replays but from a different perspective.

Cinematographer (director of photography) A title used to distinguish motion-picture photographers from still photographers. If the cinematographer in the filmmaking process is fully responsible for the artistic and technical quality of the screen images, that individual is known as the "director of photography." The director of photography, working with camera operators and other technicians, has the larger responsibility for (1) **exposure**, (2) **lighting**, (3) **color**, (4) **camera movement** and placement, and (5) **lens** choice and **framing** of the screen **image**. The film director works closely with the director of photography to achieve the desired visual compositions and moods that enhance and carry the story.

A director of photography usually works to develop a visual **style** for a film. That style may be romantic (*Win a Date with Tad Hamilton,* 2004) or harshly realistic (*Se7en,* 1995).

Cinéma verité A stylistic movement in documentary filmmaking, and a term often applied to a fictional film which presents drama in a candid, documentary-like manner. In this type of film the filmmaker either seeks to use the motion-picture camera in an improvisational way or does so out of necessity. *Cinéma verité,* meaning "cinema truth," attempts to avoid the slick, controlled look of **studio pictures. Available lighting, handheld cameras, long takes, in-camera editing,** and natural sound recordings are techniques used to achieve a newsreel-like quality on film. The cinéma verité method de-emphasizes the importance of artistic lighting, exact focus, perfect sound, and smooth camera movements in favor of an ostensibly more realistic, truthful recording of an event. **Lighting** is often intentionally "**flat,**" and **exposures** may be less than perfect. Film "grain" is often visible.

The documentaries of Frederick Wiseman have been described as *cinéma verité* films because of their starkly naturalistic photographic styles. In his studies of American institutions, *Titicut Follies* (1967), *Hospital* (1969), and *High School* (1968), Wiseman uses high-speed black-and-white film stock, natural sound, and available lighting to add a realistic impact to already-shocking exposés.

One of the intended effects of *cinéma verité* is that of having the "story" appear to develop as it is being watched, thus adding to its candor.

Cinéma verité filming techniques were widely used by the French **New Wave** film directors of the late 1950s and early 1960s. In the United States, John Cassavetes employed the approach in pictures such as *Faces* (1968), *Husbands* (1970), and *A Woman Under the Influence* (1975). The behind-the-scenes treatment of the dancers in Robert Altman's *The Company* (2003) achieves a candid quality through a *cinéma verité* style of filming.

An early instance of this technique was that seen in the "News on the March" sequence of *Citizen Kane* (1941). A jerky, handheld camera with **telephoto** lens is used to show Kane being pushed in a wheelchair about the grounds of his Gothic estate, effecting a sense of candor that resembles the *cinéma verité* school of filmmaking. See **Direct cinema, Realistic cinema**.

Cinerama A motion-picture process first used commercially in 1952. Cinerama employed three cameras and three projectors, a wide curved screen, and a complex, **stereophonic sound** system. Three separate images were projected simultaneously onto the curved screen, thus allowing the effect of peripheral vision for audience members. The Cinerama process, invented in 1935 by Fred Waller, permitted novel opportunities for audience participation in the film experience. Viewers, because of the peripheral nature of the screen images and the use of carefully controlled sound effects, felt as though they were riding in an automobile or hurtling down a rollercoaster track.

The first Cinerama release, *This Is Cinerama* (1952), was essentially a travelogue demonstration of this process, but because of curiosity the film proved to be a commercially successful venture.

Cinerama did not prove to be as successful when used to tell a dramatic story on the screen. An apparent conflict resulted between the use of a gimmick and the necessity of developing plot and characterization. Narrative films using Cinerama, such as *The Wonderful World of the Brothers Grimm* (1962), seemed hampered by the technique. This fact, coupled with the considerable expense of installing equipment to handle the process, limited the use and appeal of Cinerama. The technique has been occasionally used in certain theaters for screen spectacles and in special presentations at exhibitions and amusement centers.

Cliché An overworked dramatic concept, technique, or plotting element; also trite dialogue or stereotyped characterization which through repetitive use has lost its originality and freshness. In the late 1960s, early 1970s the filming of violent death through either **slow motion** or **pixilation** was so extensive as to approach cliché treatment. The exploitation of clichéd technique, dialogue, and character can serve as the source material for screen spoofs and parodies, for example, *Young Frankenstein* (1974), *Robin Hood: Men in Tights* (1993), and the Mike Myers' *Austin Powers* films (1997, 1999, 2002), parodies of spy movies. Cliché comes from the French word for a stereotype printing plate used in publishing.

Climax (see **Dramatic structure**)

Close-up A shot which provides a limited, magnified view of a character or an object in a scene. It is a shot that usually emphasizes the face if characters are involved and provides a principal method by which the filmmaker can achieve empathy for characters. If focused on an object, the close-up bestows dramatic or symbolic value on the isolated element.

The close-up has been recognized as a device for (1) directing audience attention, (2) establishing identification with and immediacy for screen characters, (3) isolating detail in a scene, (4) creating visual variety in film scenes, and (5) providing dramatic emphasis.

A close-up, like the **long shot**, conveys a considerable amount of information, but of a different type. Emotions, feelings, and nuances can be suggested by the close-up by merely magnifying and isolating an individual in an intensely dramatic moment. Similarly, the close-up view of an object—for example, a gun or a hand—bestows and conveys a dramatic significance which might be lost in longer scenic shots.

The duration or length of time that a close-up remains on the screen also has importance as dramatic material. By sustaining close-up shots of a character's face, it is possible for the filmmaker to suggest thought and feeling. The theorist Siegried Kracauer observed that if an object or person is left on the screen long enough it will begin to lay bare its own reality. This unique perceptual possibility that exists through the close-up is a source of expressive power for the filmmaker. In Carl Dreyer's *The Passion of Joan of Arc* (1928), close-ups are used as the predominant method of conveying the spirituality of the woman on trial as well as the intensity of the legal proceedings. Lengthy close-ups generate poignancy and introspection for Robert McNamara, the principal subject of Errol Morris' Academy Award-winning documentary, *The Fog of War* (2003).

Collage film   A film whose images are created through the overlay of assorted materials (as in an artistic collage) and photographed with the intention of achieving both visual and rhythmic effect. Experimental filmmaker Stan VanDerBeek frequently produced collage films, for example *Breathdeath* (1964), a film that employed pictures of famous people, cutouts of objects, newspaper headlines, and other material phenomena for an animated protest against war. Godfrey Reggio's *Powaqqatsi* (1988) is a feature-length collage film that brings together visual images of Third World societies and prevailing labor conditions.

Collective story film A motion picture containing one or more narrative units, and arranged so that the separate stories and characters create an expanded treatment of related ideas. D.W. Griffith's *Intolerance* (1916) and Vittorio de Sica's *Yesterday, Today, and Tomorrow* (1964) are examples. *Intolerance* spanned the course of history through four narratives and collectively conveyed the theme of human injustice across the ages. In *New York Stories* (1989) directors Martin Scorsese, Francis Ford Coppola, and Woody Allen joined together to create three stylistically and dramatically diverse tales bound together by the fact that their characters resided in New York City. An unusual variation of the collective story film occurs in *The Hours* (2003), a Stephen Daldry film that tells the stories of three women whose lives span the 20th century (Virginia Woolf, a 1950s housewife, and a contemporary New Yorker). An emotional connection between the three evolves as their separate stories unfold.

Color (film)   A film in which the **emulsion** layer has been chemically developed to respond to reflected light in such a way that color images are produced rather than **black-and-white** images. Color in a motion picture may carry both realistic and expressive values in (1) suggesting time and place, (2) conveying atmosphere, (3) underscoring theme, and (4) revealing abstract ideas. Through the use of color and lighting in *The Godfather* (1972), Francis Ford Coppola was able to evoke temporal feeling for the various parts of the picture. Colors in the early parts of the film were "warm," consisting of brown, yellow, and orange tones, which imbued the scenes with a period look. The colored images resembled the warm colors of old paintings and also had a golden glow like that seen in early color motion pictures made in the late 1930s and early 1940s. As *The Godfather* moved into the 1950s, the images became cooler—containing more blues and whites and suggesting more recent times. Its sequel, *The Godfather Part Two* (1975) also combined colors to evoke a sense of past and present. Coppola used warm, sepia colors for the nostalgic **flashback** scenes of Don Corleone set at the turn of the century. The contemporary sequences with Michael were somberly blue or starkly bright to convey both a sense of modernity and a psychological mood.

The Taming of the Shrew (1967) and *Pelle the Conquerer* (1988) were photographed with dark oil-paint colors to give these films the look of "Old Master" paintings of the Renaissance period.

A color technique known as "sepia" is sometimes used in motion pictures to depict the past. Sepia is a light brown image, which can be achieved by printing black-and-white images on color emulsions or through the use of **filters**. Its color association with brown tintypes and sepia photographs has made the technique appropriate for evocative period cinematography. The New York sequence in *Butch Cassidy and the Sundance Kid* (1969), concluding with the trip by boat to Bolivia, is photographed in sepia. The use of sepia images, combined with animated photographs, gave the sequence the quality of an old photograph album.

The overexposed, washed-out color images in the **flashback** scenes of *Marathon Man* (1976) were an effective means of indicating time through color. The images of Levy's suicide had the muted "true-color" look of color films made in the early 1950s, the time of the blacklisting which prompted Levy's suicide.

Atmospheric color. Color to convey an atmospheric or thematic climate within a motion-picture story. In the films *Raintree Country* (1957), *Elvira Madigan* (1967), and

Women in Love (1970), the lush colors of nature are emphasized with such visual beauty that they immediately set the
romantic tone of these films.

In Michelangelo Antonioni's *Blowup* (1966), scenes set
in the photographer's studio convey a bluish-white clinical
quality that enhances the searching, investigative theme of
the film. By contrast, the park scenes—where the emotionally bankrupt photographer stumbles onto a moment of
romantic intrigue—are vividly green and "alive." Colors
throughout *Blowup* are both atmospheric and psychologically suggestive. The brightly painted buildings, visible as David
Hemmings drives through the streets of London, add a mod,
contemporary look to the environment in which the photographer works and lives.

Because colors have acquired symbolic connotations,
their use in motion pictures can be entirely abstract. Federico
Fellini's *Juliet of the Spirits* (1965) used colors that were
fantastic and psychologically suggestive. The inexplicable
ambiguous nature of the story was compounded by the fantastic, brightly colored costumes and vivid surreal settings.
Color provided a visual motif for the "spiritual" nature of
Fellini's highly imaginative, non-narrative film.

The color red in Ingmar Bergman's *Cries and Whispers*
(1972) is so dominant and so ever present that its use is highly theatrical and symbolic. The color stands before the viewer at all times, providing a visual cue for the deep passions
and emotions at work in the film. Such uses of color are rare
in motion pictures where more commonly a wide range of
colors is in a constant state of flux. Bold, acrylic-like colors
often set the mood for romantic comedies such as *Win a
Date with Tad Hamilton* (2004).

Before the development of color **emulsions**, it was
common practice to hand-tint film prints for symbolic value.
A night scene would often be tinted a deep blue, romance
scenes rendered in shades of pink, war and other violent
scenes in red. See **Chiaroscuro lighting**.

Comedy   A type of light-hearted drama designed to amuse and pro-
voke laughter. Most screen comedies end on a happy note,
although the plotting situations which generate the humor
may, as Walter Kerr noted in *Tragedy and Comedy* (Simon
& Schuster, 1967), simply end arbitrarily as though the
writer suddenly decided to send "everyone off to bed." Kerr

also emphasized the fine line between the tragic and the comic. The most physical types of comedy, for example **slapstick**, have their roots in harmless cruelty. Slapstick comes from a stage device made of two pieces of bound wood that produce a loud sound when struck against a character or another object. Slapstick came to mean any form of harmless cruelty or horseplay designed for laughs. An early Lumière film, *Watering the Gardener* (1896), exploited slapstick humor when a lad steps on a water hose, enticing the gardener to look down into the hose's end just as the water is released to spray the man in the face. The Three Stooges took the physical elements of slapstick cruelty in film to a comic book extreme by effecting bodily harm on one another to the accompaniment of stylized sound effects.

Much of screen comedy depends on exaggeration of situation, language, action, and character. The screenwriter and filmmaker capitalize on incongruities within character and situation for laughter, engaging the audience in the merriment of observing the foibles and deficiencies of other human beings. Charlie Chaplin's "Little Tramp" character displayed visual incongruity in his pretentious but ill-fitted tuxedo-like costume and situational incongruity in the efforts of the tramp character to survive the social environment in which he functioned. Buster Keaton was incongruously stoic as a comic screen figure doing battle with man-made objects and the physical laws of the world. The silent screen by nature exploited the visual and physical components of comedy.

"Talking" motion pictures added verbal wit to screen comedy, ranging from the absurdist view of language evident in many of the Marx Brothers' films (for instance, the reading of an employment contract in *A Night at the Opera*, 1935) to the cruel verbal barbs of W.C. Fields. Mae West's film comedy capitalized on dialogue retorts filled with deflating sexual innuendo. On a higher level Ernst Lubitsch employed witty, urbane dialogue, obliquely innuendoed, in the creation of sophisticated romantic comedies, for example, *Trouble in Paradise* (1932), *Design for Living* (1933), and *Ninotchka* (1939).

In the late 1940s the Ealing Studios in Great Britain took advantage of the country's many gifted writers and actors to make **black comedies**, many involving crime and murder. The Ealing comedies *Kind Hearts and Coronets* (1949) and

The Ladykillers (1955) represented in subject matter and stylistic toning the nature of the black comedy at its best: droll, satiric treatment of otherwise deadly serious subject matter.

Filmmakers have continued to perpetrate the classic traditions of screen comedy, usually in a highly eclectic manner, for example, Woody Allen in *Sleeper* (1973), Charles Crichton and John Cleese in *A Fish Called Wanda* (1988), Will Ferrell's *Anchorman* (2004). Sight gags, physical slapstick humor, verbal absurdity, character incongruity, topical satire, situations, and sexual innuendo all appear as comic elements in these popular films. Mel Brooks' *Silent Movie* (1976) offered itself as a **parody** in tribute to the traditions of silent screen comedy. *Showtime* (2002), starring Eddie Murphy and Robert De Niro, was conceived as spoof-parody of television cop shows.

Commedia dell'arte An **improvisational** approach to comic performance taken from the Italian commedia dell'arte companies that gained popularity during the 16th century. The commedia dell'arte actor was permitted to incorporate spontaneously any comic details, sight gags, and antics which might possibly occur as the plot synopsis was acted out. Rough-and-tumble pratfalls, stock characters, and vulgarity were also an accepted part of commedia dell'arte. The approach was widely used by silent-screen performers, particularly Charlie Chaplin and many of the comedians at Mack Sennett's Keystone Company.

Compilation film Any film created principally from existing footage that has been reedited around a topical, historical, or visual theme. Charles Braverman's *The Sixties* (1970), a compilation film, employs television and news footage of the 1960s to evoke a sense of the social, political, and cultural temperament of that decade. Henri Erlich's *My Way* (1975) is a satirical compilation film that combines the voice of David Frye singing "My Way" with "outtake" and newsreel footage of Richard Nixon's public career.

The compilation approach has also been a vital method of **information films** and propaganda documentaries, for example Frank Capra's *Why We Fight* series (1943–1945), Paul Rotha's *Land of Promise* (1945), and television's many historical series such as *Victory at Sea* (1952–1953) and *The Twentieth Century* (1957–1964).

Composition   The use of light (including color), camera **angle**, movement, and object and character blocking within the film **frame** for photographic and dramatic expression.

The impact of these elements in a film shot depends upon certain psychological and learned facets of visual perception. Lighter objects attract the eye more readily than darker objects; therefore, light can be used as a means of achieving compositional emphasis. Mass, volume, and movement also have importance for emphasis in frame composition. A single figure separated from a crowd will usually stand out as significant. Similarly, a moving actor will draw attention away from static figures. Because of the kinetic nature of the motion picture, composition is rarely static, and, hence, emphasis and psychological impact through composition are in a state of constant flux.

A straight-on view of a scene in which actors and objects have been harmoniously arranged so as to fill with equal "weight" all areas of the screen frame are said to be **formally balanced**. In a deathbed scene, formal composition can be achieved by photographing the scene from a straight-on view taken at the foot of the bed. The placement of a nurse on one side of the bed and a doctor on the other side adds further formality to the scene, which would have been lost if both nurse and doctor had been placed ("weighted") on the same side of the bed, or if a sharp side angle had been chosen for the camera's positioning. The "balanced" arrangement of characters and objects and the straight-on photography cause the deathbed scene to appear "at rest."

Whereas formal composition connotes harmony and an at-rest feeling in a scene, a slanted, or **Dutch angle**, shot produces a sense of unrest. See **Balance, Blocking Obscured frame**.

Composition in depth The blocking or arrangement of characters and objects within the film frame to give a sense of depth to the screen imagery (photo 9). Composition in depth is effected by positioning characters and objects in the foreground, midground, and background areas of the frame so that the eye looks "in depth." See **Deep-focus photography**.

Computer film   An animated film, usually of abstract imagery, generated by computer processes. The work of John Whitney, the foremost pioneer in computer films, has been primarily in the

[COMPOSITION IN DEPTH] 9. One of the many composition-in-depth shots in *Citizen Kane* (1941).

area of motion graphics—animated designs which Whitney created with the aid of an analogue computer of his own invention. This mechanical device, which was combined with an **optical printer**, permitted Whitney to preprogram and vary the nature of the graphic designs, thus making the results of his filmed efforts more than mere happenstance. Some of the many graphic possibilities of the analogue computer were displayed in *Catalogue*, a film released by Whitney in 1961. The multivaried abstract effects of Whitney's work are vividly displayed in this demonstration film. Whitney also employed a digital computer to create radiant dot patterns that constantly change and shape.

Stan VanDerBeek is among the other independent filmmakers who have experimented with computer animation, for example, *Collide-oscope* (1966). *Antz* (1998) and *Shrek* (2001, 2004) are examples of animated feature films that have been computer generated.

Computer-generated imaging Computer-derived animated images achieved through an electronic process. In James Cameron's futuristic film *The Abyss* (1989) underwater visual effects are realized by computer imaging. In one scene aliens appear to communicate by manipulating water so that the movements resemble facial expressions. The effects are achieved by electronic computer animation and **superimposed** onto the film action. *The Abyss* received an Academy Award for its computer-generated visual effects.

Steven Spielberg's *Jurassic Park* (1993) further revealed the realistic capabilities of computer-generated animation (photo 10). In addition to the use of mechanical robots and miniature models in a stop-motion, frame-by-frame process, Spielberg employed the Industrial Light and Magic (ILM) company to help create the film's dinosaur images. Using T-rex dinosaur models as prototypes, ILM animators drew wire mesh skeletal images with a pencil-like instrument that transferred them directly to a computer screen for digital recording. Color, shadow, texture, and other necessary realistic elements were later added to the dinosaur outlines that rested on a black background so that they could be **matte processed** into *Jurassic Park*'s live action. The dinosaurs' movements were created by a software program called "Matador." The Matador program provided the same sense

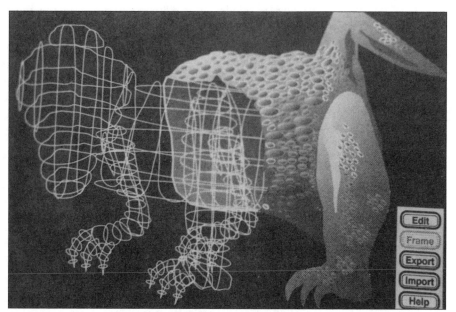

[COMPUTER-GENERATED IMAGING] 10. A computer-imaged dinosaur in the model coloring stage as it was being created for Steven Spielberg's *Jurassic Park* (1993).

of movement that is achieved through **stop-action/stop-motion** cinematography. Final integration was realized by turning the live action into digital signals so that it could be combined accurately in the computer with the animated images.

The technology of computer-generated imaging at the ILM company (founded by George Lucas in 1975) was responsible for the special effects that permitted Meryl Streep's head to spin in circles in *Death Becomes Her* (1992). The Arnold Schwarzenegger *Terminator* films (1984, 1991, 2002) took this type of special effects filmmaking to new heights.

Conceptual montage (see **Montage**)

Conflict   A term for the struggles and tensions which result from the interaction of two opposing elements in a motion-picture plot. Expressed another way, conflict is the central problem within a film story which ultimately must be resolved. It is the conflict between the protagonist (the film's sympathetic figure) and the opposing force (the antagonist) which engages the audience's interest.

Continuity   The development and structuring of film segments and ideas so that the intended meaning is clear. Continuity is another term for film construction, which includes the development of plot or idea, the editing devices, and the transitions employed to connect the film parts.

In a more specific meaning "continuity" refers to the matching of individual scenic elements from shot to shot so that details and actions, filmed at different times, will edit together without error. This process is referred to as "continuity editing." To maintain continuity within sequences the editor will often cut on character action so that the scene flows together without noticeable **jump-cuts**. Lapses in the flow of action can be avoided by **cutaways** and **transition** devices.

Music and sound are often utilized to provide a sense of continuity to a scene or sequences that may contain a variety of unmatched shots taken in different locations. In *Rocky* (1976) the song "Getting High" served as a continuity device during the highly fragmentary sequence showing Rocky in the various training preparations for his title fight. The song connected the numerous brief shots so that they appeared as a single and complete unit within the film.

Contrivance	A plotting device or story element which does not seem plausible and which detracts from a motion picture's credibility. The ending of *The Last Laugh* (1924), in which the old doorman (Emil Jannings) is relieved of his misery as a washroom attendant through an unexpected inheritance, is a contrivance. F.W. Murnau, the film's director, intended the contrivance as an ironic commentary on the differences between real life and life in motion pictures, where happy endings predominate. Charlie Chaplin effected a similar happy ending for *The Gold Rush* (1925), making note of the plot's unexpected change of fortune when "the little tramp"—wealthy and in love—moves to kiss his girlfriend and "spoils" the picture being taken by a nearby photographer. The double entendre suggested that the happy ending had spoiled the film for Chaplin admirers who knew the little tramp rarely triumphed so grandly. Most contrivances are seen as plotting flaws rather than ironic statements, for example, the arrival of a cavalry unit at the last minute to save the inhabitants of a fort from an outside attack.
Convention	An accepted dramatic element or stylistic approach or type of subject matter that is commonly associated with a kind of motion picture or with motion pictures in general. Films of a particular **genre** are characterized by the use of accepted conventions and mythic elements that are repeated from film to film. The conventions of the **western film** include conflicts involving guns and horses and climaxes that often center on shootouts and **chases**. A visual convention of the western film is the display of the open spaces of the American frontier.

Voice-over narration was a convention common in *film noir*-style detective films of the 1940s. Although the use of the voice-over narrator was eventually abandoned, the convention was revived in the remake of *Farewell My Lovely* (1975) in order to evoke a film style reminiscent of earlier versions of the Raymond Chandler story.

In a more general sense, the liberal use of **music** to underscore the actions of screen **melodramas** is a long-standing tradition. On the other hand, such conventional use of music is considered inappropriate for **realist-cinema** expression, which traditionally has avoided the use of both narration and supplied music.

Each film type, ranging from **minimal cinema** to the **epic** feature film, has its own set of established conventions.

Editing and camera techniques employed in the construction of a motion picture and accepted by audiences as indigenous to the medium's methods of expression are also regarded as film conventions, for example, **shot sequence editing,** optical **transitions, camera movement, parallel development, flashbacks**, etc.

Conventions, when overused, can become trite and ineffective, for instance, the use of **slow motion** to depict a violent death—a common convention in **gangster** and **law-and-order films** during the 1960s and early 1970s.

Cookie (cukaloris) A flat, opaque sheet with cutout patterns which will cast shadows onto the film set when placed before a strong light source (photo 11). The cookie (taken from the Greek *cukaloris*) may be used to produce non-distinct patterns for the purpose of breaking up the blandness of a set, or it may be used to cast shadows of doors, windows, trees, etc.

Costume film A motion-picture **genre** characterized by historical pageantry and **spectacle**. Since the beginning of the film narrative, the costume spectacle has been a commercial mainstay of the screen. One of the earliest films made by Thomas Edison was a brief costume drama titled *The Execution of Mary Queen of Scots* (1896). The feature-length costume drama originated in Italy with pictures like *Quo Vadis?* (1913) and *Cabiria* (1914). Bible-inspired spectacles on a much larger scale were popularized in the 1920s through the work of Cecil B. DeMille (*The Ten Commandments*, 1923, and *King of Kings*, 1927). Costume-action spectacles of a swashbuckling variety were given impetus by the great popularity of films starring Rudolph Valentino (*Blood and Sand*, 1922) and Douglas Fairbanks (*The Mark of Zorro*, 1920). The development and use of wide-screen processes in the early 1950s brought about a new rash of costume dramas displaying spectacle, color, and stereophonic sound. The genre went into demise in the 1960s after the failure of *Cleopatra* (1963). Occasionally more modern variations of the costume film appear, such as *The Three Musketeers* (1974), *Excalibur* (1981), *Robin Hood: Prince of Thieves* (1991), *King Arthur* (2004), *Casanova* (2006)—films that have brought added touches of realism along with the costume film's expected spectacle and pageantry.

Courtroom screen drama A motion picture in which the plot's highest points of dramatic tension and the ensuing climax/resolution cen-

[COOKIE] 11. In *Captain January* (1936), a film with Shirley Temple, a "cookie" produces the effect of window light being reflected onto the back wall of the set.

ter on courtroom maneuvering between trial opponents. Surprise witnesses and the psychological breakdown of a key participant are among the familiar plotting conventions of the genre. Classic examples of this popular type of motion picture include *The Caine Mutiny* (1954), *Inherit the Wind* (1960), *The Verdict* (1982), *A Few Good Men* (1992), and *The Rainmaker* (1997). A variation is *Twelve Angry Men* (1957), a Sidney Lumet film in which twelve jurors debate the justice of a hastily derived conviction. One juror leads the cause for a reconsideration of the trial facts. *The Verdict* (1982) with Paul Newman and *A Few Good Men* (1992), starring Jack Nicholson and Tom Cruise, carried forward the gratifying traditions of courtroom screen dramas with powerful climaxes.

Cover shot   A long view of a film action, taken for the purpose of establishing the location and all characters within the scene (photo 12).

[COVER SHOT] 12. A cover shot for a scene in George Stevens' *A Place in the Sun* (1951). The setting and group of characters are established in a single long-shot composition. The cover shot reveals both the environment as well as the spatial relationship of characters to each other.

Coverage   The variety of different shots—taken from various angles and perspectives—that are filmed for the purpose of providing additional options within the recorded **master scene/shot** material. Once the master scene/shot has been photographed, **close-ups, medium shots, inserts**, etc., may be taken by the director for the purpose of "covering" the action in varied detail. Coverage can serve as protection against **continuity** and acting flaws and allows the film editor extra latitude in determining tone, emphasis, and rhythm in the scene.

Craftsman director (see **Director**)

Crane shot   A moving shot that may be horizontal, vertical, forward, or backward. The motion-picture camera is mounted on a studio crane which can be smoothly and noiselessly operated by electrical means. Also sometimes referred to as a **boom shot**.

Creative geography A form of **narrative editing** where the shots taken in different locations suggest a spatial unity within a film.

In the climax of *Way Down East* (1920), D.W. Griffith used **crosscutting** among three separate but related locations to depict the **last-minute rescue** of the heroine. Griffith employed shots of Lillian Gish on a cake of ice moving down a river, shots of her boyfriend searching for her, and shots of the falls toward which her ice floe was apparently moving. For this last location, Griffith spliced in pieces of stock footage of Niagara Falls. Although the actress in reality was nowhere near that or any other falls, the audience believes her to be because the editing bound the locations together.

Lev Kuleshov, while teaching a Russian film workshop class in the early 1920s, studied the films of D.W. Griffith and then performed a series of experiments with geographic editing. In one of these, the audience saw a series of five shots: (1) a man walked from right to left, (2) a woman walked from left to right, (3) they met and shook hands, and the man pointed, (4) a shot of a white building, and (5) the two walking up a flight of steps. The audience connected these shots into a single narrative **sequence**. Actually, the two separate shots of the man and woman walking were made in different parts of the city, the white building was the White House snipped out of an American film, and the steps they ascended were those of a church in still another part of the city.

This experiment indicated how geographic unity in a film is not dependent on geographic unity in real space. The given spatial interrelationships are dissolved, and **images** are juxtaposed in such a way that their combination creates an illusion of spatial continuity.

Creative geography has become an integral part of modern filmmaking. **Special-effects films** such as *The Poseidon Adventure* (1972), *Earthquake* (1975), *Jaws* (1975), *King Kong* (1976), *Raiders of the Lost Ark* (1981), *Jurassic Park* (1993), *Spider-Man* (2002), and *Spider-Man*

2 (2004) are successful largely because of their effective use of creative geography, more often combining digitalized virtual locations with on-set action.

An unusual, psychologically effective use of creative geography occurs in a film adaptation of August Strindberg's short play *The Stronger*. In this two-character film, actress Viveca Lindfors portrays both a wife and her husband's mistress who encounter one another at a sidewalk cafe. Through creative geography which allows the dual-role approach in *The Stronger* (1969), a psychological framework is effected to suggest the merger of the two women's personalities.

Credits
The list of production personnel, including actors, who have made contributions to a motion picture. Credits for the major artists and technicians involved in the creation of a film usually appear at the beginning of the picture with a complete credit list at the film's conclusion. Until the 1960s, it was more common to include full credits at the beginning of the film rather than its conclusion. The design of introductory credits and the manner in which they are presented on the screen are often a means of setting the mood or **tone** for the film story that follows. The opening credits for *Bonnie and Clyde* (1967) are accompanied by a series of soft, fuzzy photographic shots of the Barrow-Parker gang. Throughout the film proper the gang members frequently take snapshots of one another. The credits and film photos are integrally related. Frequently the opening credits are a **superimposition** over or between **expository** scenes. In *Foul Play* (1978) credits were interspersed between scenes that went several minutes into the film story. The opening credits of *Spider-Man 2* (2004) are combined with a collage of Marvel comic book characters and images. The closing credits of *Shrek 2* (2004) include still shots of the film's major cartoon characters along with the names of the actors who created the characters' voices.

Critical focus
(see **Focus**)

Criticism
The interpretation and evaluation of film; the study and elucidation of film form and content.

Many approaches to film criticism can be taken. Films may be grouped for study according to director (as in auteur criticism), by **genre** (the **gangster**, **western**, war film, etc.), by studio (Warner Bros., Paramount, etc.), by subject matter (social themes), by technical evaluation (quality of cinematography), by time period (the **studio years**), or by nationality (French, Japanese), and lend themselves to new and differing insights in each instance. Films may also be analyzed for their cultural significance, how they serve as a mirror of or commentary upon a given society. A critical approach of this latter type is **structuralism**, an anthropological method of evaluating what films reveal about broad cultural patterns of human behavior.

Subjective film criticism judges motion pictures by their aesthetic and emotional qualities. In all cases criticism strives to enrich and deepen the film experience by increasing the understanding of what happens in a motion picture and how its effects are brought across in thematic and **cinematic** ways.

Crosscutting Cutting between two or more developing concepts or lines of action in a motion picture. Crosscutting may be used for the purpose of presenting simultaneously occurring events, or for thematic construction. Alain Resnais' antiwar film *Night and Fog* (1955) achieves its impact in part by presenting newsreel footage of concentration camps crosscut with **travelogue**-like footage of the deserted camps as they appeared ten years after the war. Whether applied to dramatic films or to films of another type, crosscutting implies that the editor has switched back and forth between units of the film. Extensive crosscutting appears in Milos Forman's *Ragtime* (1981) as the lives of several major characters are developed to reveal life in 1920s America. The film adaptation of Ruth Prawer Jhabvala's novel *Heat and Dust* (1983) employs crosscutting as its primary structural device. The story cuts back and forth between modern India and a period fifty years earlier. The crosscutting contrasts a contemporary, sophisticated young Englishwoman's life in India with that of a relative living in the country in the earlier period. The crosscuts provide insight into Indian-British attitudes toward one another, past and present. In a highly innovative use of this cinematic technique, the lives of three women, living in different periods of the 20th century, are crosscut in *The Hours* (2002) to achieve powerful emotional connections.

Cult film A motion picture of limited but special appeal to a particular group of filmgoers. Devotion to the film is such that its followers attend showings time and again, often frequenting theaters which program late-night screenings of cult favorites, for example, *Harold and Maude* (1972), *The Rocky Horror Picture Show* (1975), *Hairspray* (1988), *Trainspotting* (1996). The quirky, often outrageous nature of these films is the source of their peculiar attraction. *My Own Private Idaho* (1991), a serious film, achieved cult status through its offbeat and sometimes surreal portrayal of male-hustling and friendship in the Pacific Northwest. The film's following was limited but intense. Mainstream gay and lesbian films, in part because of their relative obscurity, also often gain cult-film status, for instance, *Desert Hearts* (1985), the story of a developing relationship between a female professor and a young woman on a Nevada ranch.

Cultural criticism/cultural studies A movement in film and literary analysis which seeks to incorporate cultural and historical context. Cultural criticism takes into account a variety of theories and critical strategies which are seen to cross-fertilize one another and, hence, may be described as interdisciplinary in intention. In its embracing of pluralism, cultural criticism has drawn upon Marxist theory, psychoanalysis, semiotics, feminism, gay-lesbian ("queer") study, among other strategies. Cultural criticism avoids any recognizable set of criteria and in this sense may be seen as a reactionary response to previously developed, hard-bound practices of analysis.

Cut The splicing together of two pieces of film to (1) maintain **continuity** (continuous action), (2) change scenes (**transition**), or (3) **insert** other relevant material into the film flow. A cut has both utilitarian and aesthetic value in film editing. By cutting on action in a scene it is possible to employ a variety of different types of shots (**long shots**, **medium shots**, **close-ups**) without disrupting the action. Most studio-era films are made up of standard cuts of this type. The use of cuts as transitions, rather than the use of **dissolves**, **fades**, and **wipes**, can affect the **pace** of the film. The cut transition is the most direct and immediate editing device for introducing new screen information. One shot is followed immediately by a cut to another shot. A cut transition may abruptly place the viewer in the middle of the action of the next scene without regard for the moment of confusion. This type of cut has been labeled "**dynamic cutting**." More commonly the film **editor** will cut to an **establishing shot**, or informational close-up, to introduce a new scene so that the viewer becomes oriented to a change in time and location before important dramatic action begins. The cut has considerable value for providing **continuity**, rhythm, **transitions**, and dramatic emphasis.

Cutaway A shot, edited into a scene, which presents information that is not a part of the first shot. The cutaway shot is usually followed by a return to the original shot, and is often used to condense time in a scene by eliminating undesired action or to cover a loss of continuity in the action. For example, a series of shots of a woman sitting alone in a room smoking a cigarette may not match correctly in editing because of the varied lengths of cigarette ash from shot to shot. A cutaway to a mantel clock, ticking away the time, would provide enough distraction to cover the loss of continuity. Or the cutaway of the clock could be **inserted** between a shot of the woman smoking a cigarette and one of the woman reading a book. The cutaway would permit the **editor** to advance the action in time.

Cut-in A shot which presents material in a scene in greater detail, usually through a **close-up** shot. A cut-in isolates and emphasizes an element of the mise-en-scène for dramatic or informational value. Each progressive movement through the shot sequence, from **long shot** to **close-up**, constitutes a form of cut-in. A cut-in made from a long shot to a big close-up can have a startling effect on the viewer because of its immediate magnification. This technique is frequently an editing method of **suspense films**. See **Insert shot**.

D

Dada

A literary/art movement founded in 1916 in Zurich, Switzerland. The descriptive term "Dada" had no logical meaning; the expressed aim of the school was to negate the traditional relationship between calculation and creativity in the arts by approaching expression in a more playful, **aleatory** manner. The Dadaists borrowed from other movements of the time such as cubism, paper **collage**, and the displaying of industrially made objects ("ready-mades") as works of art. The school was significant because of its influence on progressive artists throughout the world, and was a stepping-stone to surrealism, which developed in the 1920s **avant-garde**.

Man Ray, working in France in the 1920s, is frequently referred to as a "Dadaist filmmaker." Ray used **collage** techniques in his films, spreading materials on the **emulsion** and then processing the film for whatever results occurred (*Le Retour à la Raison*, 1923; *Emak Bakia*, 1927). The early free-flowing, rhythmic films of René Clair, for example, *Paris Qui Dort* [*The Crazy Ray*] (1923), were also inspired by the playful interests of the Dada movement.

Daguerreotype

The name given to a photographic **image** retained on silver or silver-covered copper plates, successfully realized through the efforts of Nicéphore Niépce and Louis J. M. Daguerre. Daguerre publicly displayed examples of the daguerreotype in Paris in January 1839, signaling the arrival of still photography. The development of still photography constituted an important step in the progress toward motion pictures.

Dailies A days shots, processed and viewed for quality.

Day-for-night photography A term for the photographic technique used to simulate night scenes which are shot in daylight.

Day-for-night filming requires underexposure, filtration, and a careful consideration of such factors as sky conditions, color and contrast of subject and background, and strength, quality, and direction of sunlight.

One of the most important requirements for day-for-night filming is to darken the bright daytime sky and balance it with the brightness of the objects or persons providing the foreground action.

Deep-focus photography A term for motion-picture **composition** with great **depth of field** (photo 13). In deep-focus photography the immediate foreground and the deepest parts of the background remain in critical **focus**. This range of critical focus

[DEEP FOCUS] 13. A deep-focus shot in D.W. Griffith's *Intolerance* (1916).

permits the filmmaker to work with several areas of visual information within the same shot. Deep-focus composition is often accompanied by **long-take** photography where there is little or no **cutting** within a scene. The **director** includes all essential action and important character relationships in the deep-focus **frame**. Deep-focus, long-take direction such as that devised by Gregg Toland for Orson Welles' *Citizen Kane* (1941) was in part the inspiration for André Bazin's theories of mise-en-scène analysis (analysis of the photographic image). See **Composition in depth**.

Defocus transition A type of **transition** accomplished by rolling the lens **focus** until the scene becomes blurred. Passage of time within a scene can be suggested by refocusing the shot after alterations are made in the scene: change of costume, lighting, and other **continuity** elements. The defocus device has also been frequently employed in transitions to dream or **fantasy** sequences.

Denouement   (see **Dramatic structure**)

Depth of field   A technical term, with aesthetic implications, that refers to the range of distance within which objects appear in sharp **focus**. A lens which provides great depth of field may have an object within inches of the camera in sharp critical focus as well as objects or figures hundreds of feet away also in critical focus. An object being photographed is in critical focus when each point on the object is reproduced by the lens as a single point in the film **emulsion**. When more than a single point is recorded for each point on the object, the image is said to be "soft," or out of focus. The **aperture** opening of the lens, light levels, subject-camera distance, sensitivity of film stock, and focal length of lens all affect depth of field and focus. These various factors may be manipulated so that a character's eyes are the only area of sharp focus in a **close-up**. A narrow-angle (**telephoto**) lens is most likely to produce this very limited depth of field, which focuses the viewer's attention on the subject's eyes.

On the other hand, a shot through a **wide-angle lens** provides greater depth of field and allows, sometimes demands, that the viewer choose the area of the frame on which to concentrate one's attention at any given moment. This wide-angle, **deep-focus photography** is sometimes referred to as "**composition in depth**." Orson Welles in *Citizen Kane* (1941) often used lenses with extremely wide

[DEPTH OF FIELD] 14. A shallow depth of field in this shot from Jonathan Demme's psychological thriller *Silence of the Lambs* (1990) places Jodie Foster in sharp focus while Anthony Hopkins' image is decidedly "soft." The focus differential helps convey the tense relationship between Hopkins, a psychotic killer, and Foster, an FBI trainee who is seeking information about a serial murderer.

angles of view in order to compose in depth. One shot shows Charles Kane and Susan Alexander Kane at opposite ends of a large room in Kane's palatial home, Xanadu. Susan is sitting in the foreground, playing with a jigsaw puzzle, and Kane is standing in the background at the mouth of a great fireplace. Both characters are seen in sharp focus. The creative use of the wide-angle, deep-focus lens here presents the scene in one unified view. Character relationships are clear. The huge space of the room and the considerable distance between the two characters, conveyed in one shot by the wide-angle lens, suggests the alienated nature of the Kanes' marriage and the separation these people feel even when in the same room.

A telephoto lens does not provide as great a depth of field as a wide-angle lens. If foreground shots are in sharp, critical focus in a telephoto shot, background figures usually are not. Because of the limited depth of field of telephoto lenses, it is possible to use narrow-angle lenses for compositional emphasis. In a two-character telephoto shot, one character can be placed in a plane that will put him/her out of the lens' depth-of-field range and in **soft focus**. The other character, if put within the lens's depth-of-field area, will be in critical focus and therefore more strongly emphasized than the soft-focused character (photo 14).

It is possible to have a character so out of focus as to be totally obscured. Filmmakers will often rack focus to shift the area of sharp focus from one part of the scene to another. The rack focus is commonly used to change emphasis from one character to another or to reveal blurred, indistinct material in a scene.

A popular, effective use of the rack-focus technique is to show in a **subjective shot** a scene coming into focus as though a character's eyes are focusing suddenly on essential information.

Depth of focus A technical term often confused with, and used for, depth of field. The two concepts are related, but quite distinct from each other. Expressed simply, depth of focus is a measure of the lens-to-film-plane distance. According to the *American Cinematographer Manual*, "the depth of focus is an infinitely small range between the lens at the focal plane within which the film is positioned during exposure. If the film moves out of this position, it will cause unsharp images. . . ."

Detail shot   A shot which isolates an element of detail within a scene, usually through the use of a **close-up**. A detail shot is a method of giving emphasis to material phenomena which might otherwise go unnoticed, such as a clenched fist or a revolver. When this type of shot is a detail filmed separately from the main action (for example, a close-up of a letter that a character is reading) and intended to be inserted into the action during editing, it is referred to as "**insert shot**."

Detective film   A motion picture whose plot centers on the prowess of a confident, diligent private eye. This individual is usually shown carrying out a mission of seeking evidence against, and tracking down, a criminal within a large urban environment. Cool and methodical, the detective-hero eventually gets the job done—succeeding in completing a task which local police officers and law officers could not complete.

The detective film differs from a **gangster** picture. Emphasis and sympathy within the detective film are directed toward the heroic powers of a law-enforcing intermediary, whereas in the gangster film the principal character is often an antiheroic figure living and working in the underworld. A contemporary variation of the detective film is one that has been labeled as the "rogue cop" film. The hero of the rogue cop film is a law figure with a tainted reputation who rebounds to solve difficult urban criminal activity. The popularity of the rogue hero has spawned series effort, for example, *The Dirty Harry* and *Lethal Weapon* series.

The detective film was widely popular during the 1930s and 1940s, varying in style from the lighthearted *Thin Man* series (1934–1944) to the more serious film noir effort, for example, *The Maltese Falcon* (1941). The genre has retained its popularity on long-running television series programs (for example, *Colombo, Murder She Wrote, Matlock*).

Dialectical film   A film which attempts through its methodology to present ideas for the purposes of intellectual investigation. Sergei Eisenstein created a dialectical approach in his films through an editing process known as "montage of conflict" or "**montage of collision**." In his films Eisenstein employed a variety of differing types of shots which, edited together, created new meanings. One shot (thesis) would oppose another (antithesis) to produce meaning (synthesis) which did not exist in each separate shot. This dialectical system or thought process developed from Hegelian-Marxist theories which argue that change occurs when one entity passes into and is fulfilled by an opposite entity.

The antiwar **documentary** *Hearts and Minds* (1974) employed visual, aural, and structural devices of dialectical design. Through a combination of available newsreel footage and their own interviews and on-the-spot filming, directors Peter Davis and Bert Schneider in *Hearts and Minds* develop an inquiry into American involvement in the Vietnam War. Pro and con positions are edited into the film along with scenes of the personal impact of the war on the Vietnamese people and on American veterans. The dialectical nature of *Hearts and Minds* is achieved principally through the development of ideas in conflict with one another, and thereby the work seeks to produce an understanding of the range of motivations that prompted and sustained American involvement in the war. *60 Minutes*, the long-running American television news program, has employed a structural technique of intercutting pro and con positions on a particular issue under investigation to achieve dialectical effect. The juxtaposing of opposite opinions on a newsworthy issue has been colloquially referred to as a "journalistic shootout."

Dialogue   Verbal exchange between two or more characters in a film or play. Dialogue may be presented voice-over. In the opening exchange between a French actress and a Japanese architect in *Hiroshima Mon Amour* (1959), the dialogue (two lengthy passages) is heard as the camera roams the museums of Hiroshima. More commonly, dialogue is shown in **lip sync**. The spoken lines are in synchronization with the moving lips of the characters.

Diegesis   A term for all that which exists within the world of a film or play—characters, dialogue, sounds, music. When these elements are part of the fictional narrative (the text's "world"), they are said to be diegetic. A character within the visible mise-en-scène or one who is heard or described off-screen would be diegetic. A visible phonograph or radio playing music is diegetic; thunder heard outside a home is diegetic. An anonymous voice-over narrator and supplied background music on the sound track would both be labeled non-diegetic. Extra-diegetic is used to describe elements such as voice-over narration or voice-over dialogue spoken by a character who is within the diegesis, for instance, the voice-over narration of Ewan McGregor in *Trainspotting* (1996).

Diegetic sound   Sounds, including dialogue and music, originating from an actual source within the film setting. Diegetic sound is also known as "source" sound. Non-diegetic sound is sound that has been created separately and added to the on-screen source sounds, for example, musical scoring, non-synchronous sound effects, voice-over narration.

Differential focus (see **Focus**)

Digital animation (see **Computer-generated imaging**)

Digital sound (digital signal processing, DSP) A superior fidelity sound recording system achieved through the conversion of sound into a binary stream of ones and zeroes that are computer stored for later signal conversion and amplification without risk of distortion. The computer has a capability for recording as many as forty-four thousand elements of sound per second and for signal conversion and transfer without machine-noise buildup. This technological capability results in motion picture sound of vastly improved quality over earlier recording systems. Previously in the editing/mixing process when multichannel transfer mixes occurred, sound clarity diminished progressively; in digital re-recording, however, no loss of fidelity occurs—allowing the same level of acoustical clarity from original recordings to final track, no matter how many subsequent transfers. Consequently, optically printed soundtracks, derived from digital recordings, reproduce with superior quality; and movie theaters equipped with digital playback technology display the system at its optimal best. *Jurassic Park* (1993) gained additional intensity in selected theaters where digital playback equipment had first been installed.

Direct cinema   A term most commonly applied to a type of **documentary** film made in the style of **realist cinema**. Direct cinema shares many of the same interests as *cinéma verité* filmmaking but is narrowly different because it avoids the fluid, spontaneous camera involvement usually associated with *cinéma verité*. Camera presence is minimized in direct-cinema filming. **Wide-angle** views and **long-take** scenes, filmed on a stationary **tripod**, are more commonly the recording methods of direct cinema. **Narration** is also avoided.

Because of distanced camera involvement the aesthetic interests of direct cinema involve an *actualité*-like approach to the subject matter and an emphasis on the subjects in their environment. "**Naturalism**" is a word frequently applied to the documentary style that emphasizes the subject in the environment, for example, *Farrebique* (1946) by George Rouquier and *Warrendale* (1966) by Alan King. Aesthetic distance between viewer and filmmaker in these two documentaries is maintained to such an extent that they are often cited as ideal examples of the direct-cinema technique. Ira Wohl's *Best Boy* (1979) employed direct-cinema methods to present a moving portrait of a middle-aged man whose maturity level is that of a child. Feature director Jim Jarmusch has employed direct-cinema styling in films such as *Stranger Than Paradise* (1984) and *Mystery Train* (1989).

Direct cut
An instantaneous change of shots, usually to a new locale or time frame, and executed without an optical **transition** device. The direct cut is made by splicing together the last **frame** of the outgoing shot with the first frame of the new shot, and serves to replace, dynamically, one shot with another. See **Dynamic cutting**.

Director
That individual in the filmmaking process who serves the principal function of developing the film story into an engaging experience that is artfully constructed. The artful construction of a film story involves the appropriate use of motion-picture techniques, the development of a unifying film style, and control of the dramatic elements of **acting**, **pace**, and **blocking**.

A second but equally important function of the film director is the coordination of the various technicians who must support the film's concept. The director usually confers on such important production elements as costumes, **lighting**, makeup, **camera movement**, locations, and **special effects**. Script changes, including additions and deletions, are often within the jurisdiction of the director, who in filming the story must determine whether a scene will or won't "play" and whether plot and character development are clear.

In a general way, it is possible to divide the motion-picture director into two broad types: (1) the craftsman director and (2) the personal director.

The craftsman director. That individual who is skillfully efficient at taking a motion-picture script and bringing it to life on the screen. The craftsman director knows all facets of film production thoroughly and is able to function with both dramatic and technical ease. A **shooting script** is closely followed as the director works with the actors and other technicians. The craftsman director is one employed to guide and coordinate the filming of a story with professional skill.

The personal director. An individual whose degree of involvement in the filmmaking process is pervasive. Most often this type of director selects the film idea and either alone or with other writers develops the idea into a screen scenario and eventually into a shooting script. The idea is chosen because the director has a strong artistic urge to bring the story to the screen. The personal director often both generates and develops the film idea, e. g. Woody Allen's *Match Point* (2005).

Director of photography (see **Cinematographer**)

Director's cut   A "new" release version of a motion picture which contains material not in the film as it was originally shown in theaters. Often the added material is restoration footage that was edited out of the film earlier because of corporate decision, or to control length or gain a particular **rating**. A director's cut version is of special interest to film **cineastes** who wish to see the motion picture as it was initially conceived by the director. The more important the director and the film, the greater the curiosity. Director's cuts also often contain interviews with the director and other artists involved in the production.

A "director's cut" label on a theatrical re-release of a film or on a VHS or DVD copy has served to enhance marketing of the restored version. Director's cut versions exist of older classics such as *Frankenstein* (1932), *King Kong* (1933), *Lost Horizon* (1937), and *Touch of Evil* (1958) as well as more contemporary works, such as *Spartacus* (1960), The *Godfather* trilogy (1972, 1973, 1990), *Blade Runner* (1982), *9 1/2 Weeks* (1986), *JFK* (1991), *Body of Evidence* (1993), and *The Lord of the Rings* trilogy (2001, 2002, 2003).

Ethical questions have arisen as a result of commercial exploitation of various director's cut versions which have contained little new intrinsic value for the work or its director's so-called artistic vision.

Disaster film   A type of screen **melodrama** characterized by a narrative plot that is centered on the efforts of a number of characters to escape a man-made or natural disaster. In its primary goal of providing mass-appeal escapism, the disaster film usually combines extensive action sequences with a story containing character types that are chosen to represent a broad spectrum of society. Technical virtuosity in the display of screen special effects is also a critical element in the disaster film's formulaic design. The **genre** achieved popularity during the 1930s with such works as *San Francisco* (1936) and *In Old Chicago* (1938) where an earthquake and a fire, respectively, generated calamity. Beginning with *Airport* (1970) and *The Poseidon Adventure* (1972), the disaster film experienced an impressive revival that lasted throughout most of the 1970s. *Titanic* (1997) took the disaster-film concept to new heights of popular and commercial success.

Dissolve   A gradual **transition** in which one scene fades out as the other fades in. Both the end of the outgoing shot and the beginning of the incoming shot are briefly seen on the screen simultaneously. The typical length of dissolves is two seconds, although they may be longer or shorter depending on the desired effect. In traditional filmmaking the dissolve came to be the accepted technique for indicating substantial geographic leaps from one place to another and for indicating passage of time from one scene to another or passage of time within the scene itself. This was so because the **cut** was reserved for scene **continuity** or for **crosscutting** to simultaneous action. The dissolve separates units of action by adding a note of finality to what has gone before and by offering a momentary pause in the action flow. This is usually not true of the cut transition, where new information is instantly revealed and the pace unbroken by an optical process. During the 1960s filmmakers increasingly moved away from the dissolve as a standard convention for indicating a scene change or passage of time, preferring instead the more dynamic cut transition.

The optical nature of the dissolve can carry tonal implications for a film. Extensive use of long dissolves is frequently a device for adding a lyric, poetic quality to a film story, for example, *The Summer of '42* (1971).

A dissolve slowly links two separate moments of time and therefore can be utilized for conceptual purposes. In *The Godfather* (1972), for instance, the scene in which the Hollywood producer awakens to find a severed horse head under his bedcovers ends with a slow dissolve to Don Corleone sitting at his desk in his home office. The dissolve connects the horrified screams of the producer with Marlon Brando's slight raising of an eyebrow before the Don starts a conversation with a visitor. The raising of the eyebrow, although part of a new scene that is unrelated to the one just ending, nevertheless seems also to be a subjective, knowing signal to the viewer that Corleone's will has been carried out in Hollywood.

In the days of motion-picture **censorship**, the dissolve was also a popular means of suggesting, through ellipsis, sexual activity that could not be depicted on the screen.

The dissolve may also be used in scenes of continuous action to suggest the psychological state of a character's mind or to portray fantasies. Many experimental filmmakers, such as Maya Deren, have employed the dissolve to indicate **psychological time** rather than real time. Often these dissolves are so lengthy as to become a **superimposition**, for example, the holding of two shots on the screen simultaneously.

Docudrama   A term for the narrative blending of documentary and fictional elements to create a film drama based on historical, news-inspired actuality. This form of filmmaking is also sometimes referred to as "infotainment," "faction," and "real fiction." The docudrama is most commonly thought of as a **made-for-television-movie** event, although the term has been applied from time to time to theatrical motion pictures (for example, *Not Without My Daughter*, 1990; *JFK*, 1991). Television docudramas escalated significantly in the United States in the 1980s to1990s as tabloid television (*A Current Affair*) and other types of news-simulation programming (*Rescue 911, America's Most Wanted*) also gained in popularity on the airwaves.

An essential characteristic of scripting in the docudrama is a dependence on audience knowledge of the event being treated. The script often develops well-known incidents of a news-familiar story to emotional crescendos, doing so by providing imagined glimpses of what goes on behind the scenes. In *Jacqueline Bouvier Kennedy* (1981) a moment of climactic "snooping" occurs just after John Kennedy has been narrowly elected president. Walking on a Hyannis beach with her husband the morning after the election,

Jacqueline Kennedy (Jaclyn Smith) notices a group of men in the distance following the couple and asks: "Who are those men?" Kennedy replies: "Secret Service" to which his wife responds, "Why so many?" A sense of privileged eavesdropping on the most private conversations of historically destined characters serves as the source of the docudrama's electricity and its manufactured ironies.

Because of its exploitation of news-familiar events, the docudrama strives for a close proximity of actual event to its dramatized version. Typically, production is hastily prepared, **B-picture**-quality filmmaking. *Ambush in Waco* (1993), a made-for-television docudrama of the David Koresh-Branch Davidian religious cult holdout in Waco, Texas, was aired just weeks after the ill-fated raid by government agents. The David Koresh story was actually in production at the time the final showdown occurred in Waco on April 19, 1993. Similarly, a quickly prepared docudrama *Terror in the Towers* (1993) developed a story of the World Trade Center bomb blast in New York City on February 16, 1993.

The blurring of lines between fact and fiction in the docudrama has resulted in considerable discussion of the ethics of a form of drama which exploits historical realities and which does so in a highly imaginative, emotional manner. The telescoping of events, alteration of time chronologies, and the invention of behind-the-scenes situations and dialogue are among the content elements that have helped fuel the docudrama controversy. This was the case in the controversy over a 2003 television docudrama about the private lives of Nancy and Ronald Reagan. Critics sought to suppress the docudrama because of the innuendoed, behind-the-scenes interaction between the Reagans—dramatic material that the critics argued could not be verified. Another part of the debate has centered on the docudrama's tendency to reduce complex news events to simplistic form and to replace potential social and/or political analysis with emotionally charged manipulation of the event.

The docudrama has had a literary counterpart in the so-called docunovel, represented by such works as Truman Capote's *In Cold Blood*, Tom Wolfe's *Bonfire of the Vanities*, and Joyce Carol Oates' *Black Water*.

Documentary   A nonfiction film. Documentaries are usually shot on location; use actual persons rather than actors; and focus thematically on historical, scientific, social, or environmental subjects. Their principal purpose is to enlighten, inform, educate, persuade, and provide insight into the world in which we live.

The World Union of Documentary has defined the documentary film **genre** in this manner:

"By the documentary film is meant all methods of recording on celluloid any aspect of reality either by factual shooting or by sincere and justifiable construction (reenactment), so as to appeal either to reason or emotion for the purpose of stimulating the desire for, and the widening of, human knowledge and understanding, and of truthfully posing problems and their solutions in the spheres of economics, culture and human relations."

Newsreel essays and **informational films** with unifying themes are often categorized as a type of documentary film.

A documentary, more often than not, is a recording of physical reality which the filmmaker interprets for us by the edited arrangement of the material: "a creative treatment of actuality" (John Grierson). Among the early significant creative documentary filmmakers were Robert Flaherty (*Nanook of the North*, 1922) and Pare Lorentz (*The River*, 1937). Flaherty's films dealt with humans in their environment. Lorentz in *The River* and *The Plow That Broke the Plains* (1936) produced poetic films aimed toward social persuasion about ecological problems of the decade. These films established the traditional documentary. In recent decades many sub-schools of documentary filmmaking have developed, for example, *cinéma verité*, **direct cinema, docudrama, ethnographic film**.

With the advent of television, the documentary film genre acquired the two principal elements needed to sustain the form: (1) a mass audience and (2) financial support through institutional sponsorship. On television, the genre has been seen in a variety of different orientations: (1) journalistic: information and analysis (*CBS Reports, NBC White Papers*); (2) social: documentaries designed to reveal social problems and to persuade (*Harvest of Shame*, 1960; *I Want It All Now*, 1978); (3) poetic, educational: documentaries to entertain and teach (*America*, 1972); (4) magazine: a variety of short documentaries and newsreel essays included in a single program with a studio host or hosts introducing and commenting on different segments (*60 Minutes, 20–20, Prime Time*).

A revival of and commercial viability for theatrical release of feature-length documentaries have been evident in the success of widely varied documentary effort, for example, *Roger and Me* (1989), *Hoop Dreams* (1994), *American Movie* (1999), *Winged Migration* (2001), *Bowling for Columbine* (2002), *Spellbound* (2003), *Fahrenheit 9/11* (2004), *March of the Penguins* (2005).

Dolby® Pro Logic® A patented electronic sound-steering system developed for **home cinema theater** setups that creates the effect of **Dolby** stereo acoustics found in professional movie theaters. Home videos that are Dolby-encoded reproduce the multichannel studio sound mix, providing in addition to standard side stereo speakers a center (dialogue) channel as well as an **ambient** effects component located at the rear. Additional speakers channeled to the back of the room for acoustical texture and depth are commonly called Surround Speakers. See **Home cinema theater**.

Dolby® sound (system) A patented noise-reduction sound system which is used with theatrical motion pictures as an embellishment to the screen imagery. The Dolby system makes possible high-fidelity, **stereophonic-sound** accompaniment on the optical **sound track** rather than a **magnetic sound track** as was once required for clean, noise-free reproduction. Dolby sound found wide application during the 1970s in screen spectacles as diverse as *Star Wars* (1977) and *Apocalypse Now* (1979). The system became a standard of high quality, big-budget motion pictures.

Dolly shot   A shot in which the camera, placed on a wheeled mount, moves closer to or away from a scene. The camera dollies in or the camera dollies out.

The dolly shot is an alternative to the **cut** in changing scope and **angle of view**. The camera moves dynamically and fluidly through space in a dolly, rather than jumping through it as happens in **shot-sequence editing** and cut-ins.

Because of the physical movements of the camera, the dolly in shot moves fluidly and directly into the heart of a drama. An important **reaction shot**, for example, seems all the more important and dramatic when combined with a dolly into a **close-up** of the actor's face. Such a shot occurred in *Rocky* (1976) while the boxer was being told that he is to be given a chance to fight the heavyweight champion. The sustained movement of the camera seems to allow the reaction to grow in impact. Similarly, a dolly out seems to take us away from the heart of the drama but, depending on its speed, allows some time for contemplation. Like **pans** and **tilts**, the dolly permits a director to follow action with sustained, unedited **continuity**.

Double exposure Two or more **images** which have been photographed separately but which appear over one another or side by side on the same piece of film. A double exposure may be achieved by running unprocessed film through the camera more than once or by optical printing at the processing laboratory. Georges Méliès created illusory effects in many of his early **trick films** through double exposures (photo 15). In contemporary filmmaking the technique appears more commonly in **experimental-film** efforts, for example, Marie Menken's *Hurry, Hurry* (1957) and Ed Emshwiller's *Relativity* (1963–1966).

Double feature A motion-picture marketing practice begun by the American film industry during the Depression years of the 1930s. Two pictures, one often better in quality than the other, would be exhibited for the price of a single admission. The

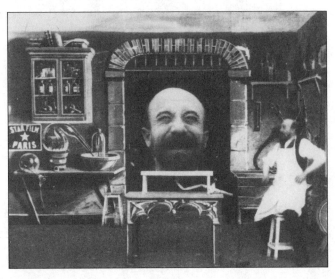

[DOUBLE EXPOSURE] 15. Through double-exposure shots, achieved by exposing the same piece of film to two different scenes, Georges Méliès produced numerous trick films—in this instance *The Man with the Double Head* (1902).

double-feature bill was a successful audience booster for almost two decades. Its demise was brought about by two major events: (1) the advent of television, which served to satisfy general audience entertainment needs and (2) the 1948 antitrust decree of the U.S. Supreme Court. The latter event forced motion-picture producers to give up their ownership of movie theaters. Without the guarantee of assured booking (block booking), emphasis had to be placed on the first-rate film; the cheaper picture, which had been made for second place on the double-feature bill, became an uncertain commodity. This fact, coupled with dwindling box office receipts in the early 1950s, killed double features as a standard exhibition procedure. Contemporary exhibitors occasionally present double-feature programs to attract audiences. Two films by a popular director are often played on a double-feature bill, for instance, two Ingmar Bergman films or two comedies by Woody Allen.

Double-system sound Sound that has been recorded on a tape recorder that is not part of the camera, and that is later added to the edited film—either as an optical or a magnetic sound track. When the sound track is recorded directly onto the film (either optically or magnetically) as the camera is filming an event, the procedure is referred to as a "single-system sound." See **Magnetic film**.

Dramatic structure Refers to the composite body of elements which function as essential plotting conventions in the development and resolution of a dramatic play or motion picture. These elements are as follows:

Exposition. Early information in a developing screen narrative that reveals character and begins to set the plot in motion.

Inciting action. A situation, usually taking place early in the film narrative, which reveals the conflict around which the plot will revolve. Sometimes referred to as an "exciting force."

Rising action. Episodes and events within the film plot, occurring after the inciting action, which increase dramatic interest as the story conflict builds to a climax. The events within the rising action are also referred to as "complications." Introduction of enhancing narrative and plot information that has occurred in the script's "past" is referred to as "back story."

Climax. The moment of greatest interest or tension in a film story—bringing about a turning point in the dramatic action. The climax usually occurs at a point of great crisis for the principal character or characters, at which time a crucial decision that affects the outcome of the dramatic conflict is made.

Falling action. Events or episodes that occur after a film's climax.

Denouement. The final moments of revelation in a film narrative during which time all loose ends, mysteries, and uncertainties unfold so that the plot is fully disentangled.

See **Anticlimax, Antagonist, Back story, Protagonist**.

Dream balloon   A method of visualizing a character's thoughts by including the desired information in a circle that usually appears above the character's head. The device was commonly used by film-makers during the medium's silent era, and was achieved either through **rear-screen projection** or **double exposure**. Edwin S. Porter inserted a dream balloon in the opening shot of *The Life of an American Fireman* (1903) to show the wife and child of the fireman as he sleeps at his desk in the fire station. See **Photographed thought**.

Dream mode   A term sometimes used to describe motion pictures or parts of motion pictures whose stories and techniques suggest the workings of the mind, resembling either dreams or situations which are derived from the imagination. Films operating in the dream mode are often so labeled because of their lack of **continuity** and the illogical, unconnected manner in which **images** come and go on the screen. *Un Chien Andalou* (1928), a surrealist film, is often described as a film which operates in a dream mode. Parts of the screen version of *Slaughterhouse Five* (1972) function within a dream mode, as do scenes in *My Own Private Idaho* (1991). Robert Altman's *Three Women* (1977), a film whose plot Altman says came to him in a dream, has continued to mesmerize because of its mysterious dream-mode elements. *Three Women* was remastered and re-released on DVD in 2004.

Important critics such as Hugo Munsterberg and Suzanne Langer have used the concept of dream mode as a distinguishing characteristic of the film medium. Langer maintains that films are like dreams, moving rapidly through space and constantly changing the images for the viewer as in a dream.

Drive-in theater A form of open-air movie theater which increased in number and popularity in the decade following World War II. The development and growth of this type of theater resulted in part from the postwar baby boom and the increasing auto culture of new family-oriented suburbanites. Drive-in theaters were designed and equipped so that motion-picture viewing would be possible from inside a parked automobile. The average drive-in theater would hold 300 to 500 automobiles and larger ones held as many as 1,500 cars. In a period when box office revenues were diminishing, drive-in theaters spurred new interest in film going by making group attendance possible at a lower cost than indoor theater ticket prices. The number of drive-in theaters continues to decrease after a peak in the late 1950s.

Dubbing The process of adding sound, **dialogue**, or **sound effects** to a film after the dramatic action has been photographed. This is possible because sound in most motion pictures is recorded on a separate system (**double-system sound**) rather than on the film itself and later edited to fit the visual images. When all desired sounds (**music, dialogue**, sound effects) have been edited and mixed into a single synchronized sound track, it is then printed on the edited film.

Some directors prefer to dub dialogue and sound effects rather than use the original on-the-set sound. This approach has become even more prevalent as **location shooting** has increased. By dubbing, it is possible to obtain better sound quality and even to change the original dialogue. "Dubbing" is also the term for converting foreign-language films to another language. The technique frequently used in dubbing a motion picture is that of **looping**. In looping, a section of film is spliced end to end so that it repeats its movement through the projector. A looped piece of **magnetic film** is interlocked into a projector-recorder system. Actors, through this double-looping process, are able to rehearse and record lines with the film images until the sound dubbing is satisfactory.

Dutch angle An angled shot in which the horizon and objects in a scene are canted (slanted, photo 16). Vertical and horizontal lines within the scene are photographed so that they are in an oblique relationship to the vertical and horizontal lines of the film **frame**. This unnatural, tilted view of a scene is disorienting and can suggest tension, confusion, and psychological imbalance. In *Arabesque* (1966), for example, Gregory Peck's loss of physical and mental orientation with his environment, after he has been drugged, is conveyed in part by a series of canted shots of his confused actions. The increasing derangement of Glenn Close in *Fatal Attraction* (1987) is depicted in occasional Dutch-angle cinematography. In contemporary documentary filmmaking, tilted, Dutch-angle close-up shots of interview subjects have gained in popularity, for example, Robert McNamara's talking-head shots in the Academy Award-winning *The Fog of War* (2003).

[DUTCH ANGLE] 16. One of several Dutch-angle compositions used by Carol Reed in *The Third Man* (1949) to depict the shattered, unbalanced world of postwar Vienna. Orson Welles portrays Harry Lime.

Dynamic cutting   An approach to film editing in which the cutting from one shot to the next is made abruptly apparent to the viewer. In **matched cutting** or **invisible editing**, the cuts are not as obvious to the viewer because these approaches adhere to continuity procedures designed to hide the edit, for instance, cutting on action. Dynamic cutting, on the other hand, is self-conscious and will often startle the viewer by moving abruptly in time or space or by rapid cutting within a scene for expressive as well as narrative purposes. Bob Fosse's *All That Jazz* (1979), Richard Rush's *The Stunt Man* (1980), and Oliver Stone's *JFK* (1991) and *Natural Born Killers* (1994) employed dynamic cutting extensively.

Dynamic frame   A term attributed to Sergei Eisenstein after the Russian director wrote an essay in 1931 in which he discussed the possibilities and values of changing **frame** size from the traditional 4 to 3 **aspect ratio** to other shapes (photo 17). In his writings Eisenstein advocated new **image** formats of any shape or size suitable to the treatment of diverse subject matter. In his own work, Eisenstein had experimented with

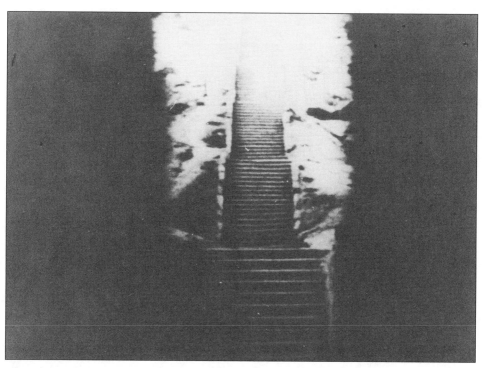

[DYNAMIC FRAME] 17. Sergei Eisenstein employed vertical masking to produce this dynamic frame in *The Battleship Potemkin* (1925).

masking (imitating D.W. Griffith) and unusual **compositions** to vary image shape.

A British film, *The Door in the Wall*, created in the 1950s by Glen Alvey, Jr., experimented with masking techniques that permitted a constantly changing image size. A narrow vertical screen image would widen as a character passed from an interior location to an exterior setting. This process, while intriguing, was too complex technically to be practical. Filmmakers continue to achieve the effect of the dynamic frame through traditional methods: composition, lighting, or set shape and design as demonstrated in the cinematography of M. Night Shymalan's *Unbreakable* (2000).

E

Editor	That individual responsible for the aesthetics of film construction in the postfilming stages. In dramatic filmmaking the editor determines cutting **style, transitions**, and the development of the narrative. Astute rearrangements of **scenes** to aid dramatic effect and enhance tempo, as well as the deletion of undesirable material, are within the jurisdiction of the film editor. It is not uncommon for the **director** and the producer to work closely with the editor in making editorial decisions or in approving both the "**rough cut**" (first assemblage) and **final cut** of the motion picture.
Emulsion	The layer of a film stock which contains light-sensitive particles of metallic silver. These particles (**grains**) at the moment of exposure are "tagged"; in **black-and-white** emulsions the film when processed produces **images** that are rendered in various shades of gray. These shades vary from light to dark according to the quality of reflected light which "tags" emulsion particles. A **color film** is one in which the emulsion layer has been chemically developed to respond to reflected light in such a way that color images are produced rather than gray ones.

Film emulsion particles are suspended in a clear gelatin substance on a flexible celluloid base (film base).

Epic A motion picture characterized by its extensive narrative form and heroic qualities. The epic film generally covers a large expanse of time as it follows in an episodic manner the continuing adventures of a hero or set of heroes. Often the heroes of epic films are boldly courageous figures whose deeds are presented in the course of great historical events (*The Birth of a Nation*, 1915; *Gone with the Wind*, 1939; *War and Peace*, 1956; *Dr. Zhivago*, 1965; *Gandhi*, 1982; *Dances with Wolves*, 1990; *Gettysburg*, 1993; *Gladiator*, 2000; *Gods and Generals*, 2003). Other epic films are more picaresque in quality, chronicling an extended portion of a roguish character's life story, for example, *Tom Jones* (1963), *Barry Lyndon* (1975), *Reds* (1981). *Cold Mountain* (2003) is an epic, picaresque treatment of a Civil War soldier who is making his way from Petersburg, Virginia, to his home in North Carolina. During the journey, extensive parallel story lines are intercut to chronicle the domestic struggles of those left behind in Cold Mountain during the war.

The production of epic films usually involves elaborate settings, authentic period costumes, and a large cast of characters. These elements are considered necessary in achieving the grand aura expected of epic films.

Episodic (story development) A quality attributed to a motion picture which contains numerous dramatic incidents in the development of the story line rather than a single line of developing action. Epic or picaresque films such as *Gone with the Wind* (1939) *Barry Lyndon* (1975), *Cold Mountain* (2003), and *Master and Commander* (2003) were highly episodic whereas *High Noon* (1952), a western whose story follows actual time and moves inexorably toward a gunfight, is not as episodic in plot construction. *Before Sunset* (2004), a largely dialogue film with Ethan Hawke and Julie Delpy, essentially occurs in real time.

Establishing shot A **shot** which establishes the location of a film story or scene. The establishing shot usually presents a long, wide-angle view of an area to identify the location either generally or specifically. Shots of the New York skyline or the Eiffel Tower are specific in establishing location. A wide-angle shot of a busy street scene will in a more general way establish the location as that of a large city. Establishing shots may also identify specific activity areas through **long shots**, for example, of a courthouse, police station, state capitol building, etc. See **Master shot**.

Ethnographic film A film of an anthropological nature which attempts to describe or visualize the social and cultural experiences of one group of people for another. The goal of interpreting one society for another distinguishes the ethnographic film from other types of **documentaries** that might be more concerned with national, social, and political issues. All of Robert Flaherty's major films are ethnographic studies: *Nanook of the North* (1922), a heroic view of Eskimo life in the Hudson Bay area of Canada; *Moana* (1926), a picture of Samoan traditions; *Man of Aran* (1934), an account of the harsh realities of life for a family living on an island off the coast of Ireland; and *Louisiana Story* (1948), a poetic view of bayou life in the southern United States.

Other early pioneering ethnographers included Merian C. Cooper and Ernest Schoedsack, whose *Grass* (1925) charted the nomadic life of herdsmen in the Middle East. Like Flaherty, these documentarists sought to record and describe the unique culture of their subjects as objectively as possible without any preconceived bias—a particular requirement of the ethnographic film. Modern ethnographers, of which there are many, follow this demand, often filming in **long shot** in a spontaneous manner so as to record accurately the raw visual data needed for cultural preservation and interpretation. John Cohen's *Queros: The Shape of Survival* (1978) employs these methods in presenting a stark ethnographic study of Queros Indians who live in primitive isolation in the Andes Mountains of Peru. Feature narrative films are often said to possess strong ethnographic qualities, for example, *Coal Miner's Daughter* (1980), *The Story of Qui Ju* (1992), *Before Night Falls* (2000).

Expanded cinema A general term referring to the inquiry into the exploration of highly technological approaches to film art. Ranging from the use of multiple projectors to **computer-generated films** to simple shadow plays, the artist attempts to create a moving, kinetic art experience and mixed-media environments which affect the senses. Often expanded-cinema artists deal with the essence of motion, which has always intrigued the filmmaker, and also seek a re-exploration of three basic principles of cinematic art: light, time, and space.

Removing itself from the popular concept of a "**canned**" film projected onto a screen in a movie house, expanded cinema seeks to make each production a totally self-sufficient and original experience. Expanded-cinema programs have included (1) mixed-media presentations including "live" performers, (2) video technology, and (3) multi-projection systems. The term expanded cinema was first used by the critic Gene Youngblood.

Experimental film A film term with a number of different meanings. The term "**avant-garde**" is generally used to describe the first experimental film movement, which began in France in the 1920s. Many of the avant-garde filmmakers were artists who came to the cinema from other arts, particularly from painting and literature. The movement began as a reaction against the narrative motion picture of the time. It was also an extension of contemporary art into the medium of cinema, where artists such as Hans Richter, Viking Eggeling, Salvador Dalí, and Fernand Léger could continue their experiments with abstract, expressionistic, and surrealistic art. Painters such as Richter and Léger were particularly interested in the motion picture as a means of bringing their abstract images to rhythmic life. In *Rhythmus '21* (1921) Richter rhythmically alternated black and white geometric shapes on film. Léger in *Ballet Mécanique* (1924) placed common objects into rhythmical and mechanical motion. These films are also commonly classified as **abstract films**.

Because they believed that the film story was too closely allied with the theater and literature, the avant-garde filmmakers experimented extensively with cinematic techniques and camera tricks—an approach referred to as *cinéma pur* (pure cinema).

Leading a second experimental film movement was Maya Deren, a Russian-born director whose important work was done in the United States in the 1940s. Her *Meshes of the Afternoon* (1943) was a subjective self-study that mixes dream and reality in an ambiguous manner. Deren's work stimulated numerous filmmakers to create highly personal self-projections on celluloid, including Curtis Harrington (*Fragments of Seeing*, 1946) and Kenneth Anger (*Fireworks*, 1947). The frank quality of these films and the necessity of self-distribution and exhibition led to the use of the term "**underground film**" in the 1950s to denote the work of experimental American filmmakers. However, by the time the term came into use the range of experimental approaches was far greater than the subjective model introduced by Deren. "Underground" came to mean: any film which was made for non-commercial, personal purpose; sought to break with the traditions of commercial cinema; treated subject matter which was taboo in commercial films; and exploited the pure-cinema possibilities of the medium.

Other terms emerged in the 1960s to denote experimental film. **New American Cinema** appeared briefly in reference to works by an organized group of filmmakers, most of whom were located in New York City. The term "**expanded cinema**" was coined by critic Gene Youngblood in reference to multimedia experiments, often including live performance. Generally speaking, contemporary experimentalists—whatever their intentions or their methods of cinematic expression—are referred to as "**independent filmmakers**." See **Psychodrama**.

Exploitation film A term used to describe a commercial motion picture whose subject matter has been chosen and developed to appeal to a particular type of audience. Sensationalism is usually a major ingredient. Two types of films falling under the label are the **sexploitation film** and the **blaxploitation film**. The term "exploitation" is to some extent redundant since a vast majority of feature-length motion pictures are designed to draw audiences through particularized appeals.

Exposition (see **Dramatic structure**)

Exposure The act in motion-picture photography of exposing a sensitized film material to light for the recording of **images**.

Exposure is the product of both time and intensity of illumination acting upon the photographic material. Exposure takes place when light from the subject, **focused** by the lens system, strikes the film **emulsion**, usually very briefly. The photochemical reaction of the light with the silver halide compounds in the film emulsion forms a latent image which is converted into a permanent visible image when the film is processed.

Exposure of film in the production of a motion picture is usually very closely controlled in order to yield shots that photographically reproduce reality as closely and consistently as possible. Deviations from what might be termed "normal" exposure usually are scrupulously avoided.

However, the ability to control the degree of exposure presents the cinematographer with valuable creative possibilities. Both underexposure and overexposure have been intentionally used in many films to enhance scenes visually and dramatically.

Underexposure. The act of exposing each frame of film to less light or for a shorter period of time than would be required to produce a "normal" exposure of the same subject. Underexposure yields a picture that tends to be dark overall, the degree of darkness depending on the degree to which the shot is underexposed. There is little or no visible detail in the shadow areas of the picture, and in **color films** colors look muddy and somewhat indistinct.

Underexposed shots have been occasionally used when it is the director's intention to keep the viewer uncertain of the identity of persons or objects in the shot, as is often necessary in mystery and suspense films. Carefully underexposed shots filmed at dusk can often simulate a later time of evening. This is called **day-for-night** photography.

Overexposure. The act of exposing each frame of film to more light or for a longer period of time than would be required to produce a "normal" exposure of the same subject. There is little or no visible detail in the highlights—the bright areas of the picture—and images appear bleached, more or less washed out.

The ***washout***. The most extreme form of overexposure is the washout. The visual manifestation of the washout is a screen that goes completely white (or very nearly). This effect can be accomplished by directing the camera at a bright light source that will wash out most, if not all, of the **frame** area, or by having the effect processed in the film laboratory.

Expressionism   A stylistic movement within film, drama, painting, fiction, and poetry which uses non-realistic, non-naturalistic methods in an attempt to reveal inner experience. In the expressionistic film, and in expressionistic drama, actors, objects, and scenic design are treated not as representational but as elements that function to convey mood, emotion, and psychological atmosphere. *The Cabinet of Dr. Caligari* (1919) is a well-known film that employs expressionistic devices (photo 18). In this German motion picture the settings are wildly distorted. The actors move in concentric circles, and

CONRAD VEIDT et LIL DAGOVER dans *Le Cabinet du D' Caligari*, réalisé par R. Wiene.

[EXPRESSIONISM] 18. Dark, foreboding shadows, distorted set designs, and stylized makeup were common elements in expressionistic films of psychological import. Robert Wiene's *The Cabinet of Dr. Caligari* (1919), shown above, is perhaps the best-known example of screen expressionism.

lighting is unusually dark and somber. The ***mise-en-scène*** of *The Cabinet of Dr. Caligari* underscores in a psychological rather than a realistic manner the film's story, which occurs in the mind of an inmate in a mental hospital. Similar in expressionistic and thematic interests is Alain Resnais' *Last Year at Marienbad* (1961), a film presenting the viewpoint of a single character. The use of stylized settings, costumes, and special effects (fast motion) also lend an expressionistic quality to Stanley Kubrick's *A Clockwork Orange* (1971). Dark, somber toning of the cardboard-like settings of *Batman* (1989) gave the production design of this Tim Burton film an expressionistic feeling. The serial-killer film *Se7en* (1995) possessed psychological and visual qualities associated with expressionism, as did *Monster* (2003), also a serial killer study.

Expressionistic sound A term for film sound which has been stylized by distortion, volume, or great presence or has been asynchronously arranged with disparate images. In Robert Enrico's *An Occurrence at Owl Creek Bridge* (1961) the sounds of footsteps, a musical pocket watch, and dialogue are all intentionally distorted through volume and technical manipulation to suggest the intense, confused awareness of a condemned traitor's mind. Ken Russell's *Altered States* (1980) employed expressionistic sound elements in presenting a science-fiction account of the uncertain world of human subconsciousness. In *Made in America* (1993), sound manipulation changes a sperm-bank clerk's voice from female to male to create a subjective awareness of this intimidating figure for a young male posing as a donor.

External rhythm   Rhythm within a motion picture achieved through editing. A form of external rhythm through editing, common in chase and action stories, is called "accelerated **montage**." Usually this effect is achieved by using increasingly shorter shots of a depicted movement. A long-distance runner, for example, can seem to be increasing his speed at an incredible pace by the editor's use of a sequence of shots which continually decrease in length. The contrast of shorter, more staccato shots following earlier shots more prolonged in length creates an illusion of accelerated movement.

D.W. Griffith employed accelerated montage in his famous **last-minute-rescue** films. In addition to rapid **crosscutting** between the beleaguered victim and the approaching rescuer, Griffith would gradually decrease the length of shots to make the action appear even more exciting.

External rhythm can also be applied to achieve a more **lyrical film** quality. In a motion picture, as in a poem, lyricism evolves in part from rhythmic patterns designed to enhance impressions of beauty, romance, ecstasy, mood, and other sensory perceptions. The editing rhythm of film images can serve essentially the same function as phrasing in poetry. Films such as Alain Resnais' *Night and Fog* (1955), Claude Lelouch's *A Man and a Woman* (1966), Barry Levinson's *Avalon* (1990), and Wong Kar-Wai's *In the Mood for Love* (2000) employ editing rhythms for a lyrical effect.

Extra   An individual appearing in a motion picture who has no speaking role or pointed dramatic significance. The extra is merely an embellishment within the mise-en-scène.

F

Fade	A transition device for moving from one scene or sequence to another in a motion picture. A fade-out occurs when the image on the screen fades to black to end the scene. The scene which follows may suddenly appear, or it may gradually fade in from black. The first is a fade-out/cut-in transition, while the second is the traditional fade-out/fade-in. The use of a fade-out/cut-in has a different effect than the slow, more contemplative movement of the fade-out/fade-in. The fade-out/cut-in gives the fade-out a feeling of finality and separation to the scene just ending, while the cut-in introduces the new action in a dynamic, attention-getting way. In *Small Change* (1976), François Truffaut uses the fade-out/cut-in transition to separate the longer sequences of his film about children. The use of this technique separates the parts of the film like movements in a musical composition or stanzas of a poem, without significantly slowing the pace of the whimsical film.
Falling action	(see **Dramatic structure**)
Fantasy	A type of film story or film experience which occurs within the imagination, dreams, or hallucinations of a character or within the projected vision of the storyteller. Siegfried

Kracauer defined film fantasy as storytelling or visual experience which is "outside the area of physical experience." The term "fantasy" is also often used to describe a work which is set in an unreal world or which includes characters that are incredible in conception. Many of the early trick films of Georges Méliès, such as *A Trip to the Moon* (1902), are fantasy films, as are *The Blue Bird* (1976) and *Star Wars* (1977). Fantasy has been used both for light entertainment (*Mary Poppins*, 1964; *Elf*, 2003) and as a vehicle for social commentary (*It's a Wonderful Life*, 1946; *Heaven Can Wait*, 1978; *Defending Your Life*, 1991; *What Dreams May Come*, 1998).

Fast motion (undercranking) A motion-picture effect which occurs when fewer than twenty-four frames per second are taken of an action and are projected at normal projector speed. The effect is that of herky-jerky, speeded-up motion. Fast motion is most commonly associated with comedy, because early screen comedies were often undercranked slightly to enhance their slapstick pace. The runaway subway-train scene in *Spider-Man 2* (2004) benefited from fast-motion cinematography.

Feature film   A full-length motion picture made and distributed for release in movie theaters as the principal film for any given program. **Shorts** were those films which accompanied the feature film and which were shown to fill out a theater's program. By tradition the feature film and the shorts have comprised a program approximately two hours in length. The evolution of the feature film in the period 1913–1916 brought with it larger, more comfortable movie theaters and refined systems for motion-picture exhibition. By the early 1920s the economic success and popularity of feature-length films had led to the development of movie-house chains owned and operated by the major Hollywood production studios.

Film craftsman   (see **Director**)
Film criticism   (see **Criticism**)
Filmic   A descriptive term that may be used interchangeably with "**cinematic**." "Filmic" is often applied in film criticism to suggest that subject matter and film methods are deemed particularly appropriate to the medium. A **chase** sequence might be described as filmic or the use of **crosscutting** in the development of plot. Like the term "cinematic," filmic is often used as an analogy for describing literary or dramatic methods which resemble the methods of the motion picture.

Film noir   A style within American filmmaking which evolved in the
1940s and whose unusual tone and atmospherics came to
be called "film noir" or, literally, "black film." This descriptive label has been applied to motion pictures, often **detective films** and crime stories of a pessimistic nature, whose
lighting schemes were heavily **low key**. The use of **black-
and-white film** stock, standard in the 1940s, allowed a wide
range of black-to-white shadings, and permitted directors to
experiment with the darker end of the scale in photographing stories and characters of a sinister, brooding quality.
Interior settings were lit to look dark and gloomy, as though
photographed at night. Exteriors were often shot at night to
add to the dreary environments. Story locations in films
noir were commonly the dark streets and dimly lit apartments
and hotel rooms of big cities. The tone of films noir is decidedly pessimistic. Character stereotypes, female and male,
abound.

[FILM NOIR] 19. An adaptation of Raymond Chandler's novel *The Big Sleep* (1946) resulted in one of the finest examples of the many film noir-style detective pictures made during the 1940s. Humphrey Bogart portrayed the cynical detective Philip Marlowe and
Lauren Bacall was his girlfreind Vivian. The unforgettable first-person, voice-over narration—a distinguishing characteristic of the genre—was written, in part, by William Faulkner.

The film noir style was found in film adaptations of Raymond Chandler novels, in many of the private-eye films of Humphrey Bogart, and in works by Howard Hawks (*The Big Sleep*, 1946, photo 19), John Huston (*The Maltese Falcon*, 1941), Robert Aldrich (*Kiss Me Deadly*, 1955), and Orson Welles (*The Lady from Shanghai*, 1948; *Touch of Evil*, 1958). The inspiration for films noir came in part from Welles' bold, expressive use of low-key lighting in *Citizen Kane* (1941) and *The Magnificent Ambersons* (1942). Films noir also had earlier precedent in German expressionism and in the psychological films of the German directors E.A. Dupont, G.W. Pabst, and F.W. Murnau, where mood was often matched by shadowy lighting and darkly oppressive settings. Interest in film noir styles and themes can be noted in many of the policeman-hero films of the 1960s and 1970s: *Madigan* (1968); the *Dirty Harry* series (1971–1976); the Raymond Chandler remake *Farewell, My Lovely* (1975); in Lawrence Kasdan's *Body Heat* (1981); in Paul Verhoeven's erotic sex-thriller *Basic Instinct* (1992); in Curtis Hanson's *L.A. Confidential* (1997); and in Stephen Frear's *Dirty Pretty Things* (2002).

Filmography   A bibliographic listing of a group of films, most commonly the listing of a director's or an actor's full body of work.

Film speed   A term used to designate a particular film **emulsion**'s sensitivity to light. Film speeds in the United States are regulated by the American Standards Association and hence are supplied with an ASA rating. The higher the number of the ASA rating (e.g., ASA 400), the faster the speed of the film or, expressed another way, the more receptive the emulsion is to recordings made where little light is available. Because high-speed films tend to show **grain** when printed, film speed becomes an important consideration in a director's choice of emulsions. As a general rule of thumb, directors will choose the slowest possible film stock for a sharply defined, low-contrast image. Higher speeds, however, may be chosen if the desired look of the processed film is intended to simulate grainy, newsreel-like footage, or where high contrast images are desired.

Filter   Usually a glass or gelatin material through which light is altered as it passes to the film **emulsion**. Neutral density filters are employed most commonly to retard amounts of light and sometimes to darken areas of the frame in **day-for-**

night photography. Neutral density filters come in varying shades of gray. Correction or conversion filters contain color values which change the light so it matches the emulsion characteristics of the film. Polarizing filters rotate so as to alter the angle of light rays as they hit the lens and thereby can function to darken sky areas in color photography and to reduce in black-and-white and color photography undesired natural reflections.

Contrast filters are filters that come in a variety of colors and are most frequently used in black-and-white photography to reproduce colors in lighter or darker shades of gray than they would reproduce without a filter by allowing the filter's color to pass through the filter and by holding back the filter's complementary color. Other types are haze filters and diffusion filters.

Final cut (fine cut) A term for the edited version of a motion picture as it will look when printed and released for exhibition. A final cut usually follows a **rough cut** version which the **director, editor**, and other members of the production team may examine with the intention of offering suggestions about the final cut. In many instances final cuts have been made after gauging audience reactions at sneak previews, or in some cases after screening a rough cut for media specialists, for example, *Nashville* (1975). Altman's work, in longer form, was shown to selected critics in advance of the final cut. See **Director's cut**.

Fish-eye lens (shot) An extreme wide-angle lens whose glass element resembles a fish eye (photo 20). The **focal length** range of fish-eye lenses varies from 1 to 7 mm in 16-mm filmmaking and of slightly greater range in 35-mm cinematography. Fish-eye lenses commonly serve as special-effect lenses because of their ability to distort objects at close proximity to the camera and to greatly expand the sense of space in longer views. An arm extended toward a fish-eye lens can appear twice its length. Horizons will have a curved quality.

Lina Wertmüller in *The Seduction of Mimi* (1975) employed a fish-eye lens for comic and dramatic effect in a scene where Giancarlo Giannini, to avenge his wife's affair with a city official, tries to make love to the official's overly large, unattractive wife. The woman's size is severely emphasized by a distorting fish-eye lens, and its use conveys in a subjective manner Giannini's repulsion while attempting to

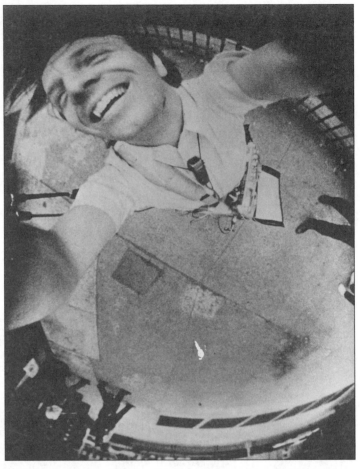

[FISH-EYE LENS] 20. The distorting qualities of a fish-eye lens are evident in this shot from Jim McBride's *David Holzman's Diary* (1967).

carry out the sex act. Fish-eye lensing is employed with surrealistic effect in Danny Boyle's *Trainspotting* (1996), most notably in the drug-withdrawal scene with Ewan McGregor.

Flashback   A scene or shot in a motion-picture story which deals with an event that has occurred prior to the film's principal time period. Flashbacks are often inserted into a story line for the purpose of recalling a situation that is relevant to the developing plot, or to clarify points of information as in the concluding scenes of a mystery film. In many films flashbacks become a principal plotting device for revealing character by **crosscutting** among scenes of past and present time. *Citizen Kane* (1941), *In Which We Serve* (1942), *Rachel,*

Rachel (1968), *The Godfather Part Two* (1975), *Fried Green Tomatoes* (1991), *Iris* (2001), and *Big Fish* (2003) are examples of motion pictures which have made extensive use of flashbacks for plot and character development. The flashback acts as the unifying narrative device in *In Which We Serve*, revealing officers and enlisted men aboard the British naval war ship *H.M.S. Torrin* in various domestic scenes. The flashbacks create a sense of unified cause in the war effort—linking national interests with community and family, and giving heroic proportions to the men on board the *Torrin*, which was downed by torpedoes off the Isle of Crete. The beginning sequences of *Cold Mountain* (2003) intercut flashback scenes of Inman (Jude Law) meeting and falling in love with Ada (Nicole Kidman) with scenes of Inman and other Civil War Confederate soldiers preparing for the Battle of Petersburg. One of the most powerful moments in *Brokeback Mountain* (2005) is a flashback scene to an embrace between Jack and Ennis that occurred in the early stages of their relationship.

Flash-forward   An editing technique where scenes or shots which occur in a future time are inserted into the developing story line of a film. Flash-forwards are often employed to anticipate a critical dramatic situation toward which the plot is progressing. The technique can also provide an element of mystery because of ambiguous relationships of the flash-forward to the film's time continuum; often flash-forwards are recognized as such only after the story has proceeded to the point of the shot (the flash-forward) which has appeared earlier in the film. *They Shoot Horses Don't They?* (1969) repeats throughout the film an ambiguous flash-forward shot of a young man as he stands in the presence of a judge. The meaning of this flash-forward does not become clear until the end of the film, after the man has committed a "mercy killing." A similar use of the flash-forward occurs in Nicholas Roeg's *Don't Look Now* (1973), where a gondola carrying a coffin is visualized a number of times before its meaning becomes clear at the end of the film.

Flash pan   (see **Swish pan**)

Flat lighting   Lighting within a motion-picture scene which is so evenly diffused across the scene that little sense of depth or visual relief is provided. Control of light quality and light placement are employed to eliminate flat lighting by increasing light and shadow contrast in the scene and by separating actors, objects, and set pieces through light modeling.

Flickers
A colloquial term for motion pictures. The term developed in the medium's formative years as a result of technical imperfections in early motion-picture projection devices. A pulsating, flickering effect accompanied the projected images, thus giving rise to the term "flickers" or "the flicks."

Flood (floodlight)
Both a type of lighting instrument and a quality of light. A floodlight is a lamp that disseminates a broad, non-directed area of light onto a scene. The uncontrolled quality of flood-lighting can give a washed-out look to a scene, and it is some-times used to create a stark effect. Floodlights, available in various sizes and intensities, are commonly used to provide the generalized light in a lighting scheme which includes other types of aesthetically controlled lamps.

Flow-of-life film
A term applied to a motion picture in which development of the narrative appears accidental and casual. The concept is often associated with **neo-realist** films and other types of **realist cinema** which have de-emphasized dramatic crisis and climax for a slice-of-life effect. Dramatic plotting evolves from the milieu in which the characters function. Common situations as the characters move through life are used to reveal the story. Often these films are set in the streets or on the road. *The Bicycle Thief* (1948), *Harry and Tonto* (1974), and *The Straight Story* (1999) all contain elements that fit the flow-of-life concept. In the last film, Alvin Straight, an Iowan in his seventies, travels three hundred miles by rid-ing a lawnmower to visit a sick brother in Wisconsin. In the course of the journey, and through the characters he meets on the journey, the nature of Straight's life and spirit are revealed to the viewer. The leisurely, contemplative pace of David Lynch's film is the basis of the film's simple but pow-erful effect.

Fluid camera
A term used to describe the constant movement of the cam-era during the filming of a motion-picture scene or shot. The camera dollies, **tracks, arcs,** or **cranes** so frequently that its use is said to be fluid. The use of fluid camera techniques marks the camera as an active participant in the recording process, usually providing a more subjective **point of view** than that acquired by a stationary camera. Fluid, roving camera techniques were popular with innovative German directors of the 1920s: E.A. Dupont (*Variety*, 1925); F.W.

Murnau (*The Last Laugh*, 1924). These directors in dealing with stories of basic human emotions—love, jealousy, loss of pride—employed a fluid camera as a means of giving dramatic importance to space. The fluid camera allows: scenes to be played out without cuts, thus providing unity in spatial relationships; the following of character movement through space, thus revealing the immediate environment; the discovery of new information through camera movements. Most film directors have employed fluid camera techniques to a certain degree; many directors make the moving camera a dominant expressive element of their shooting style, for example, Luchino Visconti (*Death in Venice*, 1970), Claude Lelouch (*Another Man Another Chance*, 1977), Stanley Kubrick (*The Shining*, 1980), Oliver Stone (*Wall Street*, 1987), Woody Allen (*Deconstructing* Harry, 1997), and Michael Mann (*The Insider*, 1999).

Focal length A lens designation usually expressed in millimeters and sometimes in inches. The focal length of a lens is the distance from the optical center of the lens to the point of the film plane when the lens is focused on a distant subject or object. Lenses of longer focal length produce narrower **angles of view**. The focal length of a lens determines whether it is a **wide-angle lens**, **normal lens**, or **telephoto lens**. A lens with a set focal length is referred to as a "fixed-focal-length lens"; a lens with a variable focal length is commonly called a "**zoom** lens."

Focus The point at which rays of light converge to form an image of a subject after having been reflected or transmitted by that subject and passed through a **lens**. A point on the subject is considered to be in focus when it is registered as a point on the film by the lens, rather than as a circle or blur of points.

Beyond its technical consideration, focus can be manipulated as a creative tool by the filmmaker interested in conveying subjective or psychological reality. Scenes intentionally shot out of focus, for instance, may show the world from the point of view of a character who is experiencing mental aberration.

Differential focus is the emphasis through sharp focus of one of several elements in the frame while other elements are intentionally out of focus.

A camera operator may **rack focus** during a shot to change the area of differential focus within the frame from the heroine in the foreground, walking down a dark alley, to the escaped killer approaching her in the background. In this way one can generate suspense or surprise or effect a transition by controlled discovery. In Clint Eastwood's *Play Misty for Me* (1971), a murderess is revealed in a scene hiding behind a bush where she is stalking two picnickers. The woman's presence, unnoticed in the early part of the scene, is made known through a slow **zoom** in to the bush that simultaneously brings the blurred background and the hidden murderess dramatically into focus.

Foley artist/sound A Foley artist is a sound technician who creates sounds and sound effects that will coordinate with the actions on the screen, for example, footsteps, doors opening, the crinkle of paper, etc. Foley artists enhance realism and enliven the mise-en-scène. The term "Foley artist" is a tribute to the gifted sound technician, Jack Foley.

Follow focus The shifting of focus within a shot so that a character or an object moving toward or away from the camera **lens** remains in critical **focus**. The lens focal ring is adjusted to keep the character or object within the **depth-of-field** area at all times. Sharpness of image is retained and the moving object is supplied with a visual emphasis.

Foreground music Another term for **source** or **diegetic music**—music which originates from a source within the film scene: a record player, a radio, or "live" musicians. The term "foreground music" (source music) distinguishes diegetic music from non-diegetic music, the latter being music which appears on the **sound track** but which has no actual relationship with the film's narrative or its scenic elements.

Formal balance The symmetrical arrangement of elements within the film frame so that both sides of the frame and the center are equal in visual attraction (photo 21). A formally balanced composition appears restful and without dramatic conflict.

Formal criticism Film criticism which examines an individual motion picture for its techniques and organization in order to illuminate the work's total effect. Formal critics separate form from content, viewing form (method and structure) as the means by which the filmmaker has expressed content. Form is seen as a vital, organic link to a film's ultimate impact. Critics applying this analytic approach often examine a particular film in relationship to the methods of other works, especially those of a similar type or **genre**.

[FORMAL BALANCE] 21. Ingmar Bergman's *Winter Light* (1963) opens with a formally composed shot of a nearly empty church—a composition which emphasizes the minister's view of his church as a place of worship that is lacking in spirituality.

Formal editing   An approach to film editing where length of shots remains consistent and unvaried, so much so that the rhythm of the film produces a formal, dignified pace in the action flow. The editing pace of Stanley Kubrick's *Barry Lyndon* (1975) was consistently ordered and formal in an attempt to convey the moods and rhythms of 18th-century life in Europe. See **External rhythm**.

Formalism   Artistic, literary, or dramatic expression in which the emphasis is on form (technique) rather than subject. Formalism emerged as a dominant factor in the theater and in cinema in the Soviet Union during the 1920s. The practices and theoretical writings of Eisenstein, Pudovkin, and Kuleshov in cinema, and Vsevolod Meyerhold in theater were based on formalist concepts. Their work was a revolt against the traditional responses that marked pre-Revolutionary treatment of narrative material. The Russian filmmakers of the 1920s approached subject matter in a highly calculated, scientific manner while Meyerhold treated the actor on the stage as a "biomechanical" puppet. Editing, pictorial composition, and auralvisual arrangements consumed the interests of the formalist filmmaker.

As a general concept, formalism has come to mean an approach to film expression or film analysis which emphasizes the importance of form over content, with the film artist or critic maintaining that it is through cinematic technique that a film's meaning is communicated and understood.

Formula film   A phrase used to describe a motion picture which has used familiar plotting devices and tested subject matter in the development of a film story. Formula films imitate successful works by following precisely the elements which characterized the more original, earlier films and which are usually recognizable as having been patterned after specific films or film types. Many film **genres**, especially the **western** and **gangster film**, lend themselves to formularized variations.

A formula film, despite its lack of originality, has often enjoyed considerable popularity because of its well-known, easily understood plot, theme, and conventions.

Frame   Each individual photograph recorded on motion-picture celluloid is referred to as a frame (photo 22). The frame is the basic visual unit of motion pictures, printed on a strip of celluloid material of varying widths: 8 mm, 16 mm, 35 mm, 65 mm, 70 mm. In sound motion pictures twenty-four separate frames are photographed and projected per second to create the effect of natural movement on the screen.

Frames per second (fps) A term used to designate camera shooting speed or motion-picture projection speed. Most sound motion pictures are photographed at speeds of twenty-four frames per second (fps) and projected at the same speed. **Slow motion** is achieved generally by photographing at speeds greater than twenty-four fps and projecting at twenty-four fps. **Fast motion** involves shooting at a slower camera speed and projecting at a faster projection speed: filming action at eight or sixteen fps and projecting at twenty-four fps.

Framing   The act of composing through the viewfinder of the camera the desired view of the images to be photographed. Framing includes choices of camera **angle, angle of view** (scope), and **blocking**. The end result of the photographed scene or shot is also referred to as the filmmaker's framing, and is an important consideration in film analysis which examines photographic style.

Free Cinema (Britain) A term coming from the New Cinema programs presented by the National Film Theatre beginning in 1956. Altogether six programs were offered between 1956 and

[FRAME] 22. Motion pictures are made up of a series of still photographs called frames, which depict a continuous action through rapid projection of the individual images. The series of film frames on the right are taken from the final war scene in D.W. Griffith's *The Birth of a Nation* (1915).

1959, consisting primarily of documentary films with personal, social points of view. Because many of the Free Cinema documentaries dealt with the realities of life for working people in contemporary Britain, the term was carried over as a descriptive label for the feature-film movement (introduced by *Room at the Top* in 1958) which similarly examined the everyday lives and ambitions of Britain's working class. The aims of the Free Cinema movement extended not only into the British film but into theater and fiction as well, appearing notably in the class-conscious works of the country's "angry young theater men" (John Osborne, *Look Back in Anger*, 1956) and in novels by such writers as Alan Sillitoe (*Saturday Night and Sunday Morning*, 1958 and *The Loneliness of the Long Distance Runner*, 1959). Both of Sillitoe's novels became important films in British cinema's transition to greater social realism. The often dreary settings of these films led to their being described broadly as "kitchen sink realism."

Freeze-frame   A motion-picture effect which stops (freezes) the motion of the film on a single frame and allows the chosen image to continue as though a still photograph. Because of its abrupt interruption of action, the freeze-frame technique isolates and emphasizes the dramatic moment within the repeated frame. The viewer examines a "frozen" action until the filmmaker "frees" the frame. The device is also often employed to give impact to the concluding shot of a motion picture, for example, *The 400 Blows* (1959), *Butch Cassidy and the Sundance Kid* (1969), and *The Apprenticeship of Duddy Kravitz* (1975). In *Small Change* (1976) François Truffaut used brief freeze-frames as a transitional device for ending scenes, as did Martin Scorsese in *GoodFellas* (1990). An unusual freeze frame occurs in Tim Burton's *Big Fish* (2003). When Ewan McGregor sees "the love of his life" at a village carnival, the background scene with the young woman and other villagers suddenly "freezes" as if time has stood still. McGregor's character remains "animated" in the foreground, with the frozen frame in the background.

French New Wave (see **New Wave**)

F-stop   An indicator for the size of the diaphragmatic opening of a camera **lens**, also often referred to as the "f-number." The size of the diaphragmatic opening controls the amount of light allowed to pass through the lens to the film **emulsion**. The larger the f-number (e.g., f/22), the smaller the opening and the lesser the amount of light that passes through the lens. A small f-number on the other hand (e.g., f/2) results in a large opening and, hence, permits a great deal of light to enter the camera. When the camera operator reduces the size of the diaphragmatic opening by adjusting the f-stop setting to a larger number, this is referred to as "stopping down." Adjusting for a larger opening (smaller number) is called "opening up."

The size of the opening of the lens diaphragm (f-number) and the **exposure** time (shutter speed) together affect **depth of field** (that range of distance in front of the camera in which elements remain in sharp focus). Shutter speeds in motion-picture photography are determined by the **cam-**

era speed, for example, 24 fps, which is standard for sound films. A large f-stop number (e.g., f/22) and a standard shutter speed will provide a greater depth of field than a small f-number (f/2) and a standard shutter speed. When camera operators wish to control the f-number to achieve a **deep-focus** shot, they may increase the amount of light in the scene or use a faster film stock that will allow the lens to be stopped down. Exposure time in motion-picture photography can be manipulated on cameras with a variable shutter, which permits an increase or decrease in the size of the shutter opening. By diminishing the size of the shutter opening, less light hits the emulsion of the film. The reduction of light aids in resolving objects at a greater distance.

F-stop numbers appearing in sequence on a lens (f/2, f/2.8, f/4, f/5.6, f/8, f/11, f/16, f/22) indicate that an adjustment from any one number to the next will either double the exposure light or reduce it by one-half. Adjusting the f-stop from f/4 to f/5.6 (stopping down) decreases the exposure by one-half; an adjustment from f/4 to f/2.8 (opening up) doubles the exposure light.

Futurism   An artistic movement, closely associated with cubism, which began in Italy in the early 1900s and characterized by an interest in giving expression to the movement and energy of mechanical processes. Futurist painter A.G. Bragaglia produced a film, *Perfido Incanto*, in 1906 that posed actors before futurist settings. Futurist interests can be assessed as closely allied with the interests of later avant-gardists, who placed objects in motion for formally expressive intentions, for example, *Ballet Mécanique* (1924). The movement also had an impact on Russian filmmakers of the 1920s.

G

Gangster film   A film classification in which story, plot, and conventions are developed around the actions of criminals, particularly bank robbers and underworld figures who operate outside the law. Like the **western film** genre, the gangster film evolved its own mythology in consideration of both locations and characterization. Prototypically, the gangster film is set in a large city where the criminal functions in a clandestine world of dark nightclubs, seedy living quarters, and speeding automobiles. The prohibition era has been a popular time placement for the American gangster film, largely because of associations of legendary underworld figures with the era.

Typical traits of gangster film characters include (1) the desire for recognition and success, (2) a tough, crude facade, (3) hints of gentleness and sensitivity beneath the toughness, and (4) an intimation that the gangsters are victims of circumstance.

Gangster films such as *Public Enemy* (1931), *Dead End* (1937), and *Angels with Dirty Faces* (1938) present characters who have grown up in neglected neighborhoods and who spend the remainder of their lives seeking to compensate for the neglect. In some instances the gangster is malicious, callous, and greedy by nature, for example, *Little Caesar* (1930).

During the late 1940s, the gangster film faded because of decreasing audience interest. In 1967 Arthur Penn's *Bonnie and Clyde* reintroduced with great popular success many of the conventions and ideas that had characterized the gangster films of the 1930s and 1940s, moving the genre to rural/small-town settings. Francis Ford Coppola's *The Godfather* (1972) and *The Godfather Parts Two* and *Three* (1975, 1990) also fell within the confines of the gangster genre, but were epic in structure. Less ambitious but also meritorious in quality were Robert Altman's *Thieves Like Us* (1974), John Cassavetes' *Gloria* (1980), John Huston's *Prizzi's Honor* (1985), Brian DePalma's *The Untouchables* (1987), Martin Scorsese's *GoodFellas* (1990), Quentin Tarantino's *Reservoir Dogs* (1992), Mike Newell's *Donnie Brasco* (1997), and Sam Mendes' *Road to Perdition* (2002).

Gaze (look)
A concept in cinematic discourse which theorizes that directed awareness and accompanying visual pleasure can be/are derived from the "gaze" of the film spectator as controlled by the camera's eye. The position of the camera onto the scene and screen characters is said to "set" the spectator's gaze (look) in such a way that responses to the character(s) are affected in an unconscious manner. Theorists have maintained that the screen gaze has traditionally been directed toward the male spectator—the camera's eye favoring male voyeurism (visual pleasure) in the perusal of screen imagery, while limiting female gaze. The theorist Laura Mulvey has asserted that the prevalent male gaze in narrative cinema in effect permits the male spectator to indirectly "possess" the female as an on-screen object. Others (for example, D.N. Rodowick) have taken issue with these assertions by arguing that the gaze may in fact render the male submissive to the screen female rather than possessive.

Generation
A reference term for various printings of motion-picture film. The film that is run through the camera is the "original" or "first-generation" film. A "second-generation" print is one made from the original print. A "third-generation" print would be one made from the second-generation print. Each successive generation affects image definition and contrast range. Film directors will sometimes print footage through several generations to achieve a non-theatrical look within

a shot or scene. Raoul Coutard, cinematographer for Godard's *Les Carabiniers* (*The Rifleman*, 1963), reprinted numerous shots several times in order to match the look of **stock** newsreel **footage** that was also included in the film.

Genre   A term for any group of motion pictures which express similar stylistic, thematic, and structural interests. There are numerous narrative film genres: the **western film**, the **gangster film**, the film noir, the **musical film**, the detective film, the **screwball comedy**. "Genre" is also often used to distinguish other film classes such as the **documentary**, the docudrama, the **experimental film**, and the **animated film**. Genre groupings are general in nature because pure, distinct classifications of film types are rare. Many so-called genre films share characteristics with other types of film. *Chicago* (2002), for example, is a musical film with noir and gangster elements. Michael Moore's *Roger and Me* (1989) is a docudrama constructed as a detective film.

The study of the various film genres has given rise to genre criticism. By isolating the various filmic elements which characterize a particular motion-picture genre, it is possible to employ those elements in evaluating a film that falls significantly within a genre. Through an examination of the manner in which the recognizable generic elements have been copied or varied, genre criticism seeks to determine how the film's thematic intentions have been achieved. Many western films, for example, have made topical statements by their varied arrangements of generic elements. *High Noon* (1952), a film about the bravery of a small-town marshal, also made a timely statement about individual courage during the McCarthy committee investigations. *Lonely Are the Brave* (1962), a western film story placed in a modern time and in modern settings, presented a statement about loss of individual freedom in a technological society, as did *The Electric Horseman* (1979).

Genre criticism   (see **Genre**)

Grain   The term commonly used to refer to the minute crystals of silver halide contained within the **emulsion** layer of a film stock (photo 23). These crystals (grains) vary in size, with the larger ones more sensitive to light than the smaller ones. Generally, emulsions with a considerable distribution of large grains result in fast film speeds (film stocks requiring less light for exposure) and tend toward "graininess." Graininess is the

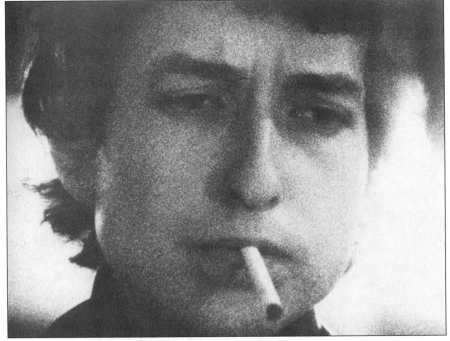

[GRAIN] 23. In D.A. Pennebaker's *Don't Look Back* (1968) large grain appeared as one of the filmmaker's realist methods of suggesting an honest, open portrait of singer Bob Dylan.

rain-like appearance, in the screen **image**, of coarse clumps of large grain. Grainy film images, when intentionally derived, can serve as a convention of **realist cinema**.

Greenscreen   (see Bluescreen)

Gross-out film   A type of outrageous and often tasteless screen comedy that developed following the abandonment of Hollywood's Production Code in 1968. In the late 1960s and throughout the 1970s, all sorts of candid material began to make its way to the screen as old, conservative restrictions were eased. In 1978, John Landis' National Lampoon's *Animal House* appeared as an early notable example of the gross-out film, a film so-labeled because of the script's emphasis on bathroom humor, sexual innuendo, and unrestrained anti-social displays that belie any resemblance to mannered human behavior (hence the word "animal" in the title). *Animal House* carried other qualities which would become conventions of later gross-out films, most notably the humorous, bawdy treatment of male ritual within a specific social context, such as a fraternity house. *Porky's* (1982) involved a group of high school friends seeking to act out their adolescent sexual urges, as did *American Pie* (1999), which transported the idea from high school to college (*American Pie II: The College Years*, 2001) to post-college marriage (*American Pie III: The Wedding*, 2003). Other films of note with gross-out qualities include *Dumb and Dumber* (1994) and *There's Something About Mary* (1998), works by Bobby and Peter Farrelly.

Group shot   **Shooting-script** terminology for a **shot** which contains several characters within the composition of the **frame**.

H

Haiku (see **Imagist film**)

Handheld camera A term used to describe a type of motion-picture filming where the camera noticeably has not been mounted on a stationary or mechanical securing device. Handheld cinematography is often intentionally used to add a spontaneous, freestyle quality to a motion picture. The technique has been employed extensively in ***cinéma verité*** documentaries and often in narrative films as well. A lengthy fight scene in Franco Zeffirelli's *Romeo and Juliet* (1968) was filmed with a handheld camera to make the camera appear a participant in the action. The introduction of the Steadicam body device in the 1970s made handheld camera work increasingly popular for following action in enclosed spaces, for example, in Kubrick's *The Shining* (1980) and Tavernier's *'Round Midnight* (1986). A verité-like quality in the social thriller *The Constant Gardener* (2005) is achieved to a significant degree by the constant use of a handheld camera. The technique is so persistent that its use is both disconcerting and dizzying, an effect which underscores the plot's dramatic intensity and edginess.

Head-on, tail-away A type of **transition** marked by actor or object movement toward and away from the camera **lens**. A character walks to the camera lens until the screen **image** is blurry and indistinct. A simple **cut** is then made to another indistinct image as the character or another character moves away from the camera to reveal a change in time and place. The head-on movement wipes away the preceding scene, while the tail-away movement reveals a new one. The head-on, tail-away can be an effective means of changing scenes while dynamically linking an individual to two different moments in time.

Heavy   Another term for a motion-picture villain, usually a male character whose amoral qualities are immediately apparent (often through physique) to the viewer. The term "heavy" is most commonly used in reference to a villainous character in a film-noir-style **gangster film** or a **western**. Many Hollywood performers became stereotyped as screen heavies, for example, Ralph Meeker, Peter Lorre, and Jack Palance.

High-angle shot   A **shot** in which the **scene** has been photographed from above (photo 24). Sometimes the camera is mounted on a boom or crane device that elevates the camera into a high-angle position. If we see the upward or downward movement of the camera into or out of a high-angle shot, it is referred to as a **crane shot** or boom shot: crane up or crane down. The boom shot usually does not provide as high an angle of view as does the crane device, which will lift the camera into an extreme high-angle position.

The essential value of a high-angle shot comes from the privileged, dominant view of the scene it produces. The famous crane shot of wounded soldiers in *Gone with the Wind* (1939) shows the dramatic use of a high-angle shot.

The scene in which Scarlett O'Hara makes her way through the hundreds of wounded Confederate soldiers at the Atlanta train station ends as the camera cranes up to a spectacular, high-angle view of the mass of soldiers. The height and scope of the shot, combined with the gradually smaller figure of O'Hara moving among the sea of war victims, suggests in one powerful image the price of war and the impending defeat of the South.

In *Psycho* (1960) Alfred Hitchcock evokes horror in one instance by the placement of a high-angle shot. As Martin Balsam climbs the stairs of the gothic house where

[HIGH-ANGLE SHOT] 24. A high-angle shot in Billy Wilder's *Sunset Boulevard* (1950) helps emphasize the oddity of a New Year's Eve party staged by fading actress Norma Desmond (Gloria Swanson). Desmond has arranged to have her lover Joe Gillis (William Holden) all to herself on a holiday evening usually celebrated in festive groups. The high-angle shot conveys the bizarre effect of an orchestra playing for a single couple.

Bates (Tony Perkins) and his "mother" live, Hitchcock employs a standard straight-on shot of Balsam's ascent. At the moment that Balsam reaches the top of the stairs, where a bedroom door stands slightly ajar, Hitchcock cuts to a high-angle shot taken from directly over Balsam's head. The bedroom door opens suddenly, and a figure leaps out to stab Balsam. The moment of the stabbing is full of surprise and shock.

Hitchcock's choice of the bird's-eye, high-angle shot adds to the intensity of the scene because of certain qualities inherent in the overhead angle of view. An overhead, high-angle shot tends to increase the amount and importance of space around a character and presents a privileged view of an environment. In situations where a character is alone or apart from others, the sense of aloneness and insignificance is often heightened by shots taken from above the figure. The "aloneness" of an individual in a large city, for example, is frequently suggested with high-angle shots of the character walking the city streets. A striking "birds-eye view" shot occurs in *House of Sand and Fog* (2003) to reveal Ben Kingsley's character, his wife, and son being held hostage in a small, family bathroom. Kingsley huddles near the toilet, while the mother and son lie together in the bathtub. The high-angle bird's-eye shot provides a surreal image of entrapment.

High-hat shot, high-hat mount/high-hat shot A high-hat is a special camera mounting device of eight to ten inches in height which permits filming at extreme low angles—seemingly directly at studio floor or ground level (photo 25). A shot taken from such a position and looking dramatically upward at the action is often referred to as a high-hat shot.

High-key lighting (see **Lighting**)

High-speed film (see **Film speed**)

Hitchcockian A reference to narrative and stylistic qualities within mystery-thriller motion pictures that recall the idiosyncratic work of Alfred Hitchcock, the master of the genre. In his silent films and in nearly four dozen sound pictures (plus a television series) Hitchcock created a body of psychologically rooted mystery-thrillers of unusual sophistication and playfulness. Tongue-in-cheek interplay with the audience—in an effort to draw the filmgoer off guard and then stun with a surprising twist—was one particularly notable Hitchcockian characteristic. In *Psycho* (1960) the film's opening plot suggested a film about embezzlement by a young bank clerk (Janet Leigh) and her lover (John Gavin). A tense encounter with a policeman as the woman drives out of the city with stolen money acts as a diversionary device to build and release suspense so that the woman—and the viewer—are lulled into a false sense of well-being. Evading possible capture, the woman drives away and toward her death by a psychopathic killer (Tony Perkins) in a lonely roadside motel room. This suspense-building method of Hitchcockian plotting as a diversionary device for more horrible circumstances was recalled by Brian De Palma in *Dressed to Kill* (1980). *Dressed to Kill*'s opening sequence developed tension around the potential consequences of sexual dalliance for a suburban housewife (Angie Dickinson) who, distracted by the possibility of a sexually transmitted disease, walks instead into the trap of a psychopathic killer in an elevator.

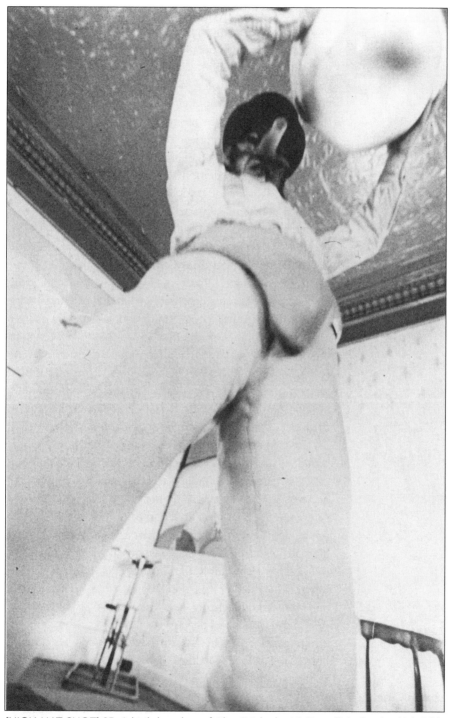

[HIGH-HAT SHOT] 25. A high-hat shot of Alex (Malcolm McDowell) in Stanley Kubrick's *A Clockwork Orange* (1971) is one of many expressionistic shots used to suggest the terrorizing gang warfare that dominates the earlier parts of the film.

Hitchcock subverted traditional approaches to the mystery thriller by implying that crime can be committed by average, respectable people in full daylight. Plotting usually explored the ironic contradictions between appearances and hidden realities—between the seemingly normal and the perverse. Criminal behavior in Hitchcock's films frequently carried psychosexual implications.

Paranoia and suspicion (often of innocent people) were essential ingredients of many early Hitchcock films: *The Lodger* (1926), *Blackmail* (1929), *The 39 Steps* (1935), *Young and Innocent* (1938), *Rebecca* (1940), *Suspicion* (1941). Later films centered more frequently on irrational, psychologically disturbed characters: *Spellbound* (1945), *Rope* (1948), *Strangers on a Train* (1951), *Psycho* (1960).

The Hitchcockian **MacGuffin** was another recognizable thriller element. The term MacGuffin was coined by Hitchcock to describe a curiosity-generating plotting device that set the narrative intrigue into motion—sometimes later forgotten altogether, sometimes seeing the story through to the end. Well-known Hitchcockian MacGuffins include the secret codes of *The 39 Steps* and *Torn Curtain* (1966), a missing governess in *The Lady Vanishes* (1938), uranium in wine bottles in *Notorious* (1946), a cigarette lighter in *Strangers on a Train*, and a lost heir in *Family Plot* (1976).

Recurring Hitchcockian cinematic devices and motifs included: subjective revisualization of a crime by a guilt-ridden character; sound-image manipulation as transitional devices; heights and steps as objects of fear; a voyeuristic camera; a minimalist approach to editing; masking and off-screen depiction of violence; murder as a correlative for sex; dramatic climaxes in familiar locations (the British Museum, the London Palladium; amusement parks, the U.S. Tennis Open, Mt. Rushmore); blond heroines; a brief, satirical appearance by Hitchcock in a fleeting role.

Those filmmakers devoted to Hitchcock's manner of creating mystery on the screen have included De Palma, François Truffaut, Claude Chabrol, and a host of other imitators.

Home Cinema Theater A home video setup incorporating visual and aural technology that brings the home cinema environment closer to that found in the professional movie theater. Large television screen (27 inches or more), a **surround**-sound system of stereophonic speakers, and an electronic amplification-steering mechanism (e.g., **Dolby® Pro Logic®**) for channeling the sound are standard components of high-technology home-cinema arrangements. Increasingly, the video **laser disc**, which is LP-sized and scanned in the manner of an audio compact disc (CD), gained in popularity in home systems over the video cassette because of greater picture resolution and an accompanying **digital** sound signal. The design of the high-technology home-cinema theater is intended to intensify sensory pleasures associated with optimal audio-visual experiences such as those realized at "live" or theater auditorium performances.

Horror film   A film whose plot is centered on strange, alarming events which threaten the principal character or characters. The terrorizing threat often occurs as a result of demonic powers (the devil in *The Exorcist*, 1974), at other times the result of scientific experimentation which gets out of hand (Proteus 4, the deviant, computerized brain in *The Demon Seed*, 1977). Conflict within the horror film pits these monsters—supernatural or man-made—against the naive and the weak. Superhuman effort of supernatural forces (the priest in *The Exorcist*) is necessary to destroy the evil that resides in the monster and which threatens those less strong. Horror films aimed at teenage audiences became highly popular in the 1970s and 1980s, often appearing in multi-sequel form, for instance, *Friday the 13th*. The gruesome murder of young people in isolated settings (summer camp, a cruise ship) typified these cheap thrillers. John Carpenter's *Halloween* (1978) is considered central in launching the teenaged horror film. *The Scream* series, beginning in 1996, paid homage to the style and conventions of the 1980s teen-oriented horror films. Jonathan Demme's *The Silence of the Lambs*, an unusually stylish and terrifying horror film, was a surprise Best Picture Oscar winner for 1990. Classic screen horror figures continue to attract filmmakers, for instance, Dr. Jekyll and Mr. Hyde in *Mary Reilly* (1996) and Count Dracula in *Shadow of the Vampire* (2000).

Horse opera   Another term for a **western** film that is intended as escapist entertainment. In such a film the standard elements of the western **genre** prevail according to audience expectations. "**Oater**" is another term frequently used to describe this type of western.

Humanistic realism "New American humanistic realism" is a phrase that was used in film criticism to describe a kind of film that evolved in the 1960s.

This phrase was applied to films whose themes are similar to those found in screen stories about alienated characters or in what might be described as "**antihero** pictures." The notable characteristics of humanistic realism are (1) the presentation of characters who are social "black sheep," or alienated from society, (2) a value scale which is concerned principally with the search for self-liberation in a milieu of social and moral decadence, and (3) an emphasis on the environment as a major thematic element.

Humanistic realism as a critical-philosophical term has been applied to *The Graduate* (1967), *Midnight Cowboy* (1969), *Easy Rider* (1969), *Five Easy Pieces* (1970), and the early dramatic films of Andy Warhol and John Cassavetes. *My Own Private Idaho* (1991) followed the traditions of humanistic realism.

Icon A pictorial representation of an object or a person; a film **image** that is taken to represent an object or person because of its similarity to the object. A photograph of a tree resembles a tree and is, therefore, an iconographic representation of a tree. The icon is one of the three principal signs or images examined in **semiological criticism**.

Iconography The imagery within a motion picture which conveys the meaning of the work; iconographic representations may be intentionally chosen by the filmmaker for specific expressive value, or the imagery may be of a random, ambiguous nature. The study of film iconography, or **icons**, is an integral part of **semiological criticism**, which examines the motion picture as a system of signs.

Image The concrete or abstract representation of filmed material as it appears on the screen. In a general sense a film image is the potential effect of any photographed material, including its artistic and symbolic manifestations. The images in motion-picture criticism are regarded to be the visual components of the film as distinguished from the aural (sound) components. Motion-picture images most often are in a constant state of kinetic motion unlike the image within a still photograph or painting, and come to the viewer through light reflection. These physical characteristics of motion and reflected light give to the film image unusual powers of expression that are both artistically and psychologically affective.

Imagist film　A type of film which employs a series of related **images** to effect a mood or to create an abstract concept. In his theoretical writing on the cinema Sergei Eisenstein discussed at some length the filmmaker's ability to use **montage** for imagist effect. Eisenstein's inspiration came from the Japanese haiku, a brief poem whose combination of images results in a psychological or emotional impression. Eisenstein likened the concentrated sequence of phrases to a shot list for a film montage, and he saw in the haiku process traits similar to those of his own editing theories.

The imagist filmmaker attempts to use visual and auditory details of related value so that the accumulation of shots and sounds for a **scene** or an entire film gives impressions of larger meaning without offering a direct statement. Imagist films go beyond the purely **abstract** or rhythmic film exercise and strive for a communication experience (often poet-

[IMAGIST FILM] 26. Natural imagery in Gustav Machaty's *Extase* (1933) acted to symbolize, through accumulative effect, erotic stimulation.

ic and lyric) that has the symbolic effect of simile or metaphor. The final sequence of Pudovkin's *Storm over Asia* (1928), in which a driving storm symbolizes the powerful force of the Russian Revolution, is one of imagist inspiration.

Gustav Machaty, a Czech director whose films were laden with symbolic imagery (for example *Erotikon*, 1929; *Extase*, 1933, photo 26) has often been described as a "pure imagist." The arrangement of naturalistic details and erotic symbols in *Extase* is highly lyrical and one which in accumulative effect becomes a representation of sexual desire. In the film a brief series of natural images (horses mating, bees swarming, and plants blowing in the wind) are used by Machaty to suggest a woman's newly discovered erotic feelings.

Makers of **experimental films** have been especially attracted to the connotative possibilities of the imagist film. *The Mechanics of Love* (1955), a short work by Willard Maas and Ben Moore, arranges Freudian symbols which, together, suggest the act of lovemaking.

Impressionism An artistic style in which the creator seeks to suggest emotions, scenic mood, and sensory impressions through a fleeting but vivid use of detail that is more subjective in intent than objective. Impressionism as a stylistic theory was first applied to the work of 19th-century painters such as Degas, Monet, and Renoir. These artists were particularly interested in the visual effects of objects and light in a painting rather than in the realistic representation of a scene.

The movement extended into literary circles and theatrical scene design and eventually had a significant impact on French silent filmmakers, including Louis Delluc, Germaine Dulac, Jean Epstein, Abel Gance, Marcel L'Herbier, and Jean Renoir.

L'Herbier's use of impressionistic methods was particularly notable in *Eldorado* (1921). In this work image distortion, **soft-focus** photography, **superimpositions**, and unusual camera **angles** were incorporated as methods for suggesting how moments in the film caught the attention of L'Herbier or one of the story's characters. As in the work of other filmmakers of the impressionist school, L'Herbier's personal impressions about the story and its characters are not hidden as would be the case with a realist, objective filmmaker.

In impressionism the director's eye is made obvious to the viewer as it explores settings and locations for subjective effect. It is this latter consideration, the creation of subjectivity from genuine settings, which separates impressionism from **expressionism**. Expressionism employs intentional artificiality and obvious distortion of the real world to project mood and a sense of inner experiences.

While impressionism as a distinct school is most often associated with the French **avant-garde** of the 1920s, impressionistic techniques have appeared liberally in the works of numerous motion-picture directors, especially those interested in the use of light, colors, and camera effects to suggest environmental or character mood. For example, Louis Malle's *Pretty Baby* (1978), a study of a young girl's life in a New Orleans bordello, is a film rich in impressionistic detail. Bertrand Tavernier's *A Sunday in the Country* (1984) resembled painterly impressionism (Renoir's *A Day in the Country*) in its portrayal of an elderly artist's Sunday visit by his children.

Improvisation   The act of spontaneous, non-scripted action and **dialogue** during the making of a motion picture. Many feature-film directors (Robert Altman, John Cassavetes, Jean-Luc Godard) are well known for their willingness to allow screen actors to improvise during shooting and thus to contribute to the development of the story. Such directors appreciate the naturalistic, spontaneous effect that can be derived from improvisation. Sometimes improvisation during the rehearsal period has been used as a means of acquiring comic or dramatic situations that are then formally scripted. Scripts for the classic Marx Brothers films of the 1930s were in part realized through improvisation during rehearsals.

The inclusion of a spontaneous, non-scripted line of dialogue into a comic or dramatic situation is referred to as an "**ad lib**." The **mockumentaries** of Christopher Guest such as *Best in Show* (2000) were created largely through the comic improvisation of Guest and co-star Eugene Levy.

In-camera editing   Editing performed within the camera itself. **Shot** and **scene** changes, as determined in the filming process, are left exactly as they have been filmed. The stop-and-start procedure of filming the various camera takes also serves as the editing process. In-camera editing has often been an integral part of **realist** filmmaking where a spontaneous quality is desired;

it is also often seen in the work of **experimental** filmmakers who prefer to leave the shots and scenes exactly as they have been filmed, without regard for subsequent restructuring or refining of the recorded material. See **Minimal cinema**.

Inciting action   (see **Dramatic structure**)

Independent filmmaker A more recent designation for the avant-garde, underground, or experimental filmmaker. The term "independent filmmaker" has come to mean any filmmaker who works outside the commercial mainstream, creating films of personal styling and expression. The resultant film may or may not be distributed for commercial purposes.

Independent film (indie) A term used to describe an American film that has been produced without the sponsorship of the Hollywood studios or produced outside an organized production house that is regularly engaged in the making of motion pictures and television programs. Hollywood studios are, however, often financial investors in independently produced film projects.

Independent productions also often utilize Hollywood technicians and well-known actors who are assembled for the production through individual negotiation.

Distribution of independently produced films frequently is handled by the major studios because of the costs involved in promoting a film and the uncertainties of film exhibition. See **American studio years**.

Index   Within **semiological criticism**, a sign which denotes meaning for an object through interrelationship (photo 27). The indexical sign offers a representation or measurement of an idea through concrete association. A thermometer is an indexical sign for temperature. The severe, emotionless settings of Woody Allens' *Interiors* (1978) are indexical signs within the film **frame** for the mother's rigid personality and subsequent unhappiness. See **Semiological criticism**.

Industrial film   (see **Informational film**)

Informational film A type of nonfiction film made for the purpose of communicating facts or ideas, usually conceived and constructed around specific points of information which the filmmaker seeks to convey with clarity to the viewer. A "how-to" film, one which visualizes methods and processes, is the most direct type of informational film (*How to Make a Simple Loom and Weave*, 1959). The television "white paper," which seeks to present facts on government-related or pub-

[INDEX] 27. In François Truffaut's *The 400 Blows* (1959) a heavy wire fence, with its strong diagonals, presents a concrete image of entrapment. Hence, the fence serves as an indexical sign of Antoine Doinel's (Jean-Pierre Léaud's) frustrations as a result of an oppressive and restricting life at home and at school.

lic issues, is another type, for example, *Cuba: Bay of Pigs*, NBC, 1964. Often specific points of information may be contained within a documentary which has also been designed to entertain, for example, George Stoney's *All My Babies* (1953), an informational film made to assist public-health nurses in teaching and supervising midwives. Stoney's film employs a liberal use of folk music and a carefully constructed narrative that communicates the film's points.

An industrial film is yet another kind of informational film, one produced specifically for the purpose of presenting information on a manufacturing business or on manufacturing processes. Industrial films may be made for general use or solely for in-house consumption. Robert Flaherty's *Industrial Britain* (1933) was an early example of this type of informational film. A more recent example is *The Factory* (1972)—a study of life in an American woodworking plant.

Ingenue   A young female character whose appeal is derived from fresh good looks and a demure personality. During the **American studio years** actresses who could portray ingenues were considered an important staple in a studio's stock company of contract players. Deanna Durbin (Universal Studios) and Loretta Young (Twentieth Century Fox) were among the many young actresses who achieved fame in ingenue roles during the 1930s.

Insert shot A **shot**, containing visual detail, that is inserted into a **scene** for informational purposes or to provide dramatic emphasis. A **close-up** view of printed material in a book, **intercut** as a character reads, is a type of informational insert. The intercutting of a close-up view of a gun resting on a desk within a room where a violent argument is occurring constitutes a type of dramatic insert. **Detail shot** is another term for "insert shot."

Instructional film (see **Informational film**)

Intercut (intercutting) A term frequently used interchangeably with **crosscutting** and **parallel development**, editing concepts which are all derived from the motion picture's ability to move back and forth among narrative elements that are occurring either at the same time or at different times. Technically, "parallel development" and "crosscutting" are more correctly used when referring to an editing structure which develops two or more narrative elements that are taking place simultaneously or within an approximately similar time period, for example, the robbery, robbers' flight, posse formation and pursuit in Edwin S. Porter's *The Great Train Robbery* (1903). Parallel development, or crosscutting, picks up simultaneously developing parts of the story.

Intercutting may be more generally used to describe editing structures that include two or more separately developing segments that have no immediate time relationship to one another. The development of the four separate stories in D.W. Griffith's *Intolerance* (1916) is more correctly called "intercutting," as is the Vito Corleone (Robert De Niro) story in *The Godfather Part Two* (1975). Coppola intercuts Corleone's earlier development as an underworld figure with the contemporary ascendance of Michael (Al Pacino) to gangster status.

A provocative form of intercutting occurs in the development of the modern and the historic romances in *The French Lieutenant's Woman* (1981) and *Heat and Dust* (1983). *The Hours* (2002) achieves its thematic impact by intercutting three character narratives that are spread across the 20th century.

Intermittent movement (camera, projector) The stop-and-go movement of a motion-picture camera or a projector that enables each

frame to be exposed or viewed and then replaced by the next frame. It is a necessary requirement of motion-picture photography and projection that only one frame at a time be exposed or projected. A continuous movement through a projector of the series of individual pictures that make up a motion-picture film would result in a continuous blur on the screen. A continuous movement of film in the camera during photography would yield an indistinguishable blur on the film itself after **processing**. Individual exposure or projection of each frame or picture combined with the **persistence-of-vision** phenomenon make possible the illusion of motion in film.

Internal rhythm   Rhythm within a motion picture achieved through the movement of actors or objects within a **frame** as distinct from **external rhythms** which are achieved through editing and length of **shots**.

Introvision   A patented procedure for special effects filming developed in the late 1970s and used to full advantage in action thrillers, e.g., *The Fugitive* (1993). Introvision employs location live-action filming, combined with studio cinematography and miniature-model filming. In *The Fugitive* Harrison Ford is shown escaping death in a violent train-bus crash. In this film, introvision specialists filmed a location train sequence (termed a "plate shot") in North Carolina. Additional filming was conducted in a studio using a replica miniature train model version of the crash that could be **matched cut** with the North Carolina footage. Harrison Ford's last-second leap away from the charging train was also re-filmed (using a stunt double) in a studio **matte** procedure and blended with the train action through interlock projection and **process** printing techniques.

Invisible cutting (editing) A method of film editing which follows precise **continuity** procedures. **Shots** are edited for the purpose of reconstructing an event, and for placing scenes in their desired chronological order. This editing is said to be "invisible" because it does not call attention to itself as does dynamic or conceptual cutting. The process of invisible cutting is sometimes referred to as "academic editing." Within a **scene**, invisible cutting is most commonly achieved by cutting on motion. A **matched cut** from a close-up to a **medium shot** is made on character movement so that the internal movement, rather than the cut, attracts the eye.

Invisible cutting may also refer to the technical process of A and B printing for the purpose of hiding splice lines which are made in assembling the film. Black, non-transparent leader is spliced to each scraped **frame** line so as to retard light when the separate rolls of film are processed as a composite print. Areas that have been scraped away from the picture frame no longer show, and thus the cutting (splicing) is invisible.

Invisible cutting can play an important role in a director's realization of film **style**. The naturalistic quality, for example, of G.W. Pabst's *The Love of Jeanne Ney* (1927) is sustained by skillful matched cutting for dramatic emphasis. Editing for a change of angle or to present a longer or closer view of a scene is performed only on a character's movement. Pabst is able to place emphasis exactly where it is desired without disrupting viewer concentration, and in so doing retains the film's naturalistic style.

Iris   A laboratory transitional effect, occurring when an existing **image** moves into a circle which rapidly decreases in size until it disappears. Often a new shot simultaneously has taken its place. If the image has been wiped to black, and a reversal of the process thus brings in a new image, this is referred to as an "iris-in/iris-out." The iris, like the optical **wipe**, is a rapid means of **transition** that sustains the pace of the story.

In the early development of the motion picture the iris served as a transitional device as well as a means of altering the shape of screen images and of isolating dramatic material. D.W. Griffith frequently employed a partial iris shot for the purpose of dramatic framing, for example, the close-up photograph of Lillian Gish in *The Birth of a Nation* (1915) as the Little Colonel pauses in the cotton fields. Griffith's framing through the iris added a subjective quality to the insert of the photograph. In Robert Wiene's *The Cabinet of Dr. Caligari* (1919), an iris shot narrows in on the young storyteller's face to increase audience awareness of his anguished state.

The iris effect frequently appears in contemporary films that have imitated earlier film **styles**, such as Herbert Ross' 1930s-style musical *Pennies from Heaven* (1981). In Volker Schlondorff's *The Tin Drum* (1978) the aging of Anna, the mother, is achieved through a transitional iris-in/iris-out.

Irony (dramatic)   A term of literary parentage referring to a meaning that is understood by the reader or audience but which often goes unnoticed by a character or characters in the work. Dialogue and dramatic situations in motion pictures are also said to be ironic when they achieve significance for the plot or for characterization through indirect methods, especially methods where the meaning occurs in the contrasting of one idea with its opposite meaning. In *Room at the Top* (1958), for example, dramatic irony is achieved at the moment when Laurence Harvey learns that his rejected lover (Simone Signoret) has committed suicide. Harvey overhears talk of Signoret's death while he is attending a party announcing his engagement to another woman, a younger woman of status whom he has pursued for social and personal gain rather than for love. Seconds after hearing the tragic news of Signoret's death, the party guests burst into a round of "For He's a Jolly Good Fellow." The contrast between the words of the song and the true nature of Harvey's character—perceived by the audience to be ambitious to a point of destroying others—provides an intense moment of dramatic irony.

For Vito Corleone's death scene in *The Godfather* (1972), Francis Ford Coppola employed objects for ironic effect. While playing with his grandson in his vegetable garden, Corleone (Marlon Brando) engages in "gunplay" with the child, using a spray gun containing insect repellent as his weapon. Later in the scene the grandfather stops to rest and eat an orange—a favorite fruit which earlier had nearly caused his death by ambush at a fruit stand. The grandfather fashions a ghoulish set of teeth from the orange peelings to amuse the child. The playful use of these objects, which are ominously perceived by the viewer as death symbols, provides Coppola with an ironic means of portending Corleone's imminent demise.

The use of irony is a primary means by which the filmmaker creates dramatic meaning in a sophisticated, satisfying manner.

Italian neorealism (see **Neorealism**)

J

Jump-cut

The cutting together of two non-continuous **shots** within a **scene** so that the action seems to jump ahead or back in time. A jump-cut is the opposite of a **matched cut**, where action appears continuous.

The jump-cut has been used widely by contemporary filmmakers for varying effect. In Jean-Luc Godard's *Breathless* (1959) extensive time **sequences** were compressed into a few moments by selecting the peaks of a conversation or action and by discarding the boring parts. The effect of this jump-cutting is similar to that of comic-strip panels where information is conveyed in a sequence of single-frame images rather than in fully played-out scenes.

The radical, time-shattering jump-cut has been extensively used in films with modern, existential themes. The contemporary look and "feel" of the jump-cut serves as an appropriate device for expressing the scrambled lifestyles of modern screen characters. In Truffaut's *Small Change* (1976) the jump-cut technique is effectively used in an eating scene at a hairdresser's home. A young boy's voracious appetite is suggested humorously by using jump-cuts as an ample meal is served and eaten.

A jump-cut may also be used to advance the action in a scene without regard for transitional devices. In Robert McKee's *A Day Off* (1974), a short, award-winning dramatic film, two men go to a phone booth and call their bosses to "report in sick." The first man makes his call with the other waiting outside the booth. After a line of dialogue by the first man in which he says that will not be in for work, there is a jump-cut to the second man in the booth saying the same thing to his boss, with the first man now on the outside. The abrupt jump-cut makes the phone call a single act of rebellion. Jump-cut editing has become a popular device in television commercials with "talking-head" plugs for a product.

A jump-cut may also occur in an unintentional editing mistake. An attempt to match action between two shots without exact continuity results in an unintentional jump-cut. A commonly recognized jump-cut occurs when, in continuous action scenes, the length of a cigarette, the volume of wine in a glass, or another detail mistakenly varies as a cut to another angle is made. These jump-cuts are the result of poor attention to **continuity** detail in filming or editing shot sequences.

Juxtaposition A term which refers to the expressive arrangement in film of any number of cinematic elements: visual and aural **images** within a **shot;** the editorial arrangement, through **montage**, of individual shots; time elements; and various color, sound, and musical elements as they come into contact with one another. A juxtaposition of past and present occurs in *The Godfather Part Two* (1974) as the stories of both Michael and his father, set some fifty years apart, are told in the same film. Sergei Eisenstein's dialectical editing, achieved through **montage** of collision, involved the juxtaposition of numerous contrasting elements. In Alain Resnais' film about German concentration camps, *Night and Fog* (1955), sharply defined color **sequences** are juxtaposed with grainy black-and-white sequences, and sound **scenes** are juxtaposed with extensive periods of silence. In Ingmar Bergman's *Cries and Whispers* (1972) the pure, white costumes of the actors are juxtaposed against the deep, passionate red of the set decoration. Bob Fosse's *All That Jazz* (1979) juxtaposes the somber realities of the principal character's illness with the theatrical world of dance. In *Sliding Doors* (1998), two narrative plots are juxtaposed against one another, one developed around the consequences for a young British woman (Gwyneth Paltrow) who misses her train home and her fate, when she is able to catch the train at the last second. The two juxtaposed narratives suggest the role of time in altering the direction of one's life.

K

Kinestasis. A filmmaking technique in which still photographs rather than moving **images** are used as the source of visual information. The word "kinestasis" is derived from two Greek words: *kine* ("movement"), implying that the images are to be projected by a motion-picture projector, and *stasis* ("static"), indicating that the images within the **frames** themselves do not move. The movement of the images through a projector gives the still photographs a rhythmic flow, hence the origin of the term "kinestasis." The technique of kinestasis was employed in the New York City and boat sequences of *Butch Cassidy and the Sundance Kid* (1969). Kinestatic interludes suggest the changing social, cultural, and political climate brought by the passage of time in the Robert Mulligan comedy *Same Time, Next Year* (1978), the study of an ongoing, annual adulterous affair.

Like the **freeze-frame**, kinestatic images can present movements in a contemplative state, rather than in a state of rapid flux. The short, award-winning, science-fiction film *La Jetée* (1964) employs kinestatic techniques entirely except for a brief moment when a character opens her eyes and blinks at the camera. *La Jetée* is a motion picture about the efforts of scientists to project human beings into the past and the future, a subject for which the technique of kinestasis seems especially appropriate.

Kinestasis is also a popular technique in many short animation films, for example, Charles Braverman's three-minute recapitulation of U.S. history, *American Time Capsule* (1968), and Frank Mouris' twelve-minute autobiographical study, *Frank Film* (1975).

Kitchen-sink realism (see **Free Cinema**)

L

Last-minute rescue A plotting-editing device common to screen **melodramas** and one in which **crosscutting** is often used extensively to build dramatic tension before a hero's rescue. Crosscutting reveals the imminent fate of the victim and the simultaneous efforts of the rescuer to reach the victim in time. The rescue occurs at the last possible moment. D.W. Griffith incorporated last-minute rescues as a standard feature of his silent films, further enhancing the buildup of tension by the use of accelerated editing within the crosscutting, as in the film *Way Down East* (1920). A form of the last-minute rescue appeared as an essential element in many of the suspense melodramas of the 1970s, for example, *Two-Minute Warning* (1976), *Rollercoaster* (1977), *Black Sunday* (1977), and *The Peacemaker* (1997). In these films a hostile individual is attempting mass violence in a highly populated area. Counterforces discover the plot and attempt to prevent the violent act—succeeding at the last minute. In film-plotting terminology, this suspense technique is often referred to as the "ticking clock" or "ticking bomb" stratgegy. *In the Line of Fire* (1993) employed cross cutting, last-minute rescue techniques in a tense drama about a Secret

Service agent (Clint Eastwood) who is racing against time to prevent the assassination of the president of the United States.

Law-and-order film A type of contemporary, action-oriented motion picture in which crime and disorder are conclusively brought to an end, often by a single individual who must take it upon herself or himself to correct societal wrongs. The law-and-order film shows individual courage succeeding in correcting crimes when law officials at large have refused to act or have been ineffective at getting the job done. During the 1970s the law-and-order film proliferated on American screens, including, for example, the Dirty Harry series (1971–1976), *Walking Tall*, I and II (1973, 1978), *Macon County Line* (1974), *Trackdown* (1976), *Lethal Weapon* (1987–1998).

Legend A narrative that has been handed down from the past and whose qualities are often mythic in proportion. *Whale Rider* (2003) was based on a New Zealand legend about a Maori girl, Pai (Keisha Castle-Hughes), whose unusual powers and instincts bring to her the respect and leadership role to which she has aspired against great odds. *The Legend of . . .* is a popular lead-in title to numerous biographical folk fables, for example, *The Legend of Tom Dooley* (1959), *The Legend of Bagger Vance* (2000).

Lens A device through which **images** are directed and focused on the film in photographing a **scene**. Lenses provide filmmakers with numerous optical and aesthetic possibilities for recording dramatic action. The choice of a lens for any given **shot** determines both **angle of view** and image quality.

Lenses are usually identified and described according to their angle of view. There are (1) **wide-angle lenses**, (2) **normal lenses**, and (3) **telephoto** (narrow-angle) **lenses**.

The wide-angle lens is one that provides a broad angle of view. It is most commonly used for long establishing shots or in situations where considerable depth of field is desired. An optical characteristic of the wide-angle lens causes moving objects to appear to speed up as they approach the lens of the camera, and, therefore, the use of the wide-angle lens for this purpose in film chases and action scenes has been common.

Another optical quality of the wide-angle lens is its ability to make limited spaces appear larger. A wide-angle lens causes the distance between background and foreground to appear greater than it actually is, and thus increases the sense of space. Wide-angle lenses, because of their tendency to distort objects in unusual ways, are also popular with experimental filmmakers interested in special effects.

The extreme wide-angle lens will distort perspective in distant shots. Horizons will appear curved, and at close range an extended arm will appear elongated. The extreme wide-angle lens is frequently employed for comic effect by distorting a character's face. For example, in a subjective **point-of-view** shot of a dentist's distorted face looking down on a terrorized patient, the extreme wide-angle lens can be used. The lens makes the dentist's face appear quite narrow, and the nose and the eyes seem to protrude sharply from the face. Because its glass element resembles the shape of a fish's eye, the extreme wide-angle lens is sometimes popularly described as a **fish-eye lens**.

The telephoto or narrow-angle lens has the opposite optical effect of a wide-angle lens. In telephoto photography, background and foreground appear compressed and the scene has a flat look. This effect is increased with extremely narrow-angle telephoto lenses.

A telephoto lens, in addition to flattening space, makes moving objects appear to move more slowly. This compression of background and foreground in a telephoto shot gives a character less visible space to move through, and therefore the action seems slower.

The principal uses of the telephoto lens have been for (1) intimate closeup views of dramatic material, (2) compositional emphasis through control of **depth of field**, and (3) the aesthetic manipulation of spatial perspectives.

A normal lens is one that provides a normal angle of view and perspective, and shows normal speed of motion as objects or figures move toward or away from the camera. A normal lens has a depth-of-field range somewhere between that of the wide-angle and telephoto classifications. It is the standard lens used for most camera setups that do not call for special angles of view.

Library footage (shot) Another term for **stock footage**—filmed material of locations and action that has been retained for use in future productions.

Lighting The control of light in a motion picture for purposes of **exposure** and artistic expression. Motion-picture light may

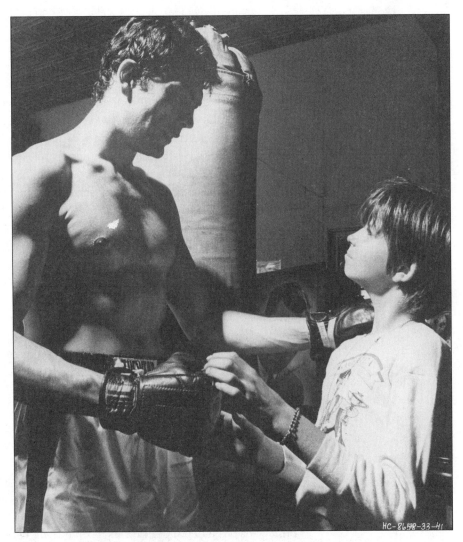

[LIGHTING] 28. (2 images) The nature of high-key and low-key lighting is shown in two shots from Haskell Wexler's *Medium Cool* (1969). The shot at left, with its heavy shadows, is an example of low-key lighting; the shot to the right—brightly lit and relatively free of shadows—shows high-key lighting.

come from either **available-light** sources or from artificially produced sources.

Available light. Light coming from an already existing
source of illumination, as opposed to that provided by the
filmmaker through portable or studio lighting instruments, is
referred to as available light.

Until interior studios and artificial lighting instruments
were developed, dramatic films were photographed outdoors
with interiors shot in box-like settings built with an open front
and no roof. The available light provided sufficient illumination for satisfactory exposures, but little creative use was
made of the light. For this reason the dramatic and documentary films made in the first decade or so of motion-picture history had a flat, bland look. In **flat lighting** the light is evenly
washed across the **scene** without artistic relief, and the light
has not been controlled to achieve a sense of depth by aid-
ing in the separation of actors or areas of interest.

To provide depth and visual dimension through lighting
in a scene, film artists control the quality, amount, and
placement (angle) of light. Light as a quality may be described
as soft light or hard light. Soft light is an evenly diffused, non-
focused light that washes softly over a scene. Hard light is a
focused, highly directed light that will produce intense shadows as it strikes objects or characters in a scene.

Set light. The combination of controlled hard and soft
light in a lighting scheme allows the filmmaker to achieve satisfactory illumination for exposure while adding artistic shadings to the setting. Architectural detail in the setting can be
achieved by throwing a hard light at a 90° angle across the
set. The hard light produces shadows at points where there
is varied texture and structural shape on the set wall. Lighting
technicians frequently begin with this setting light as the first
step in arranging light to create the desired atmosphere for
a scene. The moody, gothic quality of the Xanadu scenes in
Citizen Kane (1941) is in large part attributable to Gregg
Toland's artful use of setting light.

Actor light (three-point lighting). The characters in a
scene may also be lighted for dimensional interest and for
artistic shading. The general procedure in actor lighting with
artificial instruments is to provide the character with a **key
light**, a **back light**, and, depending upon desired mood,
additional **fill light** for purposes of general illumination.

This procedure is often referred to by film professionals as three-point lighting. The key light, generally a hard light, is the light that indicates the principal source and angle of illumination. It is the most intense light in the scene. If a character reads by a table lamp, and that is the major source of illumination, the lamp becomes what is referred to as the "ostensible" source of illumination or "apparent" source of light. Although the light in the scene might be further controlled or added to by technicians, the aesthetic guide for light quality and light angle becomes the table lamp. The *key light* will be focused on the actor to match the throw of light from the lamp. A back light, which may have no apparent source of illumination, will then be added. This light falls on the head and shoulders of the character. It comes from the back, also usually at a 45° angle, and serves to add dimension to the scene by separating the actor from the background. A *fill light*, usually a softer light than key, back, or setting light, may then be used to add some general illumination to the scene and to reduce the harsh shadows produced by the hard light sources.

High-key, low-key lighting. Terms for describing the quality of illumination in motion-picture lighting schemes (photos in 28). When a scene has a bright general illumination, the lighting is referred to as "high-key lighting." This is a lighting scheme designed so that illumination of the scene has a bright, general quality. Low-key lighting has the opposite quality. There is less general illumination in the scene, heavier shadows, and a more atmospheric quality to the scene.

By tradition, high-key lighting has been employed for comedies, musicals, and standard dramatic situations where dialogue and action are the critical concerns of the scene or film. Low-key lighting has been used to add atmosphere to dramas and suspense stories where visual underscoring of mood is a critical consideration. Whether high key or low key, in both cases the lighting sets the dramatic mood of the scene. See **Chiaroscuro lighting, Rembrandt lighting, Selective key light.**

Limbo lighting   A type of motion-picture lighting where light falls only upon the actors within a set area. Space surrounding the actors remains in total darkness. Limbo lighting removes all visual references to a physical setting and, hence, is a means of emphasizing characters exclusively. The public figures who serve as "witnesses" in Warren Beatty's *Reds* (1981) are stylistically separated from the fictionalized elements of the story through interviews with these people who were filmed "in limbo." A limbo lighting scheme or partial limbo effect is also frequently employed in film productions with limited budgets, e.g.for example, John Ford's *The Informer* (1935). Shots of Griet (Scarlett Johansson), posing for the artist Johannes Vermeer (Colin Firth) in *Girl with a Pearl Earring* (2003) are composed against a limbo background.

Lip sync   The precise synchronization of dialogue to an actor's lip movements. Lip movements and their corresponding sounds can appear out of sync because of faulty editing. Since sounds and images are usually recorded separately (double-system recording), it is the responsibility of the sound-film editor to line up dialogue and lip movements during postproduction so that the two are synchronized. Improper threading of a sound film in a motion-picture projector can also cause the sound to be out of sync, especially when the threading loop becomes too large.

Live-action film   A film with real people or animals as opposed to a hand-drawn or puppet-animated film. The term was particularly useful for the Disney Studios after the 1950s when studio output alternated between animated and live-action features and advertising distinctions had to be made between the two types of films. A live-action feature came to mean, in the Disney context, a type of narrative film or comedy designed for general audiences and emphasizing fantasy and escapism as its primary appeals, for example, *Mary Poppins* (1964). Contemporary feature films often combine live-action with animated hand-drawn characters, for example, *Who Framed Roger Rabbit?* (1988), *Looney Tunes: The Action Continues* (2003).

Location shooting (picture) The shooting of a film or film scenes in a real setting as opposed to the controlled environment of a Hollywood shooting stage or studio back lot. The term came into use after the establishment of the studio system and the arrival of talking pictures had forced film production almost entirely indoors. Better technical control of sound recording and lighting was possible within the studio setting, thus greatly diminishing the outdoor shooting that had dominated early film production.

Occasionally, important directors of the 1930s and 1940s would venture off the studio lot for location scenes, for example, John Ford (*Stagecoach*, 1939), Jean Renoir (*Swamp Water*, 1941).

Following World War II, location shooting became increasingly common, spurred by the experiences of filmmakers who had served in the armed forces during the war and by the inspirational work of Italy's neorealists who broke from the studio altogether.

With improved technology and a growth of **independent production** since the 1950s the number of films made entirely on location has continued to grow.

Long shot   A **shot** which provides a wide-angle view of a filmed area. The long shot's wide angle of view enables the viewer to delineate relative proportions with regard to various elements in a scene: their sizes, shapes, and placement. A long shot of a scene with several characters is considered necessary at some point in order to achieve viewer orientation. This type of long shot is referred to as the "obligatory **cover shot**."

The long shot also conveys basic relationships of characters to their environment and as a result can be used to reveal narrative and thematic information. In *The Joyless Street* (1925), for example, G.W. Pabst employs wide-angle long shots to convey the impoverishment of an old professor living in bleak isolation within his nearly barren quarters. These shots provide one of the film's many telling images of social injustice in post-World War I Vienna.

If a long shot takes in an unusually wide angle of view, it is termed an "extreme long shot." In John Ford's *Stagecoach* (1939) extreme long shots help to emphasize the vulnerability of the small stagecoach as it makes its way across the open plains of Monument Valley. Similar wide-angle, long-shot views were part of the Monument Valley location shooting for *Thelma & Louise* (1991).

If a long shot is used to establish locale through recognizable visual data such as the New York skyline or the Eiffel Tower, it is referred to as an "**establishing shot**."

Long take   A term describing a filming procedure in which the photographing of a **scene** or **shot** is unbroken by additional camera **setups**. The camera films the scene or shot in its duration without a repetition of the action as is the case with

master shot/coverage. A long take is distinguished from a master shot because the action of a master shot is repeated for additional angles of view. The long take serves as the desired recording of the action and is edited into the film narrative as a single **take**. A long take has aesthetic implications for film art because its use in varying degrees affects **pace, tone**, and directorial emphasis. See **Direct cinema, Ethnographic film**.

The films of British director Mike Leigh are notable for their use of long-take shots and scenes, for example, the mother-daughter scene in a High Holborn café in *Secrets and Lies* (1996). This tense, eight-minute scene consists of the two women sitting and talking in a booth and is uninterrupted by edits. Robert Altman's *Gosford Park* (2001) was notable for its numerous long-take, multi-character scenes.

Looping   The continuous running of footage while actors rehearse and match voice-to-lip movement for purposes of **dubbing**. In looping, the tail end of the scene or **shot** is joined to the head so that this loop can be run continuously through the projector until sync sound is precisely matched to the **image**. This practice is common in both feature-length films where original sound is not used and in the preparation of **sound tracks** for filmed commercials. The process of film looping occurs in a scene in *Postcards from the Edge* (1990). In this Mike Nichols' film, Meryl Streep portrays an actress who has fallen prey to drugs. In a postproduction looping session with Gene Hackman, she is able to observe herself while "under the influence."

Love interest   That situation within a motion-picture script which has been included to provide romance. Early motion-picture producers quickly discovered the popularity of romance and amply supplied their films with romantic elements; after a while audiences came to expect romance in the film story. As a result writers often seek to fulfill this expectation even when the story might be otherwise unromantic. The love interest in *On the Waterfront* (1954), a film about union corruption and courage on the docks of New Jersey, is provided by an evolving relationship between Eva Marie Saint and Marlon Brando. In *Absence of Malice* (1981), a film about newspaper ethics, the love interest occurs when Sally Field, a reporter, and Paul Newman, the subject of a criminal investigation, become attracted to each other. Motion pictures are often admired by critics when the unexpected love interest is avoided in favor of a more realistic, non-romantic treatment of the plot, for example, *Norma Rae* (1979), a film involving a textile worker (Sally Field) and a labor organizer (Ron Leibman), whose possible romantic feelings for one another do not become overt. Filmmakers often add love interest characters in adapting works of fiction to the screen, for instance, the Alec Baldwin character in *The Cat in the Hat* (2004)—a love interest for the mother. This character did not exist in the Dr. Seuss story.

Low-angle shot   A **shot** which looks up at a character or characters from a camera position set below eye level. Frequently, the ceiling of the set—if an interior scene—shows in low-angle shots.

[LOW-ANGLE SHOT] 29. One of the many up-looking, low-angle shots which appeared in *Citizen Kane* (1941).

Low, up-looking shots make a subject appear more dominant, more imposing than straight-on or **high-angle shots**. The lower angles of view allow the screen figure to tower over the viewer. A sense of arrogance and superiority can be achieved through such compositions. Much of Gregg Toland's innovative photography in *Citizen Kane* (1941, photo 29) is taken from low-angle camera positions. The approach was one ideally suited to a film, in large part about bourgeois pomposity.

In action scenes, low-angle shots taken from a 45° side angle of view are often used to add to the intensity of the action. This is especially so as moving objects or figures approach the camera position. A low-angle, "acute" view of an auto race makes the race appear more exciting than would a straight-on front view or a non-angled side view. Moving objects seem to gain speed and appear more dynamically charged in sharp, low-angle shots. The wider the **angle of view** of the **lens**, the greater the apparent increase in speed of the moving figure as it nears the camera.

An extreme example of low-angle action photography is that achieved by placing the camera in a beneath-the-surface position. For *The Birth of a Nation* (1915), D.W. Griffith filmed from holes in the ground as the Klansmen's horses charged forward toward their **last-minute rescue** of the Cameron family. Similar beneath-the-ground low-angle shots provided visual variety in *Olympia* (1936), Leni Riefenstahl's brilliant film study of the 1936 Berlin Olympics. See **High-hat shot**.

Low-key lighting   (see **Lighting**)

Lyrical film   (see **External rhythm**)

M

MacGuffin (McGuffin) A term whose origin is attributed to Alfred Hitchcock and one used to describe a plotting device for setting a story into motion. The term is frequently applied to that object or person in a mystery film that at the beginning of the plot provides an element of dramatic curiosity. The MacGuffin can be something that all the characters are trying to get their hands on, for example, a falcon in *The Maltese Falcon* (1941) or a gem in *The Pink Panther* (1963). The MacGuffin can also be someone or something that is lost and is being sought. In Hitchcock's *Family Plot* (1976) the MacGuffin is a missing heir. The ensuing search for the heir leads to a larger, more involved mystery story. Once the dramatic plot is under way in a Hitchcock film, the MacGuffin often ceases to be of major importance.

The search for the meaning of "Rosebud" in *Citizen Kane* (1941) has been described by some critics as a plotting device like that of the MacGuffin. "Rosebud" becomes the element of dramatic curiosity that motivates the mosaic investigation that helps explain the meaning of Kane's life. Michael Moore's contrived efforts to locate the chairman of General Motors in *Roger & Me* (1989) were described by critics as resembling the MacGuffin plotting device.

Made-for-television movie A motion picture made initially for television broadcast. Some made-for-television movies are released theatrically in foreign markets. The British television films *My Beautiful Laundrette* (1985), *Enchanted April* (1992), and *The Snapper* (1993) achieved popular success in international theatrical distribution. In some instances a theatrically produced film made in the United States, for instance, *Paris Trout* (1991), will debut on television and then be released to theaters abroad. *Paris Trout* was the adaptation of the award-winning novel by Pete Dexter and told the story of an unrepentant racist (Dennis Hopper) in 1940s America. Hopper's international appeal and that of co-star Barbara Hershey proved the film marketable as a theatrical release in Europe. The casting example set by *Paris Trout* in its inclusion of actors with box-office draw abroad had a significant influence on made-for-television movie producers looking for extended markets for their products.

The made-for-television movie has been standard fare on the major U.S. networks, often using popular novels (*Sins*, 1986) and nonfiction books (*Life Lines/Reason for Living: The Jill Ireland Story*, 1991) as the source of their material. Many network movies treat domestic issues in sensational ways while others strive for dramatic impact at another level. Arthur Miller's TV script *Playing for Time* (1980) looked at the ironies of World War II concentration life through the characterization of a musician (Vanessa Redgrave) who, because of her role in a camp orchestra, is spared the ultimate horror of Auschwitz: death.

With the expansion of cable and pay-per-view channel options such as Home Box Office (HBO), new revenue and outlets have served to generate more ambitious and original made-for-television movies. The Bonny Dore (Prod.)-Lindsay Anderson (Dir.) HBO film about television evangelism, *Glory! Glory!* (1989), ran for 210 minutes and was boldly satirical in its treatment of airwaves ministry. The excellence of this type of production has—along with the British films—shown the potential quality within the made-for-television mini-series.

Some made-for-television movies are created in segmented mini-series form for broadcast over an extended period of time, for example, *Roots* (1977), *The Winds of War* (1983), *Lonesome Dove* (1989), *Wild Palms* (1993).

Angels in America (2004), a three-part adaptation of Kushner's stage play about AIDS, was a highly acclaimed, award-winning made-for-television movie.

Magnetic film   A film coated with an iron oxide stripe (near the film's edge) on which the **sound track** is recorded and reproduced. With magnetic striped film, sound can be recorded directly onto the film; iron oxide is essentially the same as magnetic recording tape. The simultaneous recording of sound and image is referred to as single-system sound recording. See **Double-system sound**.

March of Time, The (see **Newsreel**)

Masking   The blocking out of the **frame** edges through devices which give emphasis to the remaining **image**. Masking has also been a popular method for varying image size and shape within the traditional frame parameters. **Irises** and black masks were frequently used by D.W. Griffith in *The Birth of a Nation* (1915) and *Intolerance* (1916) to vary image shape and to achieve dramatic emphasis. Masks are also employed to give the impression of a character looking through binoculars or a keyhole. See **Dynamic frame**.

Master shot (scene) The technique of filming a single, **long take** of a piece of dramatic action and then repeating the action for closer views. The long take or master shot provides the basic unit of action in which **medium shots** and **close-ups** are inserted. This process, common during the studio years and in filming for television, provides numerous options for the editor in placing dramatic emphasis. It also permits unobtrusive **matched cutting**. See **Coverage**.

Matched cut   An editing cut made on two identical points of action after **master shot** and **coverage filming** so that continuous action is achieved in the **scene**. Match cutting is sometimes referred to as **invisible cutting** because cutting on identical points of action draws attention away from the cut.

Matte shot   A shot in which part of the **scene** was masked so that additional action or background/foreground material could be supplied later, usually by optical printing (photo 30). Early instances of the matte shot appear in Edwin S. Porter's *The Great Train Robbery* (1903). A matte was used to show the arrival of the train outside the station window and later to show the passing landscape through the open door of the train's mail car. These matte shots have often been mislabeled as rear-screen projection.

[MATTE SHOT] 30. Three images from Victor Fleming's *The White Sister* (1933) illustrate the process of a matte shot. The top still shows the inside of a large church. The middle still reveals the chapel shot after it has been masked. The bottom shot shows the final effect of the matte process after a boys' choir has been "matted" by optical printer into the masked area. The illusion is that of a choir loft set far in the back of and above the church sanctuary.

Medium shot   A **shot** which in scope and **angle** of view falls somewhere between a close-up shot and a long shot. Generally, a medium shot emphasizes an object or subject in some detail; in a medium shot of a person, the area of view most typically shows the subject from the waist up. Medium shots isolate the subject from the environment to a greater extent than do long shots. In **shot-sequence editing** the medium shot serves the utilitarian function of a logical step between long shot and close-up. A medium shot is also often referred to as a midshot.

Melodrama   Any type of film, play, or television program characterized by a sensational plot that has been designed principally to provide thrills and to appeal to the emotions of the audience. The term "melodrama" translates literally as a "play with music," a throwback to the origins of the **genre** in English theater during the 19th century. As the form developed it became customary to include incidental music with the dramatic action to enhance the emotions and thrills, thus "melodrama."

Film melodramas in a similar manner seek to engage the emotions of the audience and provide thrills. The form has been popular in the motion picture since the evolution of the fictional film.

Metamorphosis ("Morphing") The visual effect of turning an object or a person into another thing or another person. The morphing of cyborgs in *Terminator II: Judgment Day* (1991) demonstrated this emerging visual effect as part of the film's action dynamics. Morphing is sometimes used for the sudden cameo appearances of celebrities, for example, Michael Jordan in *Looney Tunes: The Action Continues* (2003).

Metaphor   A term describing the use of imagery by which an analogy can be drawn between an object and an abstract idea so that the two are imaginatively linked. The initial idea is reinforced by its association with a concrete object.

Metaphorical expressions are possible in motion pictures through **montage** of attraction. As W.C. Fields in *The Dentist* (1932) applies his drill to a patient's mouth, an insert cut is made to a construction worker's pneumatic gun tearing at the side of a steel beam. A satirical metaphor is effected.

Metaphors in motion pictures may be of a more extended type. In *The Battleship Potemkin* (1925), for example, the battleship serves as a metaphor for the Russian state under the Czarist regime. The oppression, rebellion, and ultimate efficiency of the sailors aboard the Potemkin together represent a metaphorical account of the conditions leading to the overthrow of the Czarist regime and also suggest the subsequent public attitude of unity needed to sustain the new government.

Both the title and settings of Woody Allen's psychological film *Interiors* (1978) are associative metaphors for the characters' internal conflicts.

Method actor   A popular term used to describe actors who have studied the Stanislavski method of naturalistic **acting**. Popularized in the United States in the 1930s by director Richard Boleslavski and acting teacher Stella Adler, and eventually a principal approach at the Actors Studio under Lee Strasberg and Elia Kazan, method acting sought to combine a psychological attitude with learned technical skills. The ultimate goal was greater realism in character interpretation. Method acting began to make an impact in Hollywood with the arrival of Actors Studio graduates (Marlon Brando, Julie Harris, James Dean, Karl Malden, Kim Stanley) in the early 1950s. This new acting style coincided appropriately with a partial move in American filmmaking toward more psychological, introspective stories: *The Men* (1950), *A Streetcar Named Desire* (1951), *East of Eden* (1955), and *The Goddess* (1958).

Metonymy   A film term derived from the Greek "*metonymia*," meaning "change of name." Metonymy refers to the use of the name of an object or concept to imply something of related meaning, for example, "the brass" for "high-ranking military officers." Metonymy in the motion picture can refer to an object that serves narrative and thematic functions through implied correlation. In Vittorio De Sica's *The Bicycle Thief* (1947) a stolen bicycle acts as a metonymical device for implying the desperation of post-World War II Italians in a context greater than that of the protagonist's (Antonio) own individual plight. The missing bicycle signifies an overall sense of desperate need and can be seen as representing, metonymically, "a paradise lost."

Metteur-en-scène   A term sometimes used for "director," from the French meaning "placer-in-the-scene." The term is often applied to a director of modest talents as if to suggest that the director has essentially moved actors into their places within the **scene**. The **blocking** and **composition** are effected without noteworthy aesthetic appeal.

Mickey Mousing (music) The exact synchronization of a visual **image** in a motion picture with an associative musical sound. This technique was common in the cartoon films of Walt Disney, with musical sounds accompanying every movement of the animated characters. Hence, the technique has sometimes come to be described as "Mickey Mousing" or "Mickey Mousing the music," especially when overworked in coordinating **music** with image. Use of the technique, particularly in comedies and suspense stories, has proved an effective device for wedding sound to visual image. In *Sleepless in Seattle* (1993), musical notes are Mickey-Moused to the letter and word images on Meg Ryan's computer screen as she searches the internet for the identity of a man in Seattle whose wife has recently died.

Millimeter (mm) A measurement designation used in describing (1) the **focal length** of photographic **lenses** and (2) the width of celluloid filmstrips. The focal length of lenses ranges from approximately one millimeter to several hundred millimeters. 25 mm is the equivalent of 1 inch. Film widths used in motion-picture photography also vary: 8 mm, 16 mm, 35 mm, 60 mm, 70 mm.

Miniature A motion-picture setting or set piece which has been rendered in a scaled-down model rather than in actual size (photo 31). The miniature is a cost-saving approach to set design that, with artful photography and lighting, can provide the illusion of a real environment. Through **matte**-screen processing, and with digital computers, it is possible to combine effectively "live" foreground action with background shots taken of miniature settings. Miniatures were used extensively in *Master and Commander* (2003) for storm and battle scenes at sea. See **Introvision**.

Minimal cinema An approach to motion-picture expression where extreme realism dominates. Imagery and structure are simple and direct, in a manner reminiscent of the ***actualité*** films of the Lumière brothers made in the 1890s. Artistic intervention through varied camera **setups** as well as editing are kept to a minimum, thus reducing the film expression to a scientific-technical recording of an event. **Long-take** photography is often the principal method of minimal cinema, as in Andy

[MINIATURE] 31. Miniature settings were used to great effect in the 1940 rendering of the Arabian Nights fable, *The Thief of Baghdad*. This British production starred Rex Ingram as a genie who was capable of swelling to gigantic proportions or shrinking to a size that would fit inside a bottle.

Warhol's *Sleep* (1963–1964), *Eat* (1963), and *Empire* (1964).

Mise-en-scène   A term which generally refers to the elements within a **scene**, that is, the physical setting which surrounds a dramatic action. In a theatrical situation, the term refers to the total stage picture—the scenery, the properties, and the arrangement of the actors. In France, the term is used for the film's direction. In film criticism mise-en-scène has sometimes been used to describe an approach to cinematic art which places greater emphasis on pictorial values within a shot than on the juxtaposition of two **shots** (**montage**). According to the American critic Andrew Sarris, this theory of mise-en-scène developed as an effort to counteract the popular editing (montage) theories of Sergei Eisenstein and V.I. Pudovkin. André Bazin, a French theorist and proponent of mise-en-scène tenets, noted that the dynamic editing devices used by the Russian filmmakers did not present events on the screen fully, but only alluded to them. Bazin argued instead for dramatic actions that were more unified in time and space through sustained shots and **camera movement**. Events to him were more effectively presented when the filmmaker showed the actual waiting period in a dramatic situation; furthermore, dramatic space existing between characters or objects in the scene could be maintained so as not to lose the importance of preexisting relationships. Robert Altman explored this approach in creating multi-character scenes for *Gosford Park* (2001). An examination of film works shows that throughout the history of the cinema filmmakers have fluctuated between montage and pictorial mise-en-scène in telling their stories.

Mocumentary   A fictional motion picture which possesses the qualities of documentary film: spontaneous shooting, the semblance of real characters and actual situations. Christopher Guest's *Best in Show* (2000), a humorous account of a national dog show competition, is an example.

Monster film   A type of thriller movie in which an aberrant or alien creature becomes a threat to the immediate environment. The definitive example of the monster movie is *Frankenstein*, a horror story of scientific experiment gone awry. Since the first screen version of Frankenstein in 1931, there have been at least a dozen variations of the story. The monster-through-laboratory-error concept has undergone a variety of treatments, including the poignant David Cronenberg film, *The Fly* (1986). Steven Spielberg's *Jurassic Park* (1993) employed DNA research experimentation with a mosquito preserved in amber to create yet another variation of the laboratory-generated screen monster—this time in the form of vicious dinosaurs on the loose. The "Doc Ock" villain

(Alfred Molina) in *Spider-Man 2* (2004) is a variation of the laboratory-generated monster. Alien monster movies include such telling titles as *Monster from the Ocean Floor* (1954), *Monster from Green Hell* (1957), *Aliens* (1968), *Alien Predator* (1987), and *Alien Resurrection* (1997). Another popular type is the monster-ape movie represented by such efforts as *Godzilla* (1955) and the classic "lovable monster" ape film, *King Kong* (1933, 2005).

Montage

A French word meaning "mounting," frequently used to describe the assemblage of a film through editing. Numerous subcategories of montage have developed to denote particular methods of editing. Among them are the following terms:

Accelerated montage. The use of editing to add to the effect of increased speed of action in a motion picture. By decreasing the length of individual shots in an action or chase sequence, it is possible to impose an external pace on the rhythm of the film. The quickening of pace through editing is termed "accelerated montage." The climax to a screen chase is often accompanied by accelerated montage, where the excitement of the event seems to quicken with shorter shots and staccato editing. In D.W. Griffith's *The Lonedale Operator* (1911) accelerated montage is achieved through rapid crosscutting among three locations until a young engineer on a speeding train arrives to rescue his girlfriend from invading robbers. The scene in Godard's *Breathless* (1959) in which Jean-Paul Belmondo kills a policeman seems unusually fast because of accelerated montage. Three quick shots are cut together in a brief, four-second span of time.

American or Hollywood montage. A term sometimes used to describe a **scene** in which a series of short, quick shots are edited so as to suggest in a brief period the essence of events occurring over a longer span of time.

The cinematic cliché of newspaper headlines, presented in a rapid succession of shots, to capsulize in time the major developments in an event and to serve as a transition between dramatic sequences, is an example of American montage. *Citizen Kane* (1941) employs this type of device on several occasions. Another form of American montage occurs in *Something's Gotta Give* (2003), as Jack Nicholson tells Diane Keaton of his ill-fated effort to reconnect with younger women from his past. The young women are seen in a quick-cut American montage.

Conceptual montage. The cutting together of shots for the purpose of creating meanings that exist only by the arrangement of the various shots. The theories and application of conceptual montage were major concerns of the Russian filmmakers of the 1920s, particularly Sergei Eisenstein and V.I. Pudovkin. These filmmakers believed that montage (editing) was the very essence of film art and sought to exploit its most expressive possibilities. Eisenstein and Pudovkin were less interested in matched editing and more interested in the overall effect of an assortment of shots. They arranged their material for emotional-intellectual impact as well as for narrative flow.

In the Odessa steps sequence of *The Battleship Potemkin* (1925) Eisenstein intentionally distorts time and space by expanding the actual time of the scene and employs dramatic long shots of the fleeing victims beside close-up shots of the pounding boots of the Cossacks. The contrast provided by this editing of close shots of marching feet and helpless victims becomes a powerful visual **metaphor** for authoritarian persecution in Russia. To end the scene a shot of a soldier lifting his rifle saber to slash a baby in a pram is followed by a dynamic cut to a startled woman who has just been hit in the eye by a Cossack's bullet. The woman's shocked expression of horror becomes a realistic one for her own fate and a symbolic, conceptual one for the baby's fate, as it is edited in immediately after the stabbing which is not visualized. A larger concept of the horror and tragedy of the event is achieved by the joining of the two shots.

Montage of attraction. An editing method whereby two separate **images** on the screen become related to one another because of visual and contextual similarities.

Montage of attraction is often used for expressive or conceptual purposes. In *Ten Days That Shook the World* (1928) Eisenstein employed this method of montage of attraction so extensively as to make at times the film a virtual burlesque. For example, a shot of an arrogant Czarist politician is followed by a shot of a peacock spreading its proud tail feathers. This type of satirical, expressive editing is common throughout Eisenstein's film.

The advantages of montage of attraction for suggesting

internal feelings and ideas have also been exploited by film-makers. In the early 1920s a Russian film experimenter, Lev Kuleshov, edited a single shot of an actor's expressionless face between shots of an empty soup bowl, a dead woman in a coffin, and a child playing with a toy. In each return to the shot of the actor's face film viewers who were shown the short film said that the actor's emotions had changed. They saw hunger after the shot of the empty bowl, sadness after the shot of the coffin, and happiness after the insert of the playful child. The belief that the actor had changed expressions was a direct result of montage-of-attraction editing.

Narrative montage. The editing together of shots and scenes which have been arranged in a desired chronological order according to a prescribed **shooting script** or **master-shot** procedure. The **editor**'s goal has been to reconstruct the semblance of events and to structure the narrative flow of the film story. Narrative montage is more concerned with the development of a story, whereas conceptual montage seeks to produce ideas and effects through the joining or collision of shots.

Rhythmic montage. Editing for rhythmic variation to effect the thematic intentions of a **film** or a film scene. The length of shots, movement within a frame, and types of **transitions** employed between scenes most significantly affect editing rhythm. The actual length of shots determines **external rhythm** while movement within a frame determines **internal rhythm**. Eisenstein employed the term rhythmic montage to describe editing methods used in his films. The Odessa steps sequence, for example, combines external and internal rhythms to create a montage of powerful effect.

A short film called *Values and Interpretations*, produced by the American Society of Cinematographers, illustrates the role of the film editor in determining dramatic effect through cutting rhythms. *Values and Interpretations* shows a shot **sequence** being filmed for the television series *Gunsmoke*. The scene opens with a man assaulting a young woman and concludes with a fistfight between the man and the town marshal. The woman and various other townspeople watch the action. The **director** of the scene, Ted Post, employs a standard approach in filming the material. He begins each action with long shots and then repeats the action for closer views and reaction shots of the onlookers.

The *Gunsmoke* sequence of shots is then given to three different film editors and we are allowed to see how each edits the scene. The most striking and revealing contrast occurs between the work of the first two editors. The first editor breaks the material into short, staccato shots, frequently cutting in the middle of sentences of dialogue rather than at the end of sentences. As a result the **pace** of the action is dynamic and metronomic. Obviously this editor interprets the scene as intense and active and sought to use quick cutting to complement that interpretation.

The second editor on the other hand is less dynamic. He makes extensive use of **close-up** reaction shots and "holds on" these shots for a more extended period of time than did the first editor. Because of this less dynamic approach, the second version appears more contemplative. The onlookers seem to be absorbing the impact of the violent action rather than passively viewing it.

The length of the shots is the key difference between the tempos of the two sequences.

Russian montage. A reference to the various editing approaches of prominent Russian directors during the 1920s, namely, Sergei Eisenstein, Lev Kuleshov, V.I. Pudovkin, and Dziga Vertov. Spurred by extensive post-Revolutionary experimentation in all the arts, Russian film directors sought new methods of expression as the motion picture acted to achieve its assigned task of educating and rallying the country's citizens. Montage—expressive editing—was viewed as the very essence of cinematic art, particularly the linkage and collision of shots to produce emotional, physical, and ideological meaning. In his effort to produce socially useful statements, Dziga Vertov's early editing experiments in the *Kino-Pravda* newsreels (1922–1925) often juxtaposed scenes of the past (taken from vintage footage) with newly recorded shots of more favorable current conditions. Kuleshov's **creative geography** and **montage-of-attraction** experiments reveal how separate shots when linked together through editing could suggest geographic and emotional realities which in fact did not exist. Pudovkin developed a theory of "constructive editing" in which the precise selection and arrangement of narrative details were seen as the primary means by which the filmmaker seized

attention and guided the viewer's "thoughts and associations." Eisenstein advocated "**montage of collision**"—the
clash and contrast of shots for a dialectical effect. Montage
of collision, Eisenstein said, could be achieved through rhythmic clash, temporal-spatial conflict, and within image composition, including the clash of mass or volume. The
application of these latter methods appear most noticeably
in Eisenstein's *The Battleship Potemkin* (1925).

By employing editing as their primary means of film
expression, Russian directors of the 1920s gave new meaning to the concept of montage, while establishing themselves through their dynamic methods as important
motion-picture formalists. See **Formalism**.

Montage of attraction (see **Montage**)

Montage of collision (see **Montage**)

Motif A recurring element in a motion picture that gains in dramatic importance through its repetition. In *House of Sand and
Fog* (2003), the serving of tea, for purposes of soothing characters in tense situations (as a respite from cares), is a motif
which culminates in the film's tragic ending.

Motivation In script terminology, motivation is the name given to the
basis of character impulses and dramatic plotting as the
story is revealed and progresses to its conclusion. Actors in
preparing for a role often seek to uncover what has been
called "the character spine," that primary motivational factor that dominates at all times. Uncovering "character spine"
serves the actor as an interpretive tool. It has been said that
Colin Smith's "character spine" in *The Loneliness of the
Long Distance Runner* (1962) is one ruled by unabated *societal anger*, and hence provides understanding of a character (acted brilliantly by Tom Courtenay) who possesses an
unswerving, lifelong commitment to anti-social behavior and
criminal activity.

Multiple exposure A visual effect achieved by **superimposing** two or more
images into a shot. Multiple exposure is usually created by
laboratory printing and is often employed to reveal simultaneous actions. The device is also common in dream, hallu-
cinatory, and supernatural sequences, for example, *The
Flatliners* (1990).

Multiple-image shot A **shot** in a motion picture which includes two or more
separately recorded **images** within a single **frame**. Most
multiple-image shots are achieved through laboratory

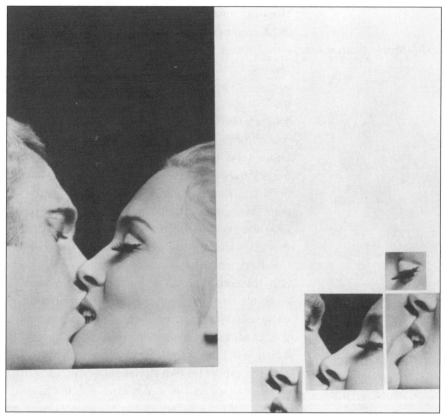

[MULTIPLE-IMAGE SHOT] 32. Unusual multi-image shots of Steve McQueen and Faye Dunaway appeared in Norman Jewison's *The Thomas Crown Affair* (1968).

processes such as **superimposition** and **split-screen** techniques. By use of multiple-image shots it is possible to present simultaneous action or several different segments of visual information, for example, *The Thomas Crown Affair* (1968, photo 32). The multiple-image technique has been popular with experimental filmmakers (*N.Y., N.Y.,* 1957) and with the producers of filmed commercials.

Multi-screen projection The presentation of a single motion-picture **image** or several different images onto more than one screen. In the concluding **sequences** of *Napoléon* (1927), Abel Gance used three separate projectors with synchronized motors and three separate screens to achieve an extremely wide panoramic view of the action. Gance called his triple-screen effect "polyvision." Experimental multi-screen presentations are often seen at amusement centers and in **expanded-**

cinema exercises for the purposes of novelty and innovative visual experiences, respectively.

Music (film music) Music appearing as a part of the **sound track** of a motion picture. Film music may be either realistic or functional, sometimes both. Realistic (diegetic) film music, generally, is music that appears on a film as a part of the story, and its source is visible, or made known, to the viewer, for example, music from a radio or record player. Functional film music, on the other hand, is most often a background **score** (nondiegetic music) designed to enhance mood, to intensify emotions and actions, and to aid film structure by supplying aural unification. In achieving these goals the music serves several expressive functions. Scenic music sets the scene for the action that will follow. The musical sound of the French Can-Can in a clichéd manner sets the scene for a Paris location; the clichéd sound of American Indian music, suggested by the rhythmic beat of a tom-tom, signals the old West while sounding an ominous note; the music coming from the flute of an Indian snake-tamer suggests India and the exotic nature of the Far East. Familiar Stephen Foster folk music often accompanies film stories set in the old South.

Time periods may also be a functional goal of film music. Film stories set in Renaissance Europe are often scored with music dominated by blaring trumpets, cornets, and other brass instruments. Later periods, set in the more genteel 17th and 18th centuries, will utilize harpsichords and harps to suggest the time. Contemporary films with modern themes, such as *Medium Cool* (1969) and *Mickey One* (1965), both set in Chicago in the 1960s, contain modern jazz scores to suggest both their contemporaneity and their urban settings.

In addition to its scenic functions, film music may also punctuate and reinforce screen action. A chase scene is often accompanied by a rhythmic, dynamic piece of music, which is coordinated to match the **pace** of the dramatic action, and is thus reinforcing. Music to reinforce action may be generally synchronized to the **scene**, or it may be synchronized precisely. This exact synchronization of visual image with an associative musical sound was a common technique in many of Walt Disney's cartoon films. Mickey Mouse and other Disney characters often had musical sounds accompany their every movement. This technique, when prominent in coordinating music with **image**, is sometimes referred to as **Mickey Mousing** or "Mickey Mousing the music."

Another function of film music has been to heighten dramatic tension and to convey mood. Music for mood and dramatic tension is common in melodramatic suspense scenes, romantic scenes, and landscape scenes. Such scenes are often intensified by unobtrusive **background music**, which will, without calling attention to its presence, become the principal element that establishes and maintains the mood of the scene.

Another function of music is to provide a musical motif (leitmotif) for a motion picture. The various parts of *Gone with the Wind* (1939) are unified by the lyrical music of "Tara's Theme." "Lara's Theme" in *Dr. Zhivago* (1965) provides a unifying musical motif throughout the picture. Musical motifs, sometimes used for character association, are often employed to bridge segments of the story while sustaining mood and film flow. In epic films such as *Gone with the Wind* and *Dr. Zhivago*, motif music plays an important part in conveying the epic quality of the story.

Film music can provide a method for structural unity in scenes that are visually fragmentary. An **American montage sequence**, which presents rapid shots of dramatic actions for the purpose of condensing a period of time into a brief, capsulized view, will usually be accompanied by a unifying piece of music. This was the case with the **kinestatic** interludes used as passage-of-time transitions in *Same Time, Next Year* (1978). The sustained quality of the music gave structural unity to the rapidly flowing photographs of famous people and historic events.

Because music is present on the filmstrip and can be coordinated precisely with any single film frame, it is also possible to use music to change dynamically the scene or the mood and to "key" essential dramatic information. Soft, romantic music may accompany a fireside living-room scene where a man and a woman are enjoying an evening together. A psychopathic killer makes his way down a corridor leading to the living room. The **editor** crosscuts between the couple and the killer's feet, and each time inserts dramatic suspense music for the feet shots and returns to the romantic music for the fireside shots. The intercutting has both visual and aural impact. The crosscutting of music serves as a means of rapidly indicating for the viewer different qualities of mood in abrupt scene changes.

The direct coordination of film music with image allows music to serve as an expressive **sound effect**. Frequently musical notes are substituted for the human voice for a stylized, comic effect.

A single, sustained musical note or combination of notes used to punctuate a dramatic moment in a film is called a "stinger" because of the aural conclusion it provides. A stinger calls dramatic attention, in a heightened manner, to a moment of information. An electronic stinger effect was used throughout John Sayles' *Passion Fish* (1992) as an abrupt transitional bridge.

Film music often conveys psychological and subjective states not communicable by pictures alone. Musical instruments in film may evoke impressions of happiness, gaiety, sadness, or depression. The film music may convey mood; it may also suggest interior states through its associative relationship with characters and with the emotional climate of a story. A confused state of mind can be conjured up by using a cacophonous, chaotic piece of electronic music. In Carol Reed's *The Third Man* (1949), the quality of life and an emerging cold-war mood in Vienna, Austria, during the period following World War II were indicated by a musical score played on a zither. Throughout the musical scoring for Oliver Stone's *Platoon* (1987), the viewer-listener can detect a persistent drumbeat—a recognizable musical sound for heading into battle.

Musical film (1) A fictional motion picture which deals in a significant manner with the subject of music and which uses musical performance as an integral part of the narrative, for example, *Yankee Doodle Dandy* (1942), *The Great Caruso* (1951), *The Buddy Holly Story* (1978). (2) A motion picture that incorporates the conventions of song and dance routines into the film story and in which the musical numbers serve as an accepted element in the film narrative (*An American in Paris*, 1951; *Hello Dolly*, 1969; *Grease II,* 1982; *Velvet Goldmine*, 1998; *Chicago*, 2002).

The conventions of the musical **genre**, in general, include liberal use of musical numbers, choreographed dance, expressive costuming and scenery, and abstract color and lighting—particularly in the song-and-dance routines.

A subcategory within the musical-film genre is the backstage musical, a type of film where the plot centers on characters who are stage performers. The dramatic plot in backstage musicals invariably develops around the intricacies and tensions of producing a successful stage musical. Integration of elaborate musical numbers into this type of film is justified by the nature of the story, for example, *42nd Street* (1933). The backstage musical was especially popular during the 1930s. An interesting variation of this type of musical was *Topsy-Turvy* (1999), a behind-the-scenes look at the operetta genius of Gilbert and Sullivan as they labored to bring *The Mikado* to realization on the stage. See **Biographical film**.

Mystery thriller   A film **genre** whose story centers on a tale of suspense that is generated by some type of strange or terrorizing adventure. Often the principal character is caught in a menacing situation from which escape seems impossible, for example, *Wait Until Dark* (1968), *When a Stranger Calls* (1980), *Cape Fear* (1962, 1991), *The Hand That Rocks the Cradle* (1992), *Panic Room* (2002). Frequently the mystery thriller revolves around the **protagonist**'s efforts to unravel a crime or suspected crime—leading the character toward an unknown menace which will ultimately become life-threatening, for example, *Coma* (1978), *Femme Fatale* (1991), *The Firm* (1993), *The Net* (1995), *Dirty Pretty Things* (2002).

Myth   A type of story, usually of unknown origin and containing supernatural elements, which has been handed down through a country's literary heritage. The myth's supernatural emphases spring from the need to examine and explain, dramatically and philosophically, deeply complex areas of human concern or thought: life, death, religion, the gods, creation, etc. Popular Greek and Roman myths have frequently been employed by modern playwrights and filmmakers in explaining personal views of life. Jean Cocteau, for example, appropriated the Orpheus myth as the dramatic framework for his motion pictures which investigate the complex existence and nature of the "poet" (artist), for example, *Orphée (1924), Blood of a Poet* (1930), *Orpheus* (1950), and *The Testament of Orpheus* (1959). Mythic figures have also evolved within certain **genre** films, for instance, the American **western**. The "loner" gunfighter (Alan Ladd in

Shane, 1953) and the prostitute with a heart of gold (Claire Trevor in *Stagecoach*, 1939) are among the familiar figures that have become a part of the western mythology.

In a more general context myth or mythology implies the full body of stories which evolve within a culture to make meaning of human endeavor, individually and collectively, and which convey it with a sense of common enterprise. **Archetypal** heroes and archetypal motifs provide much of the continuity of mythic storytelling, from the heroic pursuits within a John Wayne western or war film to the "heart of darkness" revelations of *Apocalypse Now* (1979). Because of the prominence of genre in filmmaking, screen myth has its own special meaning. This is especially so when viewed in the context of urban and western law-and-order heroes whose approach to societal disorder is direct and triumphant. Quintessentially, "Dirty Harry" Callahan suggests the mythic proportions of this kind of screen "god."

The mythology of the invincible war hero (as typified by John Wayne's screen persona) is employed as ironic counterpoint in Stanley Kubrick's anti-war Vietnam study, *Full Metal Jacket* (1987). The film's anti-war stance is developed in part by shattering the screen myth of the invincibility of U.S. soldiers in battle. See **Legend**.

N

Narration	A term for the spoken words of a person who relates information in a film directly rather than through **dialogue**. A narrator may be a character in the film, or an anonymous, unseen "voice" who narrates the action of the drama or the **documentary**. An on-screen narrator may talk directly into the camera or more commonly speak in **"voice-over"** narration.
Naturalism	A stylistic approach in literature, drama, or film with an emphasis on stark reality. Suggestions of artifice are avoided, and the environment in its fullest representative form becomes a central force in shaping social conditions and the destiny of characters. The naturalist also avoids value judgments in depicting character behavior, which is viewed as socially and biologically predetermined. The naturalistic school was greatly influenced in the 1870s by the French novelist-playwright Emile Zola with his "slice of life" approach to stage expression. A pessimistic, tragic view of everyday life dominated Zola's work and that of his follower, André Antoine at the Théâtre Libre. In cinema, naturalistic intentions have appeared in the films of Louis Delluc (*Fièvre*, 1921), Erich von Stroheim (*Greed*, 1924), G.W. Pabst (*The Joyless Street*, 1925), Jean Renoir (*Toni*, 1934), and in the

[NATURALISM] 33. A stark, naturalistic style accompanied the British film *Dance with a Stranger* (1985). The plot's narrative recounted the self-destructive story of Ruth Ellis (Miranda Richardson) who in 1955 was the last woman to be executed in Britain.

body of post-World War II Italian neorealist films. The British film, *Dance With A Stranger* (1985, photo 33), possessed strong naturalistic qualities in its treatment of the life of Ruth Ellis, a woman executed for murder in 1955.

Natural wipe   A transition technique accomplished by an element within the **mise-en-scène** rather than by a laboratory process. A character or an object is brought to the **lens** of the camera and wipes away the **scene** by completely blocking or blurring the frame. A closing door often serves as a natural wipe. The natural wipe is followed by a new scene. A **head-on, tail-away** transition is a type of natural wipe that is used to end one scene and to reveal another. See **Wipe**.

Negative image   A photographic **image** in which light and dark areas are reproduced in reverse tones. In a negative image dark areas appear light and light areas appear dark. Because of their unusual (ghostlike) appearance, negative images are sometimes employed in **fantasies**, **mysteries**, and psychological films. Negative sequences appear in F.W. Murnau's *Nosferatu* (1922), in Jean Cocteau's *Blood of a Poet* (1930), and in Jean-Luc Godard's *Alphaville* (1965).

The non-reality of negative images has been responsible for their popularity with experimental filmmakers: in the abstract, negative images of Len Lye's *Musical Poster Number One* (1939), in Maya Deren's dreamlike dance images in *The Very Eye of the Night* (1959), and in Michael Snow's sustained zoom shot in *Wavelength* (1967).

Neorealism (Italian) A film movement which began in Italy near the end of World War II. Roberto Rossellini, Vittorio de Sica, and Luchino Visconti were among those Italian **directors** of the time who produced films described as neorealistic. Their approach to technique and theme rejected the well-made studio film and the happy-ending story. Neorealism was characterized by social consciousness, simple stories of the common worker, and location shooting. Neorealism directors often used non-actors as performers and took their cameras into the street and into real settings for visual authenticity and thematic credibility. Among the outstanding films produced during the height of neorealism between 1945 and 1952 were *Open City* (1945), *Paisan* (1947), *La Terra Trema* (1948), and *The Bicycle Thief* (1948).

Italian neorealism as a film **style** developed as a result of the social unrest in Italy that accompanied the end of World War II and as a result of economic realities. Vittorio de Sica, describing neorealism's birth, wrote that the lack of an organized film industry in Italy at the end of the war and "the problem of finance . . . encouraged filmmakers to create a kind of movie that would no longer be dependent on fiction and on invented themes . . . but would draw on the reality of everyday life."

Because of the efforts of the neorealist filmmakers to place their characters in natural settings and to build their stories around "everyday life," the structure of their films led to their being described as "found stories" or **flow-of-life** films. Narrative incidents and flow of action appear so casual and spontaneous as to give the impression the filmmaker has simply followed a character and discovered the story rather than having invented it. The found-story, flow-of-life style of Italian neorealism can be seen in more contemporary films (*Harry and Tonto*, 1975; *The Straight Story*, 1999; *The Motorcycle Diaries* 2004).

The widespread influence of Italian neorealism with its interest in the personal struggles of common people, is evident in American films such as *Sounder* (1973), *Blue Collar* (1978), and *Country* (1984); in the Indian film, *Salaam Bombay!* (1988); in the Italian film, *The Stolen Children* (1992); and in the British-German film, *My Name Is Joe* (1998).

New American Cinema A term often used to refer to the **underground** or **experimental film** movement in the United States during the 1960s. It is derived from the New American Cinema Group, an organization founded in 1960 by various filmmakers and producers, including Lionel Rogosin, Peter Bogdanovich, Jonas Mekas, Shirley Clarke, and Robert Frank. Their interests included experimental and **avant-garde** as well as commercial film. The group's published statements opposed constraints on subject matter, in both underground and commercial filmmaking.

Newsreel A popular type of motion-picture **short** which appeared as a part of film programs until television brought about its demise in the 1950s. Newsreels were usually ten to fifteen minutes in length and contained a compilation of timely news stories and at their conclusion a human-interest feature.

The newsreel impulse existed from the beginning of motion-picture exhibition. Early Lumière and Edison programs (1896) were filled with short *actualitiés* of events and people, lifted from everyday life. By 1900 *actualitié*-gathering film units and exchanges had been set up in most large cities around the world to record and distribute short films of important events and famous people.

Fox Movietone News introduced the talking newsreel in 1927, showing movie audiences such dramatic events as

Lindberg's departure for his solo flight across the Atlantic and his tumultuous welcome home.

Eventually the newsreel concept was expanded into interpretive presentations of the news, with the best-known example being *The March of Time* series (1935–1951). Each supplement of *The March of Time* series was approximately twenty minutes in length and usually dealt with a single news topic in an editorial manner. This series was produced in the United States by Louis de Rochemont. The National Film Board of Canada produced a similarly styled series, *The World in Action* (1941–1945).

The newsreel served a particularly useful function during World War II when visualization of allied efforts was considered critical to national morale. This role and the other functions served by the newsreel for more than half a century would increasingly fall to television after 1948. Eventually the newer medium killed the movie-house newsreel altogether.

New Wave   A general term for a body of films which came out of France in the late 1950s and which were characterized by their break with traditional cinema. The French New Wave, or "*nouvelle vague,*" film grew out of a keen critical interest in the art of the film by important directors such as Jean-Luc Godard, François Truffaut, Claude Chabrol, Alain Resnais, and many other French filmmakers who are less well known. Although it is difficult to define precisely the methods and themes of French New Wave directors, their films were often highly personal efforts which on the one hand exhibited an awareness of film history and on the other broke with the conventional cinema in both theme and technique. Using traditional genres and often drawing on the styles of Hollywood directors, the New Wave filmmakers experimented with innovative approaches to editing and structure. Some of their films intentionally employed jump-cuts, moved ambiguously through time and space, and often alienated viewers by use of elements which were contradictory, self-conscious, or private. Others copied established film forms, finding inspiration in the work of Hollywood's **B-picture** directors. The New Wave director frequently worked with only the sketch of a script, preferring improvisation and spontaneous filming to a preconstructed shooting plan.

The themes of New Wave films were often existential in philosophy. Plots dealt with characters who live in a world of chaos and disorder. In Resnais' *Hiroshima Mon Amour* (1959) and Godard's *Breathless* (1959) characters are set against great events: the atomic bomb at Hiroshima and World War II, respectively, which they attempt to comprehend. The emphasis in each picture rests ultimately with the individual rather than with the event. The emotional recollection of lost love dominates in *Hiroshima Mon Amour* despite the memory of the atomic bomb's devastation at Hiroshima where the picture is set. In a scene in *Breathless*, Jean Seberg and Jean-Paul Belmondo pass by a parade on the Champs Elysées that involves two great World War II generals, de Gaulle and Eisenhower; the emphasis remains with the actions and feelings of the two lovers rather than with the historic figures. There is a clear indifference on the part of Godard toward the larger event of World War II.

Since its initial application to the French cinema of the late 1950s and early 1960s, the term "New Wave" has been applied to cinema revivals in other countries where activity in film production is extensive and intense, for example, in Yugoslavia, Hungary, and Poland during the 1960s, and in Germany and France during the 1970s and 1980s.

Noncamera film (out-of-camera film) A motion picture created without passing the film through the camera. Most noncamera films consist of abstract **images**, sometimes achieved by placing material on the raw stock and exposing it to light (Man Ray's *Retour à la Raison*, 1923). Other methods include the scratching of the film **emulsion** to create abstract patterns, or the drawing of images directly onto clear celluloid. In Norman McLaren's *Pen-Point Percussion* (1951) both the images and the sound track are produced by hand drawings. McLaren created the sound track by pen-point scratches at the edge of the film, then repeated these scratches frame-by-frame for the on-screen images. The use of color **filters** combined with in-printer solarization (random exposure of the film to light) has also been employed to create out-of-camera, abstract images. In *Mothlight* (1953), Stan Brakhage produced an out-of-camera film by attaching bits and pieces of mothwings to transparent mylar film tape and then printing the strip of images as a silent abstract expression.

Non-diegetic sound (see **Diegetic sound**)

Normal lens   A **lens** of certain **focal length** which produces a natural per-
                         spective of the area being photographed. The area of space
                         does not appear to increase as sometimes happens with
                         wide-angle lenses of short focal length, nor does it appear
                         to be magnified as is the case with long focal-length lenses.
                         The 50-mm lens is the standard normal lens used in 35-mm
                         filming and a 25-mm lens is standard for 16-mm filmmaking.

Novel into film   (see **Adaptation**)

Oater   Another term for a western film, especially one which follows the conventions of the **genre** closely and whose primary purpose is solely that of providing escapist entertainment.

Objective point of view (see **Point of view**)

Obscured frame   Compositional treatment within a film frame so that part of the picture is obscured by an object, an actor, or by **soft-focus** photography (photo 34). Obscured-frame composition is a device employed to direct visual emphasis to specific areas of the frame, to add visual variety and give a sense of depth to the **composition**, and to block from view parts of the screen **image**. See **Blocking**.

Offscreen space-onscreen space References for those **images** which appear within the film **frame** (onscreen) and those which are not visible but which are apparent as existing beyond the edges of the frame (offscreen). (See photos in 35)

Oppositional cinema Cinematic expression which intervenes on and opposes standard film conventions/techniques. Oppositional cinema is also a term for film content which acts to subvert or overcome stereotyped views of characters and cultural identities. Wayne Wang's film of a modern Chinese-American woman (*Dim Sum: A Little Bit of Heart*, 1985) has been

182 Dictionary of Film Terms

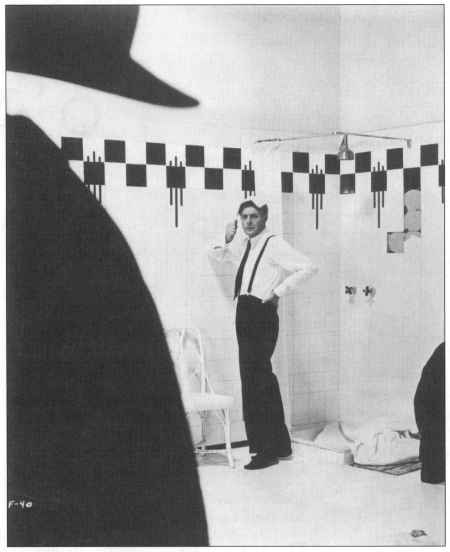

[OBSCURED FRAME] 34. An obscured frame in Federico Fellini's 8 1/2 (1963).

[OFFSCREEN/ONSCREEN SPACE] 35. The manner in which a director employs onscreen space and offscreen space carries varied dramatic possibilities. In *On the Waterfront* (1954) Elia Kazan creates an unforgettable scene in which Marlon Brando and Eva Marie Saint are chased through an alleyway by a truck. The building walls on either side of the frame close off the area so that no sense of offscreen space exists. The images suggest that a means of escape is impossible and thus the suspense is intensified. Conversely, Alfred Hitchcock in *North by Northwest* (1959) creates a chase in which Cary Grant is being pursued by an airplane overhead. By suggesting that the offscreen space (an open field) is unlimited and that there's no place for Grant to seek cover, the chase has the effect of a nightmare.

called "oppositional" because it counters the often stereo-typed view of Chinese characters on the screen.

Optical printer   A machine, consisting of a camera and projector, which is used in making additional prints from a master image or composite prints of two or more images. The projector part of the optical printer projects light through the master **image** or images to expose raw stock that is contained in the camera portion. The optical printer is also used to produce such effects as **matte shots, dissolves**, and **fades** and for reducing and enlarging image size.

Optical sound track A **sound track** appearing on the edge of the film (opposite the sprocket holes' side) and consisting of a photographic **image** of sound modulations. An exciter lamp on the motion-picture projector picks up these modulations and through electrical conversion reproduces the original sounds. An optical sound track is a standard feature on 16 mm prints that are released for distribution.

Original screenplay A screenplay developed from an idea conceived by the screenwriter, based on the writer's imagination or on an incident which provokes the writer's imagination: a historical event, a newspaper item, an interesting human being, or a story idea for a particular film **genre**. Lawrence Kasdan's black comedy, *I Love You To Death* (1990) was developed as an original screenplay from a news story appearing in an Allentown, Pennsylvania paper. Robert Altman claims to have created the screenplay for *3 Women* (1977) after having a dream about three women whose lives mysteriously cross. See **Adaptation**.

Out-of-camera film (see **Noncamera film**)

Outtake   A term for filmed material which is deleted in the editing process and which does not appear in the **final cut**. Outtake material may be removed because of flaws in the filming of a **shot** or a **scene** or simply because the film's **editor** opts not to use the material in the final cut. There is a particular fascination for outtake material because of what it can reveal about actors and the filmmaking process, often in very human or humorous ways. Consequently, outtakes are frequently screened on television programs. In a gesture of appreciation, Hal Ashby inserted closing **credits** for *Being There* (1979) over an outtake of Peter Sellers attempting to control his laughter during the filming of a scene. Sellers died before the film's release. The Will Ferrell comedy

Anchorman (2004) combined closing credits with a number of humorous outtakes. Outtake material from **documentaries** and **newsreels** is also frequently used by the makers of **experimental films** for satirical effect, as in Henri Erlich's *My Way* (1975), a humorous view of Richard Nixon made up largely of outtakes from government-produced newsreels. Michael Moore's *Fahrenheit 9/11* (2004) contains unflattering, "off-the record" shots of government officials, for example, Paul Wolfowitz wetting his comb with spittle, George W. Bush clowning before the cameras prior to a broadcast to the nation. These too constitute a form of outtake footage.

Overcrank   (see **Slow motion**)

Overexposure   (see **Exposure**)

Overlapping sound Usually a **sound effect** or speech, which continues briefly from one **shot** into the next. Overlapping sound may be a **sound advance**, where a speech or sound effect in an incoming shot is heard briefly in the outgoing shot. Overlapping sound may be used to connect dynamically two separate pieces of dramatic action or to enhance the **pace** of story development.

Over-the-shoulder shot A shot taken over the shoulder of a character or characters looking toward another character or characters (photos in 36). Most commonly, over-the-shoulder shots are taken at medium or medium-**close-up** range. By cutting between matching over-the-shoulder shots of two characters (**reverse-angle shooting**), the film **image** changes to achieve desired emphasis within an action-reaction situation. The over-the-shoulder shot also adds a sense of depth to the **frame composition** by blocking into the frame. See **Point of view**.

[OVER-THE-SHOULDER SHOT] 36. Matched over-the-shoulder shots from *A Place in the Sun* (1951). These shots avoid jump-cuts by keeping Montgomery Clift on the right side of the frame for each shot and Elizabeth Taylor on the left. Because of the position of the camera, the over-the-shoulder shot suggests a subjective point of view of the foreground character.

P

Pace
The rhythm of the film. "Pace" refers to both the internal movement of characters and objects within the film **shot**, and to the rhythm of the film that is supplied by editing. Frenetic movement within the **frame** and brief, staccato shots give a sense of considerable pace to the film, for example, in the desperate running sequences in *Run Lola Run* (1998). Little internal movement and lengthy shots add a measured, leisurely pace to the film's progress. See **External rhythm, Internal rhythm, Formal editing**.

Pan
The movement of the camera across a **scene** horizontally (left to right or right to left) while mounted on a fixed base. A pan, like the **tilt**, is frequently used to scan a scene and to follow character movement in a limited location. **Establishing shots** will often include pans, and sometimes tilts, to provide a more extensive view of an environment.

In character movement, the camera can pan to follow an actor's walk across a room and then tilt down when the actor sinks into an easy chair.

Pans and tilts, while for the most part utilitarian, allow the **director** to present a scene or follow actions fully without edits that might destroy a desired mood.

Rapidly effected pans are also often used dynamically to reveal character reactions or to reveal and emphasize important information ("revelation pans"). Pans can also be incorporated into **subjective shots** as the camera assumes the eyes of a character, and surveys a room or exterior location. The use of pans and tilts in this way makes the subjective, mind's-eye **point of view** more obvious by activating the camera. In *The Insider* (1999), this type of use of the pan tilt was a significant device in conveying the increasing paranoia of a scientist (Russell Crowe) who is fired for informing on a tobacco company. An extremely rapid pan, referred to as a **swish pan**, is a method of effecting a **transition** from one scene to another. The rapid swish pan blurs the **image**, thus wiping out the scene. A new scene then begins.

Parallel development (editing) The development of two or more separate lines of action which are occurring simultaneously. Parallel development is achieved by **crosscutting** from one location to another to pick up the action as it progresses. This technique in the early years of cinema was referred to as the **switchback** because parallel editing usually does switch back in time to visualize an event; in many instances of parallel editing, however, the crosscutting will show the event in an advanced stage of time from the point where the earlier action left off.

Parody
A motion picture which makes fun of another, usually more serious film. The intention and design of the parody are ridicule of the style, conventions, or motifs of a serious work. The comedies of Mel Brooks are often parodies of familiar American **genres**: the **western** in *Blazing Saddles* (1974); the horror film in *Young Frankenstein* (1974); the Alfred Hitchcock thriller in *High Anxiety* (1977); and the swashbuckler action film in *Robin Hood: Men in Tights* (1993). *This Is Spinal Tap* (1984), offered a screen parody of the rock documentary. See **Comedy**.

Pathos
A term derived from the Greek word for "suffering." Its application to dramatic, literary, or cinematic expression refers to the feelings of compassion or pity evoked for a character or groups of characters. In its most common application, pathos refers to aroused emotions that result from the unrelieved suffering of a helpless but dignified character. The hero is an unfortunate victim of general conditions rather than innate character flaws. The characters and their

ultimate fates in *House of Sand and Fog* (2003) and in *Mystic River* (2003) convey a powerful sense of dramatic pathos.

Persistence of vision   A physiological phenomenon whereby the human eye retains for a fraction of a second longer than it actually remains any image which appears before it. The persistence-of-vision phenomenon allows the connection of rapidly projected photographs (**frames**) so that they seem a continuous single image, thus permitting the illusion of "moving" pictures. Peter Mark Roget is noted for having presented the persistence-of-vision theory in 1824 in a paper to the Royal Society of London. See **Frames per second**.

Personal director (see **Director**)

Photographed thought The photographing and inserting into a film story shots of what a character thinks or imagines. The device is often used to suggest a character's mental and psychological state. A classic illustration of the device occurs in Alfred Hitchcock's *Blackmail* (1929) when a young woman, shortly after murdering an artist suitor, sees a flashing cocktail shaker on a sign over a pub and transposes its image into a stabbing knife. In the film *Rachel, Rachel* (1968) Joanne Woodward engages in mental fantasies as she walks to the school where she teaches. As others greet her, she imagines her skirt falling to the sidewalk. She sees a male teacher arriving in his automobile and imagines herself kissing him passionately. These imaginings are rendered as photographed thought and are given to the viewer as a means of depicting the character's mind at work. *Looking for Mr. Goodbar* (1977) also employed the technique of photographed thought to convey the principal character's fantasies. In *The Last Samurai* (2003), snippets of photographed thought appear when Nathan (Tom Cruise) reflects back on the brutal treatment of Native Americans by his Army regiment. During Jim Braddock's (Russell Crowe) big boxing fight against heavyweight champion Max Baer in *Cinderella Man* (2005), photographed thought is employed as a key dramatic element. Brief memory shots are visualized as a means of suggesting the motivation that sustains Braddock during the brutal match.

Pixilation   A type of **animated film** which employs objects or human beings in a frame-by-frame animation process. It is a descriptive label that distinguishes the animation of material objects from that of hand-drawn **images**. The process of pixilation is that of **stop-action cinematography**, where objects or subjects are moved between **frames**. Georges Méliès incorporated pixilated action in his early **trick films**. Pixilation has been a highly imaginative technique of the experimental Canadian filmmaker Normal McLaren: *Neighbors* (1952), *A Chairy Tale* (1957). It also appears from time to time in dramatic films, for example, *Nosferatu* (1922), *A Clockwork Orange* (1971), *Chaplin* (1992). In *Chaplin*, Charlie Chaplin (Robert Downey, Jr.) is shown early in his film career entering a costume room to select an outfit. In pixilated action Chaplin selects the pieces of clothing that would form his "little tramp" character. The choice of pixilated action here served as a correlative for the undercranked (16-frames-per-second) speed of silent screen comedies that Chaplin helped popularize. Pixilation is employed in Jim Sheridan's *In America* (2003), when the two young sisters are shown roller-skating in the New York loft apartment where their Irish family has recently moved.

Point of view   A term used to describe the filmmaker's relative positioning of the viewer into an objective or subjective relationship with the recorded material.

An *objective point of view* is one where the camera appears to be an uninvolved, unnoticed recorder of action. Although long, medium, and close **shots** may be taken of the action, the camera remains a viewer of the **scene** rather than a participant in it. The objective point of view attempts to call as little attention to the camera as possible or to character point of view. The filmmaker instead attempts to reproduce surface reality and movement without obvious artistic manipulation.

A *subjective point of view*, on the other hand, puts the camera into the action as though the camera lens has become the eyes or mind's eye of one of the characters.

Some **subjective shots** are more obvious than others. The most obvious is the one in which a character's eyes scan a room, followed by a camera **pan** across the room to suggest what the searching eyes can see.

The purpose of this type of subjective shot is to put the viewer into the mind's eye of a character. German directors of the 1920s, such as F.W. Murnau, E.A. Dupont, and G.W. Pabst, made extensive use of the mind's-eye, subjective camera shot to convey subtle emotions and interior feelings in films like *Variety* (1925) and *The Last Laugh* (1924).

In *Variety*, director Dupont uses the mind's-eye shot to suggest the movement of a trapeze artist through the air. The camera was actually mounted on a trapeze to photograph the effect. Later in the film, as a romance develops between Emil Jannings' wife and the new, third member of their trapeze act, Dupont employs subjective shots to show what Jannings sees as he watches the other man interacting with his wife.

Another use of the subjective-point-of-view shot was seen in one of the segments of the television series *Roots* (1977). As Kizzy (Leslie Uggams) is put on the back of a wagon, shots of both Kizzy's point of view and her mother's are **crosscut**. The camera takes Kizzy's view, showing the mother as she begins to disappear in the background as the wagon moves away. This shot was taken from a wide **angle of view**, with the camera mounted on the moving wagon to suggest both point of view and movement through space. The mother's view of the disappearing wagon was taken from a static position; the **intercutting** of the two subjective shots suggested the powerfully felt emotions of the characters, while depicting the beginning physical space that would separate mother and daughter.

A form of subjective shot occurs in certain **reaction shots**. When two characters are conversing with each other and the camera cuts back and forth between **over-the-shoulder shots (reverse angle shots)**, the editing gives the impression that we are seeing a subjective, action-reaction view of the two characters as they interact.

Point of view (abbreviated as POV) is a common designation in motion-picture shooting scripts to indicate a camera **setup** that will assume a character's angle of view.

Polyvision (see **Multi-screen projection**)

Prequel A term for a sequel in which the time period of the narrative action predates that of the original film, for example, *Butch and Sundance: The Early Days* (1979), a tale of Butch Cassidy and the Sundance Kid during early outlaw years which were not treated in George Roy Hill's 1969 classic with Paul Newman and Robert Redford. Because of strong audience associations with the original and because of the necessity of using different, younger actors in the principal roles, some prequels are disappointing. *Star Wars*

Episode I: The Phantom Menace (1999) offered a prequel to George Lucas' first *Star Wars* (1977) film. Star Wars *Episode II: Attack of the Clones* (2002) was also a prequel to the 1977 film but a sequel to *Star Wars Episode I.*

Presence (sound) An aesthetic-technical term for the relationship of an actor's voice or a **sound effect** to a recording microphone. "On-mike" presence means that the actor's voice has an immediate closeness with the microphone. When an actor's voice is away from a center of action, it is recorded away from the microphone, or "off-mike."

Presence and **volume**, the recorded level of sound, are principal means by which sounds in a motion picture are given emphasis. In a variation on standard sound-recording procedures, director Robert Altman will often record both foreground and background characters at full on-mike presence (for example, *California Split*, 1974; *Gosford Park*, 2001). The use of a multi-channel soundtrack in *California Split* was designed to convey the intense, hyper-aware world of casino life for addicted gamblers. In *Gosford Park*, the intended effect was multi-character interaction (awareness) in a British mansion where a murder occurs during a weekend gathering of assorted guests.

Presentational blocking The **blocking** of characters into a **scene** so that they appear to "present" themselves directly to the camera lens. More commonly actors are positioned at an angle (traditionally in three-quarter profile) so that their eyes do not look toward the camera lens. This angling minimizes the presence of the camera. The use of presentational blocking reduces the objective distance between viewer and dramatic action. In Ingmar Bergman's *The Seventh Seal* (1956), Death, one of the principal characters, frequently looks directly into the camera so as to bring the viewer into a more dynamic relationship with the life-death chess game occurring within the plot. Presentational moments also occur in Tony Richardson's *Tom Jones* (1963) as Albert Finney winks and shrugs at the camera to make the audience seem accomplices in his roguish capers. The entire cast of *Stevie* (1978), a British film taken from a stage play, addresses the audience in a presentational manner as the life and writings of poet Stevie Smith (Glenda Jackson) are revealed. In *Alfie* (1966) and *Shirley Valentine* (1989, photo 37) British director Lewis Gilbert gained audience immediacy with his principal

[PRESENTATIONAL BLOCKING] 37. Pauline Collins as *Shirley Valentine* (1989), a bored British housewife, "presents" herself directly to the camera throughout the film. The presentational form of personal narration serves to bring the audience and Shirley Valentine's character into a sympathetic relationship.

characters by having them interpret their lives through presentational narration aimed directly at the camera lens.

Processing   The chemical conversion of an invisible latent **image** on exposed film into a permanent visible image. The four primary steps in processing film are development, fixing, washing, and drying. Development is a chemical procedure in which the halide particles that have been exposed to form the latent image are reduced to metallic silver. Fixing is the process by which the silver halide that has not been reduced to a silver image by development is converted to a water-soluble salt complex (silver thiosulfate). Washing removes the thiosulfate salts from the film. The film is then dried, completing the processing of motion-picture film.

Process shot (process cinematography) The technical term for a motion-picture shot in which "live" foreground action has been filmed against a background **image** projected onto a translucent screen (photo 38). In process cinematography the shutters of both the camera and the rear projector are regulated by electrical means to open and close simultaneously so that frame-line flickers do not appear.

Technical considerations of process cinematography require (1) that the angle and quality of light on the set proper match that of the projected image and (2) that the projected image be absolutely stationary so as not to be discernible. Improved technology and digitized computer imaging have significantly enhanced process shot artistry by, literally, leaps and bounds. See *Stars Wars Episode I: The Phantom Menace* (1999) and *Spider-Man 2* (2004).

Process shots are common to motion-picture studio filming where unusual locations must be achieved in, for instance, boats, airplanes, and foreign settings. See **Rear-screen projection**, **Traveling matte**.

Producer (film) That individual who serves as the "executive" supervisor of a film, standing prominently beside the **director** who is the "artistic" overseer of the production. In contemporary filmmaking the producer often secures the money for the project, purchases the film script, and hires the director and other primary artists involved in the making of the film. Producers can be autocratic forces in the filmmaking process, making both logistic and artistic decisions that affect the ultimate quality of the released film. Producers such as Irving Thalberg and David O. Selznick achieved legendary status in the film world during the **American studio years**. In more recent times producers have also been able to achieve a dominant position in film production—turning out works which are considered to have their own special creative stamp, for example, Dino de Laurentis. During the 1970s, 1980s, and 1990s, increasingly more actors turned to producing as well

[PROCESS SHOT] 38. A foreground camera records a studio process shot that uses rear-screen projection to give the appearance of a couple aboard a ship at sea. The seascape is being projected onto a screen in front of the actors.

as directing films, for example, Robert Redford, *All the President's Men* (1975) and *Ordinary People* (1980), Barbra Streisand, *Yentl* (1983) and *Prince of Tides* (1991). The practice continues: Charlize Theron served as a producer of *Monster* (2003). Often actors serve as co-producers of films in which they do not appear, as with Demi Moore for

Austin Powers: The Spy Who Shagged Me (1999) and Nicholas Cage for *Shadow of the Vampire* (2000).

Production values A trade concept used in reference to the quality of set design, costumes, lighting, and sound in a particular motion picture. Usually there is a direct relationship between production values and budget expenditure. Lavish musicals, screen **spectacles**, and other types of films where a highly polished romantic look is desired usually give strong emphasis to production values.

Prosthetics Makeup which is applied to an actor's body/face in order to alter physical characteristics. A prosthetic nose was worn by Nicole Kidman (Virginia Woolf) in *The Hours* (2002). Extensive prosthetics (fake teeth, skin blotches) dramatically altered the physical appearances of Charlize Theron as serial killer Aileen Wuornos in Patty Jenkins' *Monster* (2003).

Protagonist The principal hero of a motion picture or a play; that individual or group of individuals with whom the audience empathizes. Dramatic conflict and empathy occur when another character or force (war, nature, a shark, personal weakness) challenges the protagonist, driving the hero into a crisis or series of crises. This challenging opponent force is referred to as the **antagonist**.

Psychoanalysis and cinema The application of psychoanalytic precepts to the analysis of cinematic texts. Proponents argue that interpretation of a motion picture within the context of Freudian thought (desire, sexuality, guilt, unconscious repression, etc.) can reveal multiple meanings with regard to modern culture and human experience. Cultural critic Jacques Lacan maintained that psychoanalysis of dramatic/literary texts (language) was capable of supplying new entry into exploration of the human self. Lacan's linguistic approach to textual psychoanalysis is only one of many posited in this burgeoning area of critical study. Laura Mulvey's "visual pleasure/**gaze**" readings of Hollywood films moved psychoanalytic observation into interpretive areas of gender identity and voyeurism, and into issues of power and control.

Psychodrama A term often used to describe a type of **experimental film** characterized by Freudian approaches to self-exploration. The filmmaker is frequently concerned with subconscious states and personal sexuality. A strong dreamlike, surreal quality often dominates the film experience as a result of an abrupt, fragmented flow of imagery. The term "psychodrama" is most commonly used in reference to highly personal works produced in the United States during the late 1940s, early 1950s. Maya Deren (*Meshes of the Afternoon*, 1943) inspired the psychological film movement in America, although its foundations had been laid by the first European **avant-garde**. Three California-based filmmakers earned reputations in the 1940s for their personal-experience psychodramas: Kenneth Anger (*Fireworks*, 1947), Curtis Harrington (*Fragments of Seeking*, 1946), and Gregory Markopoulos (*Psyche*, 1947–1948). Willard Maas' work on the East Coast (*Images in the Snow*, 1943–1948) was of similar Freudian character. Later work by these filmmakers often took the form of symbol-laden, ritualistic exercises, for example, Anger's *Scorpio Rising* (1962–1964).

Psychological time   A term referring to the use of filmic devices which, in the continuity of a motion-picture narrative, suggest not chronological time but time as it is perceived by a character's mind. A **dissolve**, for example, most commonly reveals a passage of time when used within an ongoing **scene**. The dissolve, by tradition, serves to exclude intervening time and action. If, however, a dissolve rather than a **cut** is used in a continuing, uninterrupted action, its unconventional placement carries psychological implications. Subjectively inspired **psychodramas** by experimental filmmakers, such as *Meshes of the Afternoon* (1943) by Maya Deren, often exploit the psychological dissolve for a mind's-time effect.

Psychological time can also be suggested by the repeated use of a piece of action. The condemned traitor's final, desperate effort in *An Occurrence at Owl Creek Bridge* (1962) to reach his wife is conveyed in psychological time by a repeated telephoto **shot** of the man running down the road to his home. He appears suspended in time and place, which in fact he is; shortly after these shot repetitions, the viewer discovers that the traitor's entire flight has been a fantasy revealed through an extended use of psychological time. A particularly engaging and sometimes bewildering use of psychological character perception occurs in *Memento* (2000), a film about a man who is searching for his wife's murderer. The search is complicated by the fact that the man has lost his short-term memory. Events come and go on the screen without their meaning being clear at first revelation.

Psychosexual (analysis) Pertaining to the emotional constituents of sexual instincts, psychosexual analysis and observation seek to relate these constituents and instincts to behavior and activity of an individual with regard to social relations. *Another Country* (1984), *Boys Don't Cry* (1999), and *Monster* (2003) were films that lent themselves to psychosexual analysis.

Pure cinema (see *Cinéma pur*)

Q

Queer cinema   A film label that emerged in conjunction with the increase in independent films that depict gay characters and gay lifestyles in free, unrestricted ways. Queer cinema moves beyond mainstream Hollywood representations of gays, and seeks to openly reveal sexual identity in all its diverse manifestations. Notable queer cinema includes both documentary and fictional accounts of gay lifestyles. *Some of Your Best Friends* (1991) was a interview-styled documentary with figures involved in the Gay Liberation Movement. *The Celluloid Closet* (1995) examined through interviews and film excerpts gays and lesbians in Hollywood cinema. Among the many significant fictional works are Donna Deitch's *Desert Heart* (1985), Todd Haynes' *Poison* (1991), Gus Van Sant's *My Own Private Idaho* (1991), Tom Kalin's *Swoon* (1992), and Greg Oraki's *Nowhere* (1997). These films reflect queer cinema's interest in exploring lesbian and gay behavior from a wide variety of personal, social, and psychological perspectives.

Queer theory studies   A theoretical-analytical offshoot of queer cinema that seeks to examine sexual identity (in films, plays, and novels) without preconceived notions or precise labels with regard to gender (male/female) or orientation (straight, transsexual, gay/lesbian). Queer studies undertake analysis of film texts, both old and new.

R

Rack focus (pull focus) The shifting of focus from one area of a **shot** to another. Through rack focus an area that is "soft" or out of focus can be brought into critical focus for the purpose of shifting emphasis or calling attention to otherwise indistinct material. Rack focus, sometimes called pull focus, or roll focus, is used most frequently in telephoto shots with limited **depth of field** so that the focus change is immediately and sharply apparent.

Rating system A mechanism for classifying motion pictures according to their perceived suitability for different age groups. The rating system was developed by the Motion Picture Association of America (MPAA) and went into effect November 1, 1968, at a time when candid material—language, violence, sexuality—was proliferating on the screen. The MPAA viewed the rating system as an indication to the public of industry concern, and also it argued that ratings would serve to prevent outside censorship of motion picture content.

As originally devised the rating system consisted of four suitability categories:

G: recommended for general audiences
M: (later changed to PG) mature subject matter; parental guidance advised

R: restricted; adult accompaniment required for anyone under seventeen

X: adult material; no one seventeen and under admitted

In 1984 a fifth category, PG-13, was added to the classifications. This new rating offered a cautionary note that a PG-13 film might contain material inappropriate for very young children and suggested that parents give special guidance for children under thirteen years of age. The demands for new, refined guidelines for the very young had intensified after such PG-rated films as *Indiana Jones and the Temple of Doom* (1984) and *Gremlins* (1984) had contained material that was thought to be particularly terrifying to youngsters. *Gremlins* had visualized small animals exploding inside a microwave oven, and *Indiana Jones and the Temple of Doom* depicted a human heart being plucked from the body of a living man.

In 1990 another revision occurred in the rating categories when the X designation was replaced with NC-17, a suitability reclassification prohibiting children seventeen and under from admission. The X rating had become tainted through years of association with sexually explicit motion pictures (the XXX film) intended for pornographic outlets. Public attitudes toward the X rating had carried over to non-pornographic films—often meaning economic doom as, increasingly, filmgoers and exhibitors shunned X-rated films.

Henry and June (1990), a psychological-sexual study of a triangular love affair involving novelist Henry Miller, his wife June, and the author Anaïs Nin, was the first feature film distributed in the United States with the NC-17 rating.

The rating system has been plagued from its inception by controversy due to the difficulty of precise categorization and an ensuing confusion over the meaning of individual categories with regard to content. At the same time film producers claimed that pressure to alter or delete material to achieve a particular rating resulted in abandonment of artistic standards to a form of internal regulation of motion-picture content.

A study conducted by the Harvard School of Public Health and released in 2004 concluded that film raters had become more lenient toward violence and sexuality on the screen. In its criticism of the rating system, the researchers accused the MPAA of providing to the public often confusing, imprecise ratings with regard to the contents of movies. A call was made for a standardized, universal rating system that could be used for film, and radio and television as well.

Reaction shot   A **shot** within a **scene** which shows a character's reaction to a dramatic situation. The reaction shot is usually achieved through a **close-up** or medium shot of the character.

Realist cinema   A **style** of filmmaking which in a general sense creates a semblance of actuality. Realist films avoid techniques that impose subjective or directed attitudes on the recorded material. Artistic lighting and expressive camera techniques usually are kept to a minimum. The realist film also often includes **long-take scenes** rather than carefully edited **sequences**.

Realist cinema stresses, most commonly, the subject in interaction with the surrounding environment. For this reason the themes of realist films often develop within a "flow of life" format, where the casualness of common events reveals their content.

The Lumière *actualités* are early examples of realist cinema in the purest sense. Italian **neorealism** approached a realist style within the narrative film. "**Direct cinema**" is a term for a type of contemporary **documentary** film that can be labeled "realist cinema."

Rear-screen projection The use of projected **images** within a motion-picture **scene** to suggest background location, in both story line and technique. Rear-screen projection, common in the "studio years," allowed the semblance of location shooting within the film studio. British special effects technicians at studios such as Pinewood helped perfect the art of rear-screen projection.

The lack of dimension in rear-screen projection required careful use of the technique; the device worked best when the projected images were atmospheric rather than sharply defined elements of the scene. "**Process shot**" is   the technical term used to describe the procedure for combining rear-projected images with "live" foreground action.

Reflexive Cinema A term applied to motion pictures which use the subject of film as the basis for narrative content and plot. Reflexive cinema derives from the grammatical term "reflexive," which designates a verb having an identical subject and object, for example, "I bathe myself." A film is reflexive when the subject treated (cinema) is the same as the medium of expression (cinema), that is, cinema treats itself.

The classic Hollywood-in-transition motion picture *Sunset Boulevard* (1950) explored the contradictions between film mythmaking and reality, developed through a faded silent-screen actress who has become captive to film's manufactured illusions. *Sunset Boulevard*'s reflexive nature was enhanced by the appearance of actual Hollywood figures (Cecil B. DeMille, Buster Keaton, Hedda Hopper, Erich von Stroheim) and by numerous references to details lifted from motion-picture history. Giuseppe Tornatore's *Cinema Paradiso* (1988) examined in largely nostalgic terms the culture of motion pictures as revealed through a young boy in a small Italian town and his friendship with the local cinema's projectionist. Robert Altman's *The Player* (1992) offered a biting satire of contemporary Hollywood business practices and the calculations involved in efforts to ensure the commercial success of a motion picture.

A special quality of reflexive cinema is the heightening of irony which occurs when subject and medium are one and the same. The viewer enjoys an ongoing intellectual interplay between message and messenger, finding pleasure in tongue-in-cheek humor, innuendo, in-jokes, and double-entendres which usually result from a film's reflexive nature. *Adaptation* (2003), the story of a frustrated screenwriter (Nicholas Cage), is a recent example of ironic, reflexive film-making.

Remake   A motion picture made from a film story which has been produced earlier. *Stagecoach* (1939) was remade in 1966. The fantasy *Heaven Can Wait* (1978) was a remake of *Here Comes Mr. Jordan* (1941) with certain plot changes being made in the 1978 version to update the story and include topical material.

Remakes have been subjected to intense critical comparison with their originals, particularly when the original is regarded as a screen classic. Such was the case with the remake of *Scarface* (1932) by Michael Cimino in 1983 and *Cape Fear* (1962) by Martin Scorsese in 1991. The growing trend toward American remakes of critically acclaimed European films was also met with a certain critical cynicism, for example, *Breathless* (1959/1983); *Cousin, Cousine* (1975)/*Cousins* (1989); *The Return of Martin Guerre* (1982)/*Sommersby* (1993); *The Lady Killers* (2004), *Alfie* (2004).

Rembrandt lighting A somewhat obscure term for a type of special-effect backlighting used in motion-picture and still photography (photo

39). Rembrandt lighting takes its name from the artist who, in painting portraits, attempted to suggest character and personality by use of light and shadow. Vivid contrasts of light on a figure, including a soft light coming from behind the person, were used by Rembrandt. The soft backlight seemed to highlight character mood in a strikingly sympathetic manner.

D.W. Griffith experimented with the expressive possibilities of Rembrandt lighting in **close-up shots** where he wanted to enhance character or add a romantic, ethereal

[REMBRANT BACKLIGHTING] 39. Rembrandt backlighting adds a romantic touch to a shot of Sissy Spacek in *Coal Miner's Daughter* (1980).

quality to a figure, usually one of his leading actresses. Rembrandt lighting in motion-picture photography usually comes from a low back-angle. This positioning causes the light to filter through the hair and to encircle the head with a halo-like effect. The same effect can be achieved outdoors by strong backlight from the sun. Ingmar Bergman frequently used strong sunlight for a Rembrandt effect.

Rembrandt backlighting, as a dramatic and romantic lighting effect, was particularly common in the studio films of the 1930s and 1940s. The effect is seen frequently in filmed television commercials where romance and glamour are important. In *Spider-Man 2* (2004), Kirsten Dunst appears near the end of the film in the doorway of Peter Parker's apartment, having fled her impending wedding to another man. This tender reunion scene is enhanced by a Rembrandt backlight on Dunst's hair.

Reverse-angle shot A **shot** which changes the **angle of view** and reveals subject matter from the opposite direction. The switching between **over-the-shoulder shots** for varying points of view in a two-character **scene** is achieved through reverse-angle shooting.

Reverse motion (shot) A trick visual effect in a motion picture achieved during editing by reversing the head and tail of the **shot**. By so doing, any motion in the shot will appear in reverse. Eisenstein employed the reverse-motion technique in *Ten Days That Shook the World* (1928) so that a fragmented statue magically appears to reassemble itself. In Jean Cocteau's *Beauty and the Beast* (1946), reverse motion is used to show Beauty being drawn backward through a wall (made of paper) which then seems to reseal itself.

Rhythmic montage (see **Montage**)

Ripple dissolve A type of **transition**, characterized by a wavering **image**, that is usually employed to indicate a change to **flashback** material, commonly a character's memory of an event. Sometimes the ripple dissolve is used as a transition to an imagined event or action. See **Photographed thought**.

Rising action (see **Dramatic structure**)

Road picture A name first given to a type of film where characters and narrative plot are centered on situations that develop within exotic locations. The "road" concept was derived from a series of light entertainment films involving international intrigue combined with musical numbers and starring Bob

Hope, Bing Crosby, and Dorothy Lamour, for example, *Road to Singapore* (1940), *Road to Morocco* (1942), *Road to Rio* (1947), *Road to Hong Kong* (1962). The term "road picture" has also been used to describe films in which the principal characters travel across the American landscape, discovering certain social, political, and cultural realities in the process of the journey, for instance, *Easy Rider* (1969), *Harry and Tonto* (1974), *Thelma & Louise* (1991). *Y Tu Mamá También* (2001) was a Mexican youth-initiation film structured around a road trip.

Rogue-cop film   (see Detective film).

Rough cut   An early version of an edited film in which **shots** and **sequences** have been placed in general order. Precise cutting points have not yet been made. When the latter step has been completed, the edited film is referred to as a "**final cut**." The rough cut is an important phase of the film editing process since it gives the **editor**, **director**, **producer**, and musical composer a sense of how the final version will look.

Running gag   A repetitive comic element in a motion picture. The running gag has long been recognized as a standard ingredient of **slapstick comedy**, and may be either a repeated comic line of **dialogue** or a repeated comic action. In *Silent Movie* (1976) Mel Brooks repeats the gag of a newspaper vendor being constantly knocked down by a bundle of newspapers that are thrown from a delivery truck. Each time that one of these slapstick incidents occurs, a **close-up** of the bundle of newspapers also reveals through a headline a new development in the film's zany plot. Thus the repetition serves as a running gag and an informational device. The fate of dogs on their daily walk is one of the slapstick running gags in *A Fish Called Wanda* (1988). A running gag with characters stepping in dog poop occurs in Robert Altman's *Ready to Wear* (1994).

S

Scene A unit of a motion picture usually composed of a number of interrelated **shots** that are unified by location or dramatic incident.

Science-fiction film (sci-fi film) A motion-picture **genre** characterized by a plot that involves scientific fantasy. The story is often a tale set in a future time that is visualized through a lavish display of imagined settings and gadgets, and sustained in part by spectacular special effects. Georges Méliès' *A Trip to the Moon* (1902) was an early notable, albeit primitive, science-fiction film which visualized future space exploration. Fritz Lang's *Metropolis* (1927) told a science-fiction tale about an autocratically run city of the future and extended the genre into the area of social and philosophical commentary. Similarly, Stanley Kubrick's *2001* (1969) offered philosophical rumination on a futuristic world where the impact of new technology places the fate of humankind in question. Science-fiction films such as *Star Wars* (1977) and *The Empire Strikes Back* (1980) presented futuristic adventure stories which also functioned as mythic morality tales about confrontations between good and evil. The continuing popularity of sci-fi at the box office is evident in the success of

The Matrix films (1994, 2003), Men in Black (1997, 2002), AI: Artificial Intelligence (2001). The ability of sci-fi producers to create believable, imaginary worlds has been significantly boosted by new computer technology, and by the diligence of special-effects artists.

Score   Music which has been composed or arranged for a motion picture.

Screen-direction continuity An early standard method of achieving continuity by establishing patterns of movement within the film **frame**. A series of **shots** with constant screen-left to screen-right movement by a performer can suggest a continuous journey without a loss of viewer orientation. In early practice it was thought that if a screen-left movement of the performer was followed by a screen-right movement, confusion would result. Traditional continuity procedures prescribed a neutral movement directly toward or away from the camera prior to reversing established direction patterns. In screen-direction continuity procedures, a character might enter and exit the frame in a constant pattern as a means of rapidly advancing the character through different geographic locations. The entrance-exit pattern established progressive continuity, although the backgrounds were constantly changing. Often an **editor** would follow a character's exit from the frame with a new shot of the character already in the center of the frame moving through another location. The character fully exited the first shot and was seen moving in the same direction in the subsequent shot.

Contrasting screen-direction patterns of two different characters could also be employed to indicate that the two were traveling to meet each other.

Although filmmakers often deviate from constant screen-direction patterns for varied effect, the rules for directional continuity were considered essential in establishing the visual logic of chases, journeys, and complex action. A rooftop chase between Clint Eastwood and John Malkovich in In the Line of Fire (1993) uses consistent screen right-to-left movements.

In another screen-direction continuity convention, an airplane or ship traveling east in an American film is usually shown moving toward screen right; a movement toward screen left indicated westward travel, resembling the patterns of map reading. One can observe these patterns in the east-to-west, west-to-east air flights in Annie Hall (1977).

Screenplay   A fully developed and thorough **treatment** of a film story. The screenplay contains character **dialogue**, describes action **sequences**, and becomes the basis for the **shooting script**. Also called a "master-scene script."

Screwball comedy A brand of comic film which originated in the mid-1930s, characterized by a zany, fast-paced, and often irreverent view of domestic or romantic conflicts which ultimately are happily resolved. Witty repartee and unlikely situations were also elements of the screwball comedy. This type of film offered pure escapism for Depression-era audiences.

Frank Capra's *It Happened One Night* (1934) is often cited as the film which introduced the **genre**. Its plot involved Claudette Colbert (a wealthy heiress) who, running away from home, encounters Clark Gable (a disguised newspaperman) on a bus traveling from Miami to New York. The newspaperman's strong confidence and the heiress's uppity ways and hesitancy lead to witty battles and eventually romance.

Capra and Howard Hawks were considered the masters of the screwball comedy. In Hawks' *His Girl Friday* (1940) Rosalind Russell, a star reporter, and Cary Grant, a wise-cracking editor, are also caught up in the sex-antagonism game, hurling verbal barbs at one another but eventually succumbing to romance.

Peter Bogdanovich revived the elements and style of the screwball comedy for *What's Up Doc?* (1972), a film starring Barbara Streisand and Ryan O'Neal as a couple engaged in sexual confrontations of the zany, eccentric kind reminiscent of the 1930s. Lawrence Kasdan's *Continental Divide* (1981) script also contained screwball elements in its story of a brash young newspaperman's (John Belushi) encounter with a beautiful ornithologist (Blair Brown). *Anchorman* (2004), with its egotistical 1970s television newscaster (Will Ferrell) and its upstart female co-anchor (Christina Applegate) draws on the professional and romantic conventions of the screwball comedy.

Selective key light A type of special-effect lighting achieved by control of the key light. Rather than allowing the key light to fall fully onto the face, the light often will be regulated as to fall only on the eyes or a part of the face (photo 40). The effect, achieved by special attachments on the lighting instruments, isolates and emphasizes facial features or throws the face into areas of light and shadow. The technique can be an effective

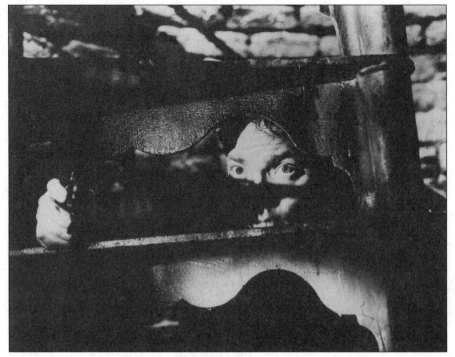

[SELECTIVE KEY LIGHT] 40. Orson Welles as Harry Lime in Carol Reed's *The Third Man* (1949) attempts to escape a manhunt by descending into the sewers of post-World War II Vienna. Selective key light falling just across Welles' eyes adds to the suspenseful chase through the darkened sewers.

means of suggesting terror, fright, or psychological states in a **close-up shot**. Selective key lighting is often employed to heighten important psychological moments in Luchino Visconti's study of passion and guilt, *Ossessione* (1942), and in John Schlesinger's *Marathon Man* (1976), a thriller whose **back-story** connects the villain (Laurence Olivier) to Nazi Germany.

Selective sound   The process in sound mixing of emphasizing certain aural elements for dramatic effect. In most films background sound and scenic **sound effects** are environmental rather than expressive. **Foley artists** work to supply expected on-screen and off-screen environmental sounds. If, however, it is to be suggested that a character is intensely conscious of the environment, sound effects of a ticking clock and a dripping faucet may be given greater **volume** and sound **presence** to suggest an interior, heightened state of mind. In Alfred Hitchcock's *Blackmail* (1929) the psychological effect of selective sound is conveyed during a lengthy monologue by a woman who talks non-stop about a murder that has occurred the night before. The young woman (Anny Ondra) who has committed the murder is overhearing the monologue; by selective sound recording/mixing only the word "knife" remains audible on the soundtrack—appearing nearly a dozen times. The other words of the monologue are muted. Selective isolation of the word "knife" reveals the young murderer's heightened anxiety. See **Expressionistic sound**.

Semiological criticism (semiotics) The consideration of film as a language or linguistic system comprised of interpretive signs which include the icon, the index, and the **symbol. Icons** are photographic representations of objects. The **index** is a sign that suggests a functional role for the object (icon) as it appears in the film. A symbol is a sign that suggests a meaning or concept apart from the inherent meaning of an object itself, for example, a cross symbolizes Christianity, the Star of David symbolizes Judaism.

In the analysis of a motion picture through the study of its signs, semiologists attempt to reveal specific meaning as well as the mode of communication of the film. Peter Wollen, Charles Sanders Pierce, and Christian Metz are among the prominent originators of theories of semiological analysis. Semiological critics have tended to emphasize the study of the narrative film because of a professed interest in textual analysis. See **Structuralism**.

Sensurround A motion-picture sound system designed for special-effects purposes and most commonly used to enhance action films, for example, *Earthquake* (1975), *Midway* (1976), *Rollercoaster* (1977). In the Sensurround process stereophonic-amplification speakers are placed in the front, rear, and sometimes on the sides of the theater auditorium; through high volume and modulation controls, **sound effects** are regulated to give the sensation of pervasive sound within the auditorium. Sensurround was essentially a technical gimmick like the **3-D process** and usually appeared only in selected action sequences of a motion picture, such as the bombing sequences in *Midway*. The effect of Sensurround in simpler applications is now standard in most up-to-date film theaters with speakers spread throughout the viewing auditorium. Many film soundtracks are now designed to channel sound elements to various speakers for a surround effect.

Sequel

A motion picture which continues in narrative development a story begun in a previous motion picture. Sequels usually are inspired by the success of an earlier film and seek to capitalize on the established appeal of the earlier work. The sequel has remained a staple of production studios where guaranteed mass-audience appeal has always been of utmost consideration. With fewer films being produced during the 1970s/1980s, the number of film sequels increased significantly, for example, *The Godfather* and *The Godfather Parts Two* and *Three*, *Jaws* and *Jaws II* and *Jaws The Revenge*, *Walking Tall* and *Walking Tall Part II*, *True Grit* and *Rooster Cogburn and His Lady*, *The French Connection* and *The French Connection II*. Sequels have followed *The Terminator* (1984) and *American Pie* (1999). In 1979, production began on the *Star Trek* series, and by 2002 ten feature films had been released. *The Lord of the Rings* (2001, 2002, 2003) trilogy represented another type of series filmmaking. See **Remake**, **Prequel**.

Sequence

A unit of film composed of a number of interrelated **shots** or **scenes** which together comprise an integral segment of the film narrative. In *Citizen Kane* (1941) the opera-related scenes—rehearsal, performance, and review scenes—together constitute a sequence. In *The Godfather* (1972), the extended visit of Michael (Al Pacino) to Italy is commonly referred to as the "Sicilian sequence."

Serial

A type of "short subject" motion picture which developed as early as 1905 (*Mirthful Mary*) and which was characterized principally by the episodic development of a story which was presented in installments over a period of several weeks. The serial engaged audience interest in a hero or heroine whose exploits reached an unresolved crisis at the end of each episode. This plotting gimmick sustained interest from week to week. The predominant **style** of the serial was melodrama, and plot lines were usually variations of popular film types: **science fiction** (*Flash Gordon*), the **western** (*The Lone Ranger*), romance (*Gloria's Romance*), action-adventure (*The Perils of Pauline*), **mystery thriller** (*Charlie Chan*). Serials remained popular with motion-picture audiences until production of them ceased in the early 1950s, a time when the serial became a mainstay of television programming (*The Lone Ranger, Superman*). A desire to revive the appeals and special qualities of the serial, and to incorporate them into a single film, resulted in *Raiders of the Lost Ark* (1981) and its sequels, *Indiana Jones and the Temple of Doom* (1984) and *Indiana Jones and the Last Crusade* (1989).

Series films   Motion pictures, usually of feature length, which repeat characters from film to film, employing stories of similar **style** and type. Series films enjoyed their greatest popularity during the studio years of the 1930s and 1940s. Because of their previous success, they were regarded by American producers as film products with an assured audience. Stylistically, the series films were highly formulaic although they were of varied type: comedy-romance (the *Andy Hardy* series); mystery (the *Thin Man* series); children's adventures (the *Lassie* series).

The series-film concept became a standard television programming format and to a limited extent still exists in theatrical filmmaking: the Billy Jack films, the *Pink Panther* comedies, and the enormously popular James Bond series which began in 1962 with *Dr. No*. George Lucas conceived the *Star Wars* (1977) saga, which included *The Empire Strikes Back* (1980) and *Return of the Jedi* (1983) as a series/installment concept, later followed by the *Stars Wars Episode I* and *II* (1999, 2001) prequels.

Setup   A term used to describe the readying procedure for each **shot** within a film. The placement of the camera and **lens** on the **scene**, the setting of lights and microphones for the purpose of recording a shot are together referred to as a setup. The term is sometimes used in film criticism to refer to a director's individualized **style** in composing shots and recording the action in a scene.

Sexploitation film (see **Exploitation film**)

Shooting script   A script containing **dialogue** and action as well as important production information for the **director** and the **cinematographer**. Included in this production information are **shot** descriptions (scope of shot); shot numbers, location, and time notations; and indications of where special effects are required. The director works from this script in the filming of the story. The shooting script can also become an assembly guide for the film **editor**.

Shorts (short subjects) Brief films shown as a part of a theatrical motion-picture program, usually preceding the presentation of the **fea-**

ture film. Shorts, along with previews and **cartoons**, were used extensively as filler material when motion-picture programs were repeated every two hours and the standard length of the feature was approximately ninety minutes. After 1960 shorts became rarer in motion-picture houses as programming concepts changed and as exhibitors reacted to the extra cost of renting short-subject films.

Shot
The basic unit of film construction. A shot is the continuous recording of a **scene** or object from the time the camera starts until it stops. In the edited film it is the length of film from one splice or optical **transition** to the next.

Shot-sequence editing A process of film construction which adheres rigidly to the conventions of **master scene/coverage filming**. The **editor**, in reconstructing a **scene**, moves through the **shot sequence**—beginning with a **long shot** (**cover shot** of the scene) then proceeding to **medium shots** and **close-ups**. This once-standard editing process is now common in dramatic material that has been filmed for television.

Simultaneity
The process in film construction of combining story elements and events which are occurring at the same time. A simple type of simultaneity occurs in the cinema through **parallel development** of separate lines of action. In a more complex manner, simultaneity is the aesthetic process employed by Sergei Eisenstein in the Odessa steps sequence of *The Battleship Potemkin* (1925). The short event is fully extended through simultaneity so that it can be perceived in its full impact.

Single-frame/stop-motion filming The process of shooting motion-picture material a **frame** at a time for the purpose of **animation**, **pixilation**, or a time-lapse effect. A person can appear to be flying four feet above the ground through single-frame filming, as in Norman McLaren's *Neighbors* (1952). This effect is achieved by taking a single frame each time the actor leaps into the air and repeating the leaps hundreds of times. Cartoon animation is achieved by photographing a hand-drawn action **sequence** frame by frame (cel animation), with the illusion of movement then occurring in the continuous projection of the individually recorded **images**. See **Time-lapse cinematography/stop-action cinematography**.

Single-system recording (see **Magnetic film**)

Slapstick comedy Comedy derived from broad, aggressive action, with an emphasis often placed on acts of harmless violence. The term comes from a theatrical device developed for comic effect and consisting of two pieces of wood (a "slapstick") which produced a resounding noise when struck against an actor. Early evidence of slapstick comedy in the motion picture is found in the Lumière film, *Watering the Gardener* (1895). See **Comedy**.

Slow motion A motion-picture effect in which **images** are shown at a moving speed that is slower than that of natural movement. The usual method of achieving slow motion is through the technique of **overcranking**, or photographing more than twenty-four frames per second and then projecting the images at sound speed (24 fps).

As a unique cinematic device, slow motion has enjoyed a considerable degree of popularity with filmmakers, originally in an experimental way, and more recently as a standard device in narrative films.

Georges Méliès first made use of slow motion in his film fantasies as another exploration by him of film's "trick" possibilities.

In later periods of film history, filmmakers utilized slow motion to suggest dreams and dreamlike states. Screen fantasies often employed slow motion, as did experimental, psychological films such as *Un Chien Andalou* (1928) and the dream films of Maya Deren. Experimental film artists of the 1920s and 1930s, who attempted to rid film of its theatrical and literary elements, utilized the innate cinematic quality of slow motion as a nontraditional way of viewing the world.

The dramatic use of slow motion in contemporary cinema has been varied and extensive. Lyric, poetic movements in a film story are often conveyed through slow motion. In the horror film *Carrie* (1976), Brian De Palma makes use of extreme slow motion in the prom **sequence** of the picture. The effect intensifies and draws out the heroine's brief moment of glory.

Slow motion is employed as a means of dramatic contrast in *The Reivers* (1969). A horse race involving the lad in the story is declared a default because of cheating on the winner's part and the race must be rerun. The first race was photographed in natural motion and edited to provide an accelerated view of the action. Director Mark Rydell photographed the second race in slow motion, allowing the event to be shown with a different dimension of reality. The action is captured in intense slow-motion photography rather than achieved through editing dynamics. As the two riders cross the finish line, with the lad the winner the second time, a cut is made which returns the action to natural motion. The dynamic return to natural motion punctuates the moment of victory. Similar cutting between slow motion and natural motion occurs in the final battle sequence of *The Last Samurai* (2003).

Slow motion lends to all movement a more precise and balletic quality, no matter how frenetic the action. The familiar death sequence in *Bonnie and Clyde* (1967) had a choreographed, balletic quality because of Arthur Penn's use of slow-motion photography to record the event. The drawn-out, agonizing desert race in *Bite the Bullet* (1975) contained numerous sequences shot in slow motion. Similarly, Stanley Kubrick employed extensive slow motion in *Full Metal Jacket* (1987), both in the exhaustive Parris Island basic training segments and in the combat sequences in Vietnam.

Smash cut   Another term for **dynamic cut**—a cut which is abruptly obvious to the viewer.

Social drama/film A screen story that is developed around a societal problem and the unresolved issues entailed in exploring the problem. In the 1930s and 1940s, Warner Bros. Studios was known for its social dramas, such as *Wild Boys of the Road* (1933), a film about the travails of unemployed boys in the early years of the Depression; and *The Black Legion* (1936) a study of the organized hatred of foreigners. A classic screen social drama, *To Kill a Mockingbird* (1962), examined racial relations in the South as did *In the Heat of the Night* (1967). Contemporary social dramas include: *Boyz n the Hood* (1991), a screen study of black urban life and parenting; *Philadelphia* (1993), a film about HIV/AIDS discrimination; and *Traffic* (2000), drug trafficking and youth drug addiction.

Socialist realism A term given to the style of filmmaking in Russia advocated by the Stalin government after 1928 as a replacement for the more formalistic methods of post-Revolutionary filmmakers, for example, Eisenstein, Pudovkin, Vertov. Socialist realism called for simpler, everyday views of life in the new Soviet state. It was believed by the government that this approach would be more useful and instructive for the masses than the formalistic, art-for-art's sake methods of the 1920s. The call for socialist realism stultified film experimentation in Russia, although **directors** like Eisenstein turned to inspirational stories about historical figures and were able to bring to the screen impressively executed epics, for instance, *Alexander Nevsky* (1938), and *Ivan the Terrible*, Parts One and Two (1944, 1946).

Soft focus A photographic **image** which lacks sharp definition. Within a single **frame** image some parts of the area of view may be in critical focus while others are "soft." The soft images are those outside the **depth-of-field** zone, either intentionally to emphasize a particular part of the **scene** or simply because greater depth of field was not possible for the chosen **lens**, film stock, and lighting conditions.

Sound advance/sound bridge The advancement of a sound, to be heard in a new **shot** or **scene**, into the end of the preceding scene. Sound advances, common in modern films, are usually combined with cut **transitions** to pull the action of the story forward in a dynamic manner. Alfred Hitchcock fairly well patented the sound advance in his 1929 classic *Blackmail*. A young woman (Anny Ondra)—wandering the streets of London in shock after killing a man—comes upon a drunk lying on the pavement—his arm extended in the same manner as the artist just murdered by the woman in his studio apartment. The image of the arm seems to precipitate a scream from the young woman. A cut, however, reveals the scream coming from a landlady who has just discovered the dead artist's body in his apartment. The sound advance also has conceptual, satirical, and dramatic possibilities. In *Five Easy Pieces* (1970) the unexpected sound of a bowling ball rolling down a bowling lane is heard in the final seconds of a scene in a motel room where Jack Nicholson has taken a girlfriend. Just as the ball strikes the tenpin, a cut is made to a new scene where Nicholson is bowling with the woman. The combined sound advance and the cut transition together serve as a sexual **metaphor**. See **Asynchronous sound**.

Sound effects Noises and sounds on the motion-picture **sound track** which have been added to supply realism, atmosphere, and dramatic emphasis to a film **scene**. This work is done by sound technicians called **Foley artists**. Sound effects may be either onscreen effects or they may be offscreen sound effects. Onscreen effects (diegetic) originate within the visible action of the scene. Offscreen effects occur outside the scene and like music are often used as a means of creating mood, atmosphere, or drama. The sound of a coyote howling in the distance has become a clichéd means of suggesting the loneliness of life on the western frontier. Distant foghorns and train whistles have been similarly used in other environments to convey a sense of atmospheric loneliness. In *The Diary of Anne Frank* (1959) considerable dramatic tension was achieved by the distant sound of gestapo police sirens interspersed throughout the picture. As described above, these onscreen, offscreen sound effects have a logical environmental source of origin and are termed diegetic.

The stylized use of sound effects to convey mood or drama represents a form of **selective sound**. The sounds may originate in the location (diegesis) and may be synchronous, but their dramatic importance is emphasized through volume or selective isolation from other sounds.

In *Thieves Like Us* (1974), Robert Altman employed radio sounds which served as an expressive motif throughout the picture. While the small-time bank robbers wait outside a bank during one of their unexciting holdups, they listen to a dramatic broadcast of *Gangbusters*. The young robber and his girlfriend listen to a concert of classical music, broadcast from New York, while sipping Coca-Colas and swatting flies on the back porch of their Mississippi hideout. When the two make love, a radio adaptation of *Romeo and Juliet* is heard in the background. The radio, while always a realistic (diegetic) part of these scenes, is employed by Altman as a means of contrasting the common lives of the bank robbers with those which come over the radio. By so doing, Altman is also able to intensify through the supplied selective sounds an awareness of the quality of the environment in which the characters live. In *21 Grams* (2003), in the climactic hotel scene, all interior diegetic sound is briefly eliminated to produce an eerie, muted rendering of the explosive action.

Sound track   The optical or magnetic track at the edge of the film which contains music, **dialogue**, narration, and **sound effects**. In most instances these various sound elements are mixed and synchronized to the desired **image**. When a sound track consists of non-synchronous sounds, it is referred to as a wild sound track. Most sound tracks are photographed on the edge of the film (optical sound) and these are technically referred to as variable-density sound tracks. A sound reader responds to the printed images to produce sound output. See **Dolby® sound**.

Source music Music which originates from a source within a film **scene**— a radio, phonograph, live orchestra, etc. See **Diegetic sound**.

Special-effects film Any film which incorporates a wide variety of special optical effects and trick photography into the story. Special-effects films exploit the unusual possibilities of the motion picture for fantasy and **spectacle**, for example, *Mary Poppins* (1964), *The Poseidon Adventure* (1972), *Star Wars* (1977), *Close Encounters of the Third Kind* (1977), *Terminator 2: Judgment Day* (1991), *Death Becomes Her* (1992). Action thrillers, such as the *Spider-Man* films and fantasies such as the *Harry Potter* series are magical entertainment because of their extensive use of special effects. See **Trick film, Computer-generated imaging**.

Spectacle A film characterized by elements which include lavish production design, epic theme, and grand scope. Screen spectacles consist of many types: dramatic films involving high adventure and heroic characters, *Intolerance* (1916), *War and Peace* (1956), *Ben Hur* (1959), *Star Wars* (1977); grand eye-catching musicals, *The Gold Diggers of 1935* (1935), *My Fair Lady* (1964); special-effects films designed to display novel motion-picture processes such as **Cinerama** in *This Is Cinerama* (1952), **3-D** in *Bwana Devil* (1952), and **Sensurround** in *Earthquake* (1975).

Spinoff A term used to describe a motion picture whose concept was inspired by another film—usually a highly successful work which enjoyed wide audience appeal. The popularity of *Young Frankenstein* (1974), for example, inspired a number of spinoff comedies including *Sherlock Holmes' Smarter Brother* (1976) and *Old Dracula* (1976). Unusual spinoffs from characters created for *Saturday Night Live* resulted in *It's Pat* (1994) with Julia Sweeney, and in *A Night at the Roxbury* (1998) with Chris Kattan and Will Ferrell as the Butabi brothers.

Splice The piecing together of two shots or sections of film during the editing process by taping, gluing, or other means of adhesion as the film is being assembled for laboratory processing.

Split-screen process A type of laboratory effect in which the **frame** has been divided by a sharp line into two or more separate areas of visual information (photo 41). Separately recorded **images** are printed onto various parts of the frame that may be divided horizontally, vertically, or diagonally. A diagonal split-screen **shot** was used as early as 1915 by D.W. Griffith to depict the burning of Atlanta in *The Birth of a Nation*. Extensive use of the split-screen technique appeared in *The Thomas Crown Affair* (1968) and *The Boston Strangler* (1968). A variation of the split-screen technique allows an actor to play two or more roles on the screen simultaneously, for example, Nicholas Cage as twin-brother screenwriters in *Adaptation* (2002). The effect is achieved by the use of bluescreen or greenscreen processes that allow the actor to be filmed on one side of the set, and then on the opposite by moving the greenscreen and actor and refilming. See **bluescreen/greenscreen**.

Star system   A system, essentially American, for obtaining financial backing for the production of a motion picture, and for the commercial marketing of the picture, by exploiting the popular

[SPLIT SCREEN] 41. Introductory split-screen images are used to reveal Ron Howard as he looked in *American Graffiti* (1973) and as a young man five years older when the story continued in *More American Graffiti* (1979).

appeal of the star or stars who appear in the film. The system developed in Hollywood in the first decade of feature-film production and led to enormous salaries for the most popular screen actors. The Metro-Goldwyn-Mayer Corporation in particular was built around its company of actors, labeling its studio as a place with "more stars than there are in the heavens."

The domination of stars in film production and marketing remained strong until the early 1960s when a shifting economy and new approaches to film producing brought about significant changes in industry procedures. To a significant degree, however, American film producers still depend on the popular appeal of familiar entertainment personalities—a fact corroborated by the numerous television actors brought to Hollywood from the 1970s onward, including most prominently the comedians on the popular television show, *Saturday Night Live*, for example, Chevy Chase, John Belushi, Bill Murray, Gilda Radner, Will Ferrell; from *Cheers*, Ted Danson and Woody Harrelson; and from *Friends*, the full cast of principal actors.

Steadicam   A lightweight, portable motion-picture camera mount which was put into wide use during the 1970s and which is remarkable for its steadying abilities when the camera is handheld or placed into motion. The Steadicam permits smooth follow shots that earlier were possible only with the use of heavy dolly devices and motorized vehicles. The Steadicam's capabilities were well displayed in the many action-training scenes in *Rocky* (1976), as well as in the dynamic moving shots of Kubrick's *The Shining* (1980).

Stereophonic sound Sound or music that has been recorded on two or more separate tracks and that, when played back on two or more separate speakers, gives an effect of three-dimensional sound.

Stereoscopic viewer/imagery A "three dimensional" viewing device which gained wide popularity in the mid-19th century. To achieve the three-dimensional effect two photographs of a **scene** appear side by side on a viewing card—one image on the left side and the other on the right. A frontispiece containing two **lenses** permits, as in natural vision, the left eye to focus solely on the left image and the right eye on the right image, thus creating the illusion of depth and dimension. Three-dimensional motion pictures, introduced commercially in 1952, worked on the same principle.

Stills   Photographs taken of a film **scene** for promotional purposes. These are usually called production stills since they are taken on the set during the rehearsal or filming of the picture. Because they are to be used in publicizing the motion picture, production stills are usually posed for the best possible quality. A photograph taken from an actual **frame** of the finished motion picture is called a frame still.

Stinger   (see **Music**)

Stock footage (shot) A **shot** or **scene** in a motion picture which is taken from existing film material, as opposed to new material which is shot specifically for a particular production. Stock footage may be incorporated in the film to avoid the expense of hard-to-derive shots: foreign locations, war scenes, airplanes in flight, etc. Major studios and other archives hold expansive stock libraries that contain every imaginable type of unusual scenic material, as well as **documentary** and newsreel footage of important historical events. The blending of stock shots with newly filmed material requires careful technical attention to avoid detection. Stock footage is often used as the background element in **rear-screen projection** and **traveling matte** shots.

Stop-action cinematography, stop motion The photographing of a scene or a situation for trick effect through a stop-and-start procedure rather than through a continuous run of the camera. The stopping of the camera in the middle of a continuing situation for a period of time before resuming filming adds an elliptical quality to a scene. Moving objects such as clouds or automobiles appear to advance in a pixilated manner. This effect is also referred to as **time-lapse cinematography**. Also, in stop-action cinematography, actors or objects can be added to or deleted from the scene while the camera is stopped, then filming of the action is resumed. This stop-start process gives the effect of the sudden appearance or disappearance of the objects or actors when the film is projected. The visual trickery of the stop-action process was often used in the magic and fantasy films produced by Georges Méliès at the turn of the century, as well as in films with miniature figure models such as *King Kong* (1933) and *Jurassic Park* (1993). The animation of real objects and people to give the impression of self-locomotion is achieved through single-frame stop-action cinematography and is often referred to as **pixilation**. See **animatronics**.

Stopping down	(see **F-stop**)
Street film	A term which usually refers to a type of motion picture produced in Germany during the 1920s and 1930s, so called because much of the action takes place on a city street. In this kind of film, German **directors** often used the street as a setting for revealing social realities for characters. G.W. Pabst's *The Joyless Street* (1925), a study of inequities in post-World War I Vienna, epitomized the German street film. A single Vienna street and its inhabitants offer a somber view of the ruin and degradation that accompanied the times. Bruno Rahn's *Tragedy of a Street* (1929) is another example of the German street film. Perpetuation of the street film concept has carried over into such American films as *Midnight Cowboy* (1969), *Mean Streets* (1973), and *Taxi Driver* (1976).
Structural cinema	A general term for a type of experimental film which places emphasis on sustained or repeated views of filmed material. A film in which a single wide-angle shot of an atomic-bomb explosion is repeated for forty-five minutes without variation is an example of structural cinema (*Atomic Explosion*, 1975). The camera in another film, Paul Winkler's *Brickwall* (1976), pans back and forth across a brick wall for nearly half an hour.
	In structural cinema, editing is kept to a minimum. The filmmaker usually chooses a single structural approach to the material to be filmed—a zoom, a pan, a wide angle of view, a **close-up**—and the approach becomes the sustained, unvaried method of exploring the photographed materials. In some instances, the repeated **images** are supplied with laboratory effects such as solarization techniques, tinting, and **superimpositions**. Michael Snow's *Wavelength* (1967) consists of a single **zoom shot** (the structural device) toward a window. The zoom takes forty-five minutes to complete. During the zoom, Snow varies image through changes in color temperature, filters, and exposure.
Structuralism	A theory of film analysis closely associated with **semiological criticism** because of its systematic approach to film analysis. Structuralism, however, emphasizes **ethnographic** interests rather than linguistic (semiological) approaches in the study of film. The principles of structuralism were in part inspired by the work of anthropologist Claude Lévi-Strauss. Lévi-Strauss studied the oral rituals and mythology

of certain South American Indians and by so doing isolated previously invisible patterns within these forms of communication. These polarized patterns, according to Lévi-Strauss, revealed how certain perceptions of the Indian tribes came to exist.

In a similar manner structuralist principles have sometimes been applied to the full body of a film director's work in order to detect patterns that will reveal social and cultural meanings and allow a better understanding of the artist under examination. In this sense, structuralism is also related to **auteur criticism**. Similarly, structuralism has been applied to a specific film **genre** or an individual film.

Studio lighting   (see **Lighting**)

Studio picture   A motion picture made principally on a shooting stage rather than on location, and usually characterized by exact technical control of lighting, setting, and sound. A studio picture often conveys a romantic quality because of controlled lighting and decor. Studio pictures also have decided advantages for expressionistic and atmospheric underscoring of theme, for example, *The Cabinet of Dr. Caligari* (1919), *Broken Blossoms* (1919), *The Informer* (1935), *New York, New York* (1976), *Moulin Rouge* (2001), *Chicago* (2002). See **American studio years**, **Lighting**.

Studio years   (see **American studio years**)

Style   The manner by which a motion-picture idea is expressed so that it effectively reveals the idea as well as the filmmaker's attitude toward the idea. Style is the filmmaker's individualistic response to the treatment of an idea. The filmmaker's style may be: realistic (Vittorio de Sica, *The Bicycle Thief*, 1948); impressionistic (Federico Fellini, *Roma*, 1972); expressionistic (Stanley Kubrick, *A Clockwork Orange*, 1971); abstract (Alain Resnais, *Last Year at Marienbad*, 1961); surrealistic (Luis Buñuel, *L'Age d'Or*, 1930); formalistic (Peter Greenaway, *The Draughtsman's Contract*, 1982). Because style is a reflection of the individuality of the filmmaker, no two directors' styles are exactly alike. Hence, style analysis is often a major emphasis in film criticism.

Subjective shot   A **shot** within a motion picture or television program which suggests the **point of view** of a character. The camera becomes the eye of the character, revealing what is being seen as the character moves through or surveys a **scene**. A combined **pan** and **tilt** shot is a commonly used method of

[SUBJECTIVE SHOT] 42. Throughout *The Lady in the Lake* (1946), the camera takes the subjective point of view of the principal character (Robert Montgomery). Since the camera view represents what Robert Montgomery is seeing, Jayne Meadows, shown above, must look directly into the camera lens. Montgomery is seen by the audience only in reflected mirror shots.

suggesting a character's surveillance of an area; a moving-camera shot conveys in a subjective manner a character's movement through space. A quick **cut-in** to an element in a film scene as a character glances toward it might also be considered a subjective shot since the cut indicates the character's subjective awareness of the detail. Subjective shots are common in the psychological film and in film mysteries. An extreme use of the subjective shot occurred in *The Lady in the Lake* (1946, photo 42), a film photographed entirely from a single character's point of view.

Subplot   A secondary complication within a motion-picture story, usually touching on and enriching the main plot. A subplot in Robert Redford's *Ordinary People* (1980) involves the fate of a young woman who, like the film's principal character (Timothy Hutton), is struggling to recover from a mental breakdown. Eventually the young woman commits suicide, an act which temporarily threatens Hutton's progress toward recovery.

Superimposition   An optical technique in which two or more **shots** appear within the same **frame**, one on top of the other (photo 43). It is a popular device in **trick films**, experimental films, and fantasies, where unusual views of reality are desired. Georges Méliès employed superimpositions in trick films as early as 1896. The device was also a common element in the impressionistic and epic work of Abel Gance in France. In his classic **spectacle** *Napoléon* (1927), Gance freely incorporates superimpositions, including a shot of Napoleon spinning a globe that contains a superimposed portrait of Josephine. The device dynamically links Napoleon's desires to conquer the world to his love for Josephine.

[SUPERIMPOSITION] 43. A superimposition permits the ghostlike appearance and disappearance of Dracula in F.W. Murnau's *Nosferatu* (1922).

Surrealism   A modern movement in painting, sculpture, theater, film, photography, and literature, originating in France in the early 1920s, that seeks to express subconscious states through the disparate and illogical arrangement of imagery. Early surrealist filmmakers, Man Ray, Salvador Dali, and Luis Buñuel, captured on film a variety of material phenomena and arranged the imagery in incongruous ways so as to effect subjective, dreamlike meanings. The classic example of an early surrealistic film is *Un Chien Andalou* (1928,

[SURREALISM] 44. The disparate and illogical arrangements of material objects, a principal characteristic of screen surrealism is evident in this shot from *Un Chien Andalou* (1928).

photo 44). Surrealism was born in a revolt against realism and traditional art. According to an early manifesto written by its leader, André Breton, surrealism is defined as "pure psychic automatism by which an attempt is made to express, either verbally, in writing, or in any other manner, the true function of thought." See **Avant-garde**.

Suspense film (thriller) A motion picture whose plot creates a high level of anxiety and tension through concern for the fate of the principal character or characters. In the suspense thriller life itself is often threatened—usually as a result of the principal character's unsuspected or knowing involvement in dangerous, potentially deadly situations. As the plot builds toward its resolution, the threat and, thus, suspense increase. Alfred Hitchcock is often referred to as the master of the suspense thriller, for instance, *Rear Window* (1954) and *Psycho* (1960). *Marathon Man (1976), Black Sunday (1977), Coma (1978), When a Stranger Calls (1979), Fatal Attraction (1987), The Hand That Rocks the Cradle* (1992), and *The Panic Room* (2002) are other examples of suspense thrillers.

Sweeten (sound) To embellish an element of a **sound track**, usually by giving the sound greater presence or clarity. The term is most often applied to the work of documentarists, including *cinéma verité* filmmakers, who enhance elements of the sound track for the purpose of adding atmosphere or thematic impact. In Frederick Wiseman's *High School* (1969) a Simon and Garfunkel song being played on a tape recorder by an English teacher is "sweetened" so that the thematic relevance of the song's lyrics is not lost to the viewer. The song is given full presence so that it has the clarity of high fidelity rather than the sound of a piece of music picked up in a classroom.

Swish pan A type of film **transition** achieved by panning the camera rapidly across a **scene**. The speed of the camera movement blurs the **image** and serves to wipe out the preceding scene. A new scene follows. The swish pan, because of its dynamic visual quality, is most frequently employed to link two scenes without a loss of momentum. See **Camera movement**, **Pan**.

Switchback An earlier term for **parallel development**, the process of including in a film through editing arrangement two or more events which have taken place at approximately the same time. Following the development of one action to a point in time, the **editor** "switches back" to pick up the action of another event. Most commonly in this type of story development, the separate elements eventually coalesce. D.W. Griffith frequently referred to this editing method as the "switchback device" and employed the technique extensively as a means of narrative construction in his early silent-screen **melodramas**, for example, *The Lonely Villa* (1909).

Symbol An object or **image** which both represents itself and suggests a meaning that is apart from its own objective reality. The object carries a literal reality and a suggestive meaning of a more abstract reality. In *The Birth of a Nation* (1915) the playful fighting of a kitten and two puppies is introduced by Griffith as symbolic representation of increasing hostilities just prior to the Civil War. Here the symbolic relationship of the animals to the war is created by plot association. In other instances symbols may contain references that are universally or conventionally accepted as such. The white hat is a conventional symbol of the **western** hero figure, the black hat of the villain. Light (white hat) also carries universal connotations of "good," while dark (black hat) has long been a symbolic representation for "evil."

In semiotic criticism the symbol is one of the signs that, along with **index** and **icon**, is examined in the systematic analysis of the motion-picture narrative. See **Metaphor**.

Synchronous sound A film term which refers to the use of **images** and their corresponding sounds as they have apparently occurred simultaneously in real life. In **lip sync** a person speaks and there is a precise coordination of voice sounds and lip movement.

Synchronized sound for the motion picture involves not only speech but noises (**sound effects**) and music as well. A type of synchronous sound occurs in a street **scene** where the typical noises of the city are heard. Music, skillfully composed to match exactly the moods and editing rhythms of a motion picture, can also be described as an evocative use of synchronous sound. "**Mickey Mousing**" of music, for example, requires exact synchronization.

The goal of synchronous sound in recording a dramatic scene is usually to present an accurate appraisal of sound originating in the environment. See **Dialogue**, **Lip sync**, **Realistic sound**, **Sound advance**, **Voice-over**.

Synecdoche A type of metaphor in which a part is used to indicate the whole or the whole is used to imply the part. "Hand" is a synecdoche for "laborer"; "wheels" is a synecdoche for "automobile." The whole for a part is evidenced in the use of "the dying year" for "fall."

In the motion picture, synecdochic imagery is common. The use of a close **shot** of synchronized marching feet is a synecdoche for military power; in a more conventional manner an **establishing shot** of the Eiffel Tower is synedochally representative of Paris.

The synecdoche has specific relevance for film analysis because of its relationship to semiotic criticism, and in particular to indexical analysis of motion-picture content. An awareness of the way various parts represent the whole allows a deeper understanding of methods of effecting connotative meaning within the context of a film. In Eisenstein's *The Battleship Potemkin* (1925), the feet of Cossack soldiers marching methodically down the Odessa steps is a part that stands for the "whole" of Czarist oppression. In the final section of Potemkin the well-oiled, smoothly moving parts of the ship's engine are synecdochally representative of the "whole" efficiency of the ship, by then under the command of the rebel sailors, that is, the "new" Russian state.

The metaphorical nature of the synecdoche derives from a connotative relationship of imagery to the film idea.

T

Tableau	A static grouping of live characters within the film **frame** (in theater, within the stage picture). Although more common in theater than in the motion picture, tableaux were often used for dramatic effect by film directors during the era of silent pictures. D.W. Griffith, for one, was fond of the tableau as a means of introducing scenes or providing a visual contrast with action shots, for example, *A Corner in Wheat* (1909, photo 45.) Christopher Miles uses a tableau in *The Virgin and the Gypsy* (1970) to present the stifling formality of a young woman's family when she sees them for the first time after returning home from boarding school. Tableaux are used extensively in Terence Davies' *Distant Voices, Still Lives* (1988) to convey photo-album-like family groupings.
Take	A run of the camera for the purpose of filming a shot or a scene. Each run of the camera from start to finish is referred to as a "take." See **Long take**, **Shot**.
Teaser	A scene which precedes the opening credits of a motion picture and which is designed to develop audience interest in the story that will follow the credits. Often in contemporary film, the credits will be superimposed over the teaser mate-

[TABLEAU] 45. The tableau, as seen here in D.W. Griffith's *A Corner in Wheat* (1909), permits a stylized grouping of characters for dramatic and symbolic effect. Griffith suggests the plight of common workers who are caught in a world of spiraling food prices.

rial. "Precredits grabber" is another term sometimes used for the teaser scene.

Technicolor   A color-film process developed by Herbert T. Kalmus and Robert Comstock during the years 1916–1918. Initially the Technicolor system produced color images through two color negatives: red-orange-yellow colors on one negative, and green-blue-purple colors on a second negative. The two separate negatives were then wed to create a scale of color values of less-than-accurate renderings; it was the color process utilized by major Hollywood studios after 1924 in a variety of films: *Cythera* (1924), *The Phantom of the Opera* (1925), *The Black Pirate* (1926). Technicolor was a popular embellishment for costume-action and romantic films.

Eventually the Technicolor Corporation replaced the two-color negative lamination process with a three-color process. *Becky Sharp* (1935) and *The Garden of Allah* (1936) were among the first Hollywood films to be photographed with the three-color process. The quality of color reproduction in these films was significantly improved although the process tended to emphasize the "warmer" colors (yellows, oranges, and browns) of the spectrum, giving the films a golden look.

The Technicolor process held an exclusive monopoly on color filming until the development of new processes in the late 1940s and early 1950s by Eastman Kodak, Warner Bros., and other competing laboratories.

Telephoto lens A **lens** of long focal length with a narrow angle of view. The telephoto lens is one that magnifies the subject or object being photographed at least 50 percent more than does the **normal lens** for any given camera. Telephoto lenses are characterized by a shallow depth of field and by their tendency to compress foreground and background areas. They also appear to decrease the speed of objects and people as they move toward or away from the camera. A telephoto shot is any shot taken with a telephoto lens and recognizable as such.

Three-dimensional (3-D) film A motion picture produced to allow a stereoscopic effect. In a 3-D, stereoscopic process two pictures of a scene are taken simultaneously from points slightly apart from one another, and through the use of eyeglasses the viewer is able to combine the projected images so that the effect of depth and solidity are achieved. The three-dimensional film was introduced to American audiences in 1952 with the release of *Bwana Devil*. After a brief period of curiosity the 3-D film lost its novelty for audiences and except for an occasional film, for example, *The Stewardesses* (1974), *Comin' at Ya* (1981), and *Jaws 3-D* (1983), use of the technique is rare.

Three-point lighting (see **Lighting: Actor Light**)

THX An acoustical monitoring concept for evaluating newer, improved motion-picture sound systems. Developed by producer-director George Lucas and sound engineer Tomlinson Holman, THX involved systematic assessment of theater performance of new film soundtracks to make certain that the theatrical reproduction of sound was commensurate with the superior tracks. The concept called attention to the increasing seriousness attached to sound and sound reproduction in the motion-picture experience.

Ticking clock/bomb A suspense-building plotting strategy in which the protagonist(s) acts to avert an impending tragic event, for instance, the urgency to get a child passenger to a dialysis machine in

Airport 75 (1974), the frantic effort to prevent a roller-coaster explosion in *Rollercoaster* (1977), and the race to defuse a nuclear warhead in *The Peacemaker* (1997).

Tilt The movement vertically (up or down) of the camera resting on a fixed base.

Time-lapse cinematography A method of filming which involves interrupted runs of the camera so that the lengthy progress of an actual event can be revealed in a brief period of time. Time-lapse cinematography has both scientific and experimental possibilities. The growth of a flower from seedling to full bloom can be observed on a few seconds of film which has used the time-lapse method. For *Coney Island* (1976) Frank Mouris employed a time-lapse method of filming to present in only three minutes a full day and evening at an amusement park. In time-lapse cinematography the flow of images, when projected, usually possesses an animated or pixilated quality since the process is quite similar to the single-frame methods of film animation. Godfrey Reggio's *Koyaanisqatsi* (1988) is a feature-length time-lapse film that explores American vistas, accompanied by the music of Phillip Glass. *Koyaanisqatsi* (Hopi for "life out of balance") continues to be shown, often with Glass performing his musical score "live."

Tinted film Generally a back-and-white film to which color has been added by hand, dye solution, or laboratory processing. Tinting for visual effect or symbolic value was common prior to the expanded use of **Technicolor** processes in the 1930s. Edison programs included tinted footage as early as 1896. Georges Méliès in France often applied elaborate hand tinting and coloring to his highly imaginative screen fantasies.

Todd-AO A commercial name for a **wide-screen process** introduced by Mike Todd Associates. Todd-AO employed a film width of 65 mm and unlike Cinerama, another wide-screen process, required only a single camera and a single projector. *Oklahoma!* (1955) and *Around the World in Eighty Days* (1956) introduced Todd-AO, which was later purchased by Twentieth Century-Fox and used in its film **spectacles** of the 1960s.

Tone A term which refers to one's responses to a particular motion picture as a result of various stimuli which are contained within the film. The filmmaker's attitude toward the treatment of subject matter produces a film's tone. That tone may be ironic, comic, serious, playful, brooding, cheerful, light-hearted, somber, and so forth. The tone of an individual film can be consistent throughout, as in Woody Allen's *Interiors* (1978), a somber work from beginning to end. Or the tone of a film may shift constantly, as in François Truffaut's *Shoot the Piano Player* (1960), a work whose tone is alternately comic, serious, playful, and tragic.

Tracking shot   A term used interchangeably with **trucking shot**—a moving camera shot where the camera and its mount are moved to follow action. In a tracking (trucking) shot the camera may travel in front of, behind, or beside the moving action. In the opening scene of Robet Altman's *The Player* (1992) an eight-minute tracking shot follows the action on the grounds of a Hollywood studio complex. The camera tracks through a variety of different vignettes, including one viewed through an office window where a screenwriter (Buck Henry) is "pitching" a sequel to *The Graduate* (1967).

Transition   Any one of a number of devices by which a film editor moves from one scene or **sequence** to another. A transition usually involves a passage of time, and can affect the **tone** and flow of a motion picture. The **cut, dissolve, fade**-out-/fade-in, **washout**, optical wipe, **natural wipe**, and **iris** are types of transition available to the filmmaker. See **Ripple dissolve, swish pan**.

Travelling matte   A laboratory process for combining two separately recorded images into a single shot (photo 46). Most commonly the traveling-matte system is a technique for combining a foreground scene with a separately recorded background scene. Traveling-matte shots should not be confused with **process shots,** which consist of live foreground combined with **rear-screen projection**. In the traveling-matte system, foreground scenes are photographed against a solid-color background, usually indoors on a studio shooting stage. A silhouette of the foreground action, called a matte shot, is produced on high-contrast film and combined in the optical printer with the background action. In the initial printing of the silhouette matte, the silhouetted foreground area because it is opaque retards light and remains unexposed. In a second run of the film through the optical printer, the foreground action can be printed onto the unexposed area for a composite of the two. Because the silhouetted matte can and usually does change while being printed, it has been labeled a

[TRAVELING MATTE] 46. A traveling matte makes possible the visualization of leprechauns in the Disney production *Darby O'Gill and the Little People* (1959).

"traveling matte." The "gunshot" traveling matte, named after its British creator George Gunn, was so perfected that in the ballet film *Red Shoes* (1948) Moira Shearer appears in a *pas de deux* with a dancing newspaper.

Travelogue   A type of **documentary** film which presents, primarily for entertainment purpose, views of interesting places and events—often exotic or historic locations abroad, frequently colorful events surrounding holiday celebrations in different parts of the world. Until the mid-1950s the travelogue often appeared as a **short** in theatrical motion-picture programs.

Treatment   A complete narrative description of a film story written as though the author were visualizing the action as it develops. The treatment is eventually developed into a film script, with the precise description of the narrative giving indication of how the story should be "treated" in the script itself. See **Writer**.

Trick film (shot)   A film or a film shot which has been derived through the special optical possibilities of the motion picture. The magical feats of stop-action filming, of filming at **fast** or **slow motion**, of animating objects or people through **single-**

frame filming, and of **double-exposure** images are among the many optical tricks available to the filmmaker. A film whose design makes extensive use of these special characteristics for the effect of optical illusion or fantasy is often referred to as a trick film. The films of Georges Méliès, for example, *Conjurer Making Ten Hats* (1896) and *A Trip to the Moon* (1902), are thought of as trick films. Filmed-for-television programs such as *Topper* and *I Dream of Jeannie*, where characters constantly and magically appear and disappear, follow in the tradition of the trick film as do such experimental works as Norman McLaren's *A Chairy Tale* (1957).

Trigger film A recently developed concept for a short film that has been designed to generate discussion on an issue-oriented topic. The trigger film's method is that of creating a dramatic dilemma (usually staged) that is centered on a timely issue such as teenage drug use, and then ending the film before the dramatic situation is resolved. This open-ended approach is intended to trigger discussion among audience members about the nature of the dilemma and its possible resolution. The trigger-film concept originated in the 1960s at the University of Michigan in a series of films designed for discussion of problems related to highway safety. Numerous other educational filmmakers have since adopted the trigger-film approach.

Triple-take filming Another term for **master shot/ coverage** procedures used to describe the filming of motion-picture subject matter, usually dramatic material, through a process of repeated action in order to acquire long views, medium views, and close-ups of the scene. Actors repeat movements and lines of dialogue for each separate **take** so that a **matched cut** will be possible. The process also presents the editor with a variety of shots in a dramatic action, thereby allowing numerous options in the reconstruction of a film scene: in establishing and controlling the **pace** of a scene; in placing dramatic emphasis; in extending time by including in the film two or more different views of the same action.

Triple-take filming was common in feature filmmaking during the studio years when the more intimate 3:4 aspect ratio of motion-picture formats permitted extensive editing within a film scene. With the introduction of wide screens in the 1950s, triple-take filming gave way to longer runs of the camera and a new emphasis on visual scope rather than on selective editing. Triple-take filming remains a popular method in the production of dramatic material for television.

Trucking shot A shot in which the camera moves alongside a moving character or object for the purpose of following the action. A trucking shot which moves the camera in a circular pattern is called an **arc shot**.

If the camera moves ahead of characters or moving objects in a scene described above or follows them from behind, it is usually referred to as a **tracking shot**. The characters are following in the tracks of the camera, or it follows in their tracks. The tracking and trucking shots have been popularly employed for action and chase scenes and also frequently used for **subjective shots** to show what a character sees while walking or riding in a moving vehicle.

Two-shot The designation for a shot composition with two characters. The term is used in a **shooting script** to indicate that in a scene containing two characters both are to appear in one composition rather than through intercutting between single shots of the two. An **over-the-shoulder** or **reverse-angle shot** is a type of two-shot.

Typecasting Selecting an actor for a certain role because of physical or professional qualities which make the actor ideally suited to play the character. In the motion-picture medium, where physique is all important, typecasting has been the rule rather than the exception. Once an actor has developed an appealing screen persona, the tendency has been to repeat that image from film to film. Major stars as well as character actors have sustained their motion-picture careers through typecasting. Inclination toward typecasting has been ongoing even for actors capable of widely divergent screen roles. Debra Winger's penchant for portraying a dying woman (*Terms of Endearment*, 1983) was again exploited in *Shadowlands* (1993). Laura Linney's successful characterization of a woman caught in a difficult brother-sister relationship (*You Can Count on Me*, 2000), resulted in being cast in a similar role in *Love, Actually* (2003).

In some instances directors will cast against type in order to give a role a new dimension, for example, Paul Newman in *The Mackintosh Man* (1973).

U

Underexposure   (see **Exposure**)

Underground film A term which was widely used during the 1940s and 1950s to describe films which: (1) Were personal, non-commercial films. (2) Sought to break away from the established traditions of the feature, narrative film. (3) Dealt with personal, taboo themes not permitted in commercial films. (4) Sought to elevate "pure" cinematic techniques—**superimposition, slow motion**, speeded action, pixilation—over the story film.

   The underground-film movement had its greatest raison d'être when Hollywood pictures were more traditional in form and technique. In the 1950s and 1960s, as feature films became more personal and innovative, many of the goals, intentions, themes, and techniques of underground film-makers were absorbed into the commercial cinema. See **New American Cinema**.

Urban drama   A motion picture in which the narrative focuses on the issues and problems confronting contemporary urban life. A strong sense of social consciousness often develops as an assortment of city dwellers interact with one another. John Sayles' *City of Hope* (1991) interwove the lives of a large cast of characters in its dissection of the problems of a city

[URBAN DRAMA] 47. Spike Lee appears in the provocative urban drama *Do the Right Thing* (1989), a film he also wrote and directed. The picture examines African-American life in the Bedford-Stuyvesant section of Brooklyn during a hot, tense summer day.

in turmoil. Lawrence and Meg Kasdan's *Grand Canyon* (1991) presented a sprawling, multicultural study of urban concerns in a tense Los Angeles as did *Crash* in 2005. John Singleton's *Boyz n The Hood* (1991) analyzed the lives of young black urban males growing up in a violent-prone inner-city environment. *Do the Right Thing* (1989, photo 47), a Spike Lee film, examined racial tensions in the Bedford-Stuyvesant section of Brooklyn, New York. Urban screen dramas are often provocative and controversial exercises, and can be traced back at least to such films as *The Joyless Street* (1925)—a German-made film directed by G.W. Pabst. *The Joyless Street* takes place in post-World War I Vienna and uses conditions of life on a single dark street to reveal the effects of war on the inhabitants of a large cosmopolitan city.

V

Variable focal-length lens (see **Zoom shot**)

Visual effects/effects shots A term for any number of special-effects components which are used to give the appearance of reality in a
motion-picture shot, such as the tornadoes and tornado
destruction in *Twister* (1996), the ocean swells in *The
Perfect Storm* (2000), and the storm-tossed ship in *Master
and Commander* (2003). A shot with special-effects manipulation is referred to in the film industry as an "effects shot."
Effects shots may involve miniature models (*Titanic*, 1997;
Master and Commander), computer-generated imagery
(the water faces in *The Abyss*, 1989), matte painting (*End
of Innocence*, 1990; *Gangs of New York*, 2002), and blue-
/greenscreen traveling mattes (*Adaptation*, 2002). Fog,
mist, and wind are visual elements which are used extensively in *House of Sand and Fog* (2003) in order to supply an
aura of mystery and significance to the contested house on
the California coast. *Master and Commander* contained
more than 700 different types of effects shots. Commercial
leaders in the field of visual effects include George Lucas'
Industrial Light and Magic (ILM), Digital Domain, and Sony
Imageworks.

VistaVision   A **wide-screen process** first attempted as early as 1919
                         and redeveloped at Paramount Pictures in 1953. The
                         VistaVision system was designed to permit the projection of
                         sharp, wide-screen images without the addition of new
                         equipment. In the filming process, picture **frames** were
                         photographed horizontally in the camera, rather than verti-
                         cally, allowing for a frame size almost three times the width
                         of a 35-mm frame. The strip permitted ordinary methods of
                         screen projection for higher and wider images. *White
                         Christmas* (1954) and *Strategic Air Command* (1955) suc-
                         cessfully utilized the VistaVision method.

Voice-over   The use of film narration, commentary, subjective thought,
                         or dialogue in which the speaker or speakers remain unseen
                         (photo 48). The most frequent use of voice-over occurs in
                         documentary and instructional films which are said to be
                         "narrated." The device is also used in dramatic films for
                         narrative exposition and, frequently, to suggest a person's

[VOICE-OVER] 48. An unusual instance of voice-over narration occurs in Billy Wilder's
Sunset Boulevard (1950). The narrator (William Holden) in effect narrates from the grave
since he is already dead when the film begins; his body, seen above, floats in the swim-
ming pool of his deranged lover (Gloria Swanson).

thoughts while that person is shown on the screen. In *Bread and Chocolate* (1978) Italian director Franco Brusati engages the principal character, Nino, in a conversation with his wife and father-in-law who are never seen in the film. This is achieved by the use of dialogue that combines Nino's **lip-sync** words with the voice-over dialogue of the unseen characters. Ewan McGregor's voice-over is a key dramatic device in the 1996 screen adaptation of John Irvine's novel, *Trainspotting*. See **Narration**.

Volume (sound) The level of amplification of motion-picture sound. Volume may refer generally to the projected level of amplification through a theater's sound system or it may refer to the **sound track'**s aural elements which, in the making of the film, were recorded at varying levels for dramatic effect. Volume and sound **presence** serve as the primary means by which an aural element can be given aesthetic or dramatic emphasis. In *Reds* (1981) the steadily increasing volume of "The Internationale" serves to highlight a culminating moment in Russian history and to bring the first half of Warren Beatty's film to a stirring musical climax. Later, near the conclusion of the film, the same anthem appears again on the sound track, but at an extremely low volume. In this instance, the music suggests memory and a fading dream for John Reed (Beatty), the film's principal character. Sound volume, at low or high levels, is a common method of conveying memory and subjective states. High volume is also an ever-present element in intense battle and crowd scenes in screen epics, for example, *Gladiator* (2000), *The Gangs of New York* (2003).

W

Washout

An optical **transition** used for editing purposes that are similar to the motion-picture **fade**.

Unlike the fade-out where the images fade to black, in a washout the images suddenly start to bleach out or to color until the screen becomes a frame of white or colored light. A new scene will then follow. Ingmar Bergman made extensive use of the washout in his psychological film *Cries and Whispers* (1972). Bergman varied the technique for both the purpose of transitions and for continuing his expressive use of color in that picture. The washouts would bring a single, rich color to the end of a scene to symbolize the emotions and psychological passions at work in the story.

Washouts were also effectively employed in the fantasy sequences of *Catch 22* (1970). *Monster* (2003) concludes with a washout as Aileen Wuornos (Charlize Theron) leaves the courtroom following her death sentencing. See **Exposure**.

Western

A descriptive label for a type of motion picture that is characteristically American in its mythic origins. Motion pictures classified as westerns share a number of common qualities and film conventions. Generally, westerns are set on the

American frontier during the latter part of the 19th century. Plotting conventions usually center on the classic conflict of maintaining law and order on the rugged frontier. The villains of western films conventionally use guns or other forceful means to take what they want; they are characters without any sense of moral compunction. The western hero on the other hand exhibits great courage in dealing with the evil forces and reveals a simplistic sense of duty and honor. A common characteristic of both hero and villain is the willingness of each to use guns in protecting themselves. Showdowns, shoot-outs, and gunfights on horseback, on trains, or in stagecoaches are common to plot resolution in the western film.

The format of the western genre as it has evolved in American filmmaking is simple and direct. The mise-en-scène draws on the romantic appeal of the open, untamed edges of the frontier, on lonely isolated forts and ranch houses, and on the stark facade of still-forming frontier towns. The forces or evil in these locations, often a gang of men, are quickly introduced through dramatic actions which display their dastardly deeds: a bank robbery, a train or stagecoach holdup, cattle rustling, or human massacre. Equal attention is given early on to suggesting the rugged qualities of the hero who must contend with the villains. The hero may be a local law-enforcement officer, a territorial marshal, or a skilled gunfighter who is brought in from another frontier location. Eventually a showdown occurs as in, for example, *High Noon* (1952), *Shane* (1953). In some instances, the hero may be a group of men—a posse—that organizes against the gang of villains. Still another variation of the western plot makes it necessary for the hero to pursue the villains into the unpopulated hinterlands beyond the frontier edges; in this variation of format the dramatic conflict centers on an extended "search and destroy" mission, for example, *The Outlaw Josey Wales* (1976), *Rooster Cogburn and His Lady* (1976), *Unforgiven* (1992), or *The Missing* (2003).

The appeal of the western film is derived from its fast-paced action, its romantic use of locations, and its clean, simple development of plot where dramatic conflicts, moral codes, and story conventions are easily understood.

Certain distinctions have been made between the serious western film and the western film of more benign intentions. To be a serious western, critics have claimed that the hero and villain must be equally committed to the killing of men in maintaining their positions on the frontier. Westerns of the other type, usually those made with a series hero such as Gene Autry or Roy Rogers, involve courageous deeds, but not to the point of death. Novelist Larry McMurtry sought to "renovate" the western cowboy in fiction which was adapted into film (*Hud*, 1963, *The Last Picture Show* , 1971) and television (*Lonesome Dove*, 1989). Appropriately McMurtry was chosen as co-writer for the screen adaptation of Annie Proulx's shortstory *Brokeback Mountain* (2005).

Whodunit   A colloquial term for a mystery or detective film whose plot is centered on efforts to solve a crime.

Wide-angle lens   A lens which provides a broad angle of view, employed most commonly in long shots and in situations where a great focus range is a consideration. Wide-angle lenses can also be used to make small space appear larger, distort perspective, and provide a sense of increased speed for moving objects or persons as they come in close range of the lens. Extreme-wide-angle lenses, often referred to as **fish-eye lenses**, produce even greater distortion.

Wide-screen processes Motion-picture screen formats with aspect ratios wider than the once-standard 3 by 4 (1:1.33) height-to-width ratio. **Cinerama, CinemaScope**, SuperScope, and Panavision were commercial names of wide-screen processes introduced by American studios in the early 1950s. Cinerama was a multi-projector, peripheral-vision wide-screen process with an aspect ratio of approximately 1:2.85. CinemaScope, SuperScope, and Panavision employed an **anamorphic lens** for an aspect ratio of approximately 3 by 7 (1:2.55). The now-standard wide-screen aspect ratio results in a 16-to-9 shape.

Wipe   A transitional device which occurs when one shot moves across the screen from left to right or right to left and appears to wipe away the preceding shot. A flip wide achieves the same effect but reveals the new shot in a manner similar to flipping a card that has a new image on the opposite side. These types of wipes are usually achieved through laboratory processes and are considered to be slick transitional techniques, used to effect a change of scene without a slowing of dramatic pace. They are also often used to recall an earlier era of filmmaking when the device was more common.

Richard Attenborough's *Chaplin* (1992) employed a variety of fast-paced transitional wipes, including vertical, horizontal, diagonal, circular, and diamond-shaped laboratory optical wipes.

A wipe that is achieved by using objects or characters to wipe out a shot or scene is known as a **natural wipe**. In *The Battleship Potemkin* (1925) a woman who is fleeing the Odessa steps massacre rushes toward the camera with an open umbrella. The umbrella is brought right up to the lens until it wipes out the shot. A new action then follows this natural wipe. A natural wipe occurs in *Something's Gotta Give* (2003) when the closing of the elevator doors "wipes out" a scene in New York City after Jack Nicholson steps into the elevator. Conversely, the next scene is revealed (a "wipe in") with the opening of elevator doors as Jack Nicholson emerges in Paris, France, where the film's final sequence occurs. See **Head-on/tail-away**.

Writer (screen)

The role of the motion-picture writer in the filmmaking process includes the major responsibility of providing a film scenario or film script which ultimately will become a **shooting script**. A **treatment** is a narrative description of a film story usually developed in a form similar to a short story. Characters and plot are described, scene-by-scene, so that the dramatic flow of the story, as it will appear on the screen, is clear.

A *film script* is a more fully developed and thorough treatment of the story. The film script contains dialogue and action sequences, and becomes the basis for the shooting script.

The shooting script contains, in addition to the dialogue and action description, important production information for the director and the director of cinematography. Included in this production information are shot descriptions (scope of shot), shot numbers, location and time notations, and indications of where special effects are required. The director works from this script in the filming of the story. It can also become a guide for the film editor.

The screenwriter may be involved in one, two, or all three phases of film scripting. Often more than one writer is involved.

The extent to which the film writer's work remains intact throughout the shooting period varies greatly. Many directors view the film script as merely a blueprint for building the film story, and proceed to embellish, delete, and rewrite parts of the script as they see fit. The script for Robert Altman's *Nashville* (1975), for example, underwent great change during filming, with both the director and the actors contributing to plot development and dialogue. In modern filmmaking this is frequently the case. Director Alfred Hitchcock, on the other hand, is said to have deviated rarely from the film script, having finalized the script earlier in story conferences with the writer or writers.

A film script usually falls into one of two categories: (1) the original screenplay or (2) the adapted screenplay.

Great screenwriters have contributed significantly to great films: Herman Mankiewicz to *Citizen Kane* (1941), Dudley Nichols to *Stagecoach* (1939), Robert Towne to *Chinatown* (1974), George S. Kaufman and Morrie Ryskind to *A Night at the Opera* (1935), Graham Greene to *The Third Man* (1949). Other screenwriters are not so well known, even some of those whose films have become highly successful. Because film scripts are translated into visual images, the exact role of the film writer cannot always be immediately evaluated. Yet, it is always possible to assess the quality of the script in terms of (1) idea, (2) story originality, (3) dialogue, and (4) power of theme, and to view the writer as a major contributor to each of them. These dramatic qualities are innately related to the contributory function of any writer who is assigned credit for a film story.

Z

Zagreb School of Animation (see **Animated film**)

Zoëtrope (Wheel of Life) A 19th-century animating device developed by William Horner and used to illustrate the persistence-of-vision theory. The effect of continuous movement was achieved by placing on the inside of a cylindrical drum a sequence of images of a figure in the progressive stages of a simple action. Each strip of images (contained on a length of paper) was called a "program." Slits cut through the outside of the drum produced a shutterlike mechanism, permitting momentary intervals between the passage of each image as the viewer peered into the revolving Zoëtrope to see the figure in an animated state. A version of the Zoëtrope was first patented in 1867.

Earlier animating devices include the stroboscope, the Phénakistoscope, and the Thaumatrope. The Stroboscope, demonstrated in Germany in 1832 by Simon Ritter von Stampfer, achieved the same effect as the Zoëtrope by spinning a slitted paper disc in front of a revolving image disc. Joseph Plateu's Phénakistoscope (later renamed Phantascope) places the slits and images on a single disc with the viewer peering through the slits toward a mirror reflection of the spinning images. The Thaumatrope, or "wonder turner," appeared in the 1820s as the simplest demonstration of a persistence-of-vision device. Separate objects, drawn on opposite sides of a circular card (a lion and an empty cage, for instance) seemed to blend into a single image when the card was spun by attached strings. The lion appeared to be seated in the cage. The invention of the Thaumatrope is attributed to Dr. John Paris.

Zoom shot A shot which changes the **angle of view** from a closer to a longer shot and vice versa. The zoom shot looks somewhat like a **dolly shot** because it appears to move closer to or farther away from a scene in a fluid continuous movement. In a zoom shot, however, the change of view is achieved without physically moving the camera as in the dolly shot.

The widening or narrowing of the angle of view in a zoom is possible because the lens used has a variable focal length. The lens used in zoom shots is referred to as a zoom lens or as a variable focal-length lens. The lens can be adjusted to change from a long shot (wide angle of view) to a close-up (narrow angle of view), or vice versa.

An optical difference exists between the zoom shot and the dolly shot because a dolly shot does actually seem to move through space, providing a dimensional perspective on objects or figures it passes in the scene. In a zoom shot all objects of the scene are magnified or diminished equally, and the space traversed is less noticeable and less dynamic than in a dolly shot.

The principal advantages of the zoom shot in filmmaking are the speed with which it permits a change in angle of view and its use in punctuating character reactions and revealing important information in startling ways.

Term Index

Topical Index

Experimental Film

Film Types

Optical Effects and Processes

Artist Index

Index of Films (& Television Shows)